Neutralism and Nationalism in France

NEUTRALISM and NATIONALISM in FRANCE

A Case Study

by

John T. Marcus
Hofstra College

BOOKMAN ASSOCIATES
New York

Library of Congress Catalog Card Number: 58-14295

WITH SPECIAL THANKS TO MY COLLEAGUE AND FRIEND
NORMAN KURLAND

WITH LOVE TO A. S. M., P. C. M.
AND RUTH

MANUFACTURED IN THE UNITED STATES OF AMERICA BY
UNITED PRINTING SERVICES, INC.
NEW HAVEN, CONN.

Preface

In May, 1958, a chronically sick French Republic came to face its darkest hour of crisis. Charles de Gaulle, who had represented the Liberation in 1944 and authoritarian conservatism in 1948 now became, by grace of the French Army in Algeria, the symbol of national unity and of national honor. The issue which had brought France to this dramatic crisis is one of the themes of this study; the rising of nationalist passion in a country which felt itself increasingly "cornered" by the movement of history. This national frustration vented itself in a desperate, stiffening defense of the last shreds of empire—or overseas territiories—and in a deepening resentment of the role of the United States.

This book was completed a few months before the crisis of 1958; it has been left the way it was originally written. The historian cannot be a prophet, and the analysis of France refers to past events as they had occurred prior to the time of writing, not to predictions of developments that were then still in the future. Some of the trends which earlier sequences of events had indicated did not materialize. Most notable among these was the growing sympathy of Communists for General de Gaulle, seen by the extreme left as a bitter foe of the United States, at worst a potential wrecker of NATO and at best a factor of instability in the Western alliance. Yet in the final showdown the Communists allowed these considerations of international affairs to take a secondary place compared with their instinct of self-preservation as an original movement in France, and they consequently sought to block the General's rise to quasi-dictatorial power.

Even this development was not fundamentally surprising. This study will show that the collaboration of Gaullists and Communists in foreign policy at the time of the Mendès-France government was necessarily short-lived as Gaullism was forced to return to its anti-Communist origins where its supporters had always remained. But if the old animosity between de Gaulle and the Communists now reappeared, it was significantly tempered by the suspicion on the part of the extreme left that Moscow would not encourage more than shadow-boxing with the General.

The probable course of events indicated by the pattern of previous developments was essentially confirmed by the May crisis. Foremost among these trends is the central theme of this study: the merger of neutralist and nationalist sentiment in France, and the spreading appeal of a nationalist neutralism from small circles of intellectual non-conformists to major, and perhaps dominant, portions of the population. In addition, the discussion of Gaullism in these pages emphasizes the decline of the movement as an organized political force and its increasing transformation into a mystique of national union, in which form the name of de Gaulle had greater rather than less appeal. The events of 1958 substantiate this analysis. The insurrectionary movement which, starting in Algeria, called for his return to power invoked the prestige of the erstwhile leader of the Free French rather than the political figure—whose Rally of the French People had collapsed by 1955. Indicative of public opinion, elections on April 27th, after the crisis of government had begun, showed a further decline of Gaullist voters from already decimated ranks. When the crisis entered its critical phase, the parliamentary groups lined up at first in an overwhelming majority against a Gaullist accession to power. The General received the premiership on his own terms not because the democratic opposition was won over but because it yielded to the superior force of extra-legal pressures. In short, the successful movement to return the war hero to the control of national affairs was not the result of the *political* force of his supporters in parliament, let alone of a nation-wide *political* mandate, but rather of the concerted action of army officers imposing their will upon a discredited National Assembly and capitalizing on the emotional connotations of the Gaullist myth.

It will be seen in the following chapters that the RPF, which had as its *raison d'être* the expression of sentiment of the French right, could not survive, as it once tried to do, in the form of the New Left. In May, 1958, with the plot-character of the new Gaullist faction and the determinant role of the army evident, those on the neutralist left-center who had come in the mid-fifties, when the RPF no longer presented a threat, to view the General with some respect naturally returned to their earlier suspicions and fears. Thus the ephemeral nature of the Gaullist-left-center coalition and the return of former RPF elements to their rightist inclinations was clearly evidenced by the May crisis. It appears that even the introduction of new variables into the French equation such as the virtual secession of the French in Algeria and the efforts of the army to impose a new authoritarian regime on Paris generally continued the trends rendered probable by previous circumstances.

This study is concerned with the causes and consequences of an explosive neutralist-nationalist combination. At a time when developments point to a renewal, or heightening, of nationalist-neutralist tendencies in France it is hoped that the following analysis may prove informative and meaningful.

June, 1958

Acknowledgments

My sincere thanks go to *The Review of Politics* (Notre Dame, Ind.) for the kind permission to make use of material which appeared originally in that journal. I wish to express my grateful appreciation to Mlle. Renard and Mme. Lien of the French Embassy's *Service de Presse* in New York for their great help in locating rare items of information.

I am indebted to Professors Thomas Helde and Robert Schwarz of Carnegie Institute of Technology for their patient reading of the manuscript and to Professor Edward W. Fox of Cornell University for his most helpful critical comments. My colleague, Dr. Robert Sobel, of Hofstra College generously carried out the onerous task of proof-reading.

The publication of this study was made possible by a generous grant from Hofstra College for which the author is very grateful. While the publication of the manuscript is in itself a measure of his debt to them, the general support he has received from the College, and in particular from Professor Gerrit P. Judd, IV, Chairman of the Department of History, has been especially gratifying and encouraging.

Contents

Introduction

A Matter of Definitions

What is neutralism? The term can be defined in one of many different ways. Neutralism is a relatively new word in the sense that it did not come into current usage until the postwar period. It can be found in the dictionary, but the definition given there does not correspond to its present meaning. Consequently, we are dealing with a term which connotes only a very vague set of ideas and which is used as an epithet to cover a multitude of sins. The student of neutralism thus is left to evolve his own definition in the context of certain general ideas and of the particular purpose of his investigation.

It is easy to see that the word is derived from the terms "neutral" and "neutrality." Occasionally, neutralism is intended to signify the idea or the policy of advocating neutrality, but this usage ignores the decisive implications of the word in connection with the Cold War. Indeed, within the framework of East-West relations—to use another ill-defined term which can scarcely stand up to either logical or geogaphical analysis —neutralism has acquired a political and ideological significance which goes beyond the simple desire of staying outside the two camps and remaining "neutral." One does not, for example, think of the governments of Sweden and Switzerland as being "neutralist." Why? Because for them neutrality is a traditional policy which does not involve political or ideological considerations peculiar to the Cold War.

What specific concepts, then, do characterize neutralism in the present context? Generally speaking, one can answer as follows: disagreement with the aims and policies of both sides as a result of which the neutralist wishes to become or remain closely involved with neither. However, since most of the countries—or groups within a country—which stand for "neutralism" had been considered as forming part of the Western camp, and since their defection, or even resistance, for ideological motives would weaken that camp, neutralism has in a sense come to take on the tangential meaning of fundamental opposition to American policy. (That is to say, the opposition outside of the Communist element.) As far as those who call themselves neutralists are concerned, the policy and objectives of neither side actually merit their full allegiance which, they believe, will be the crucial fact in maintaining peace. It follows that they do not simply want their country to remain outside the fighting in some future war—or to be "neutral" in the traditional sense—but that they believe their policy will go as far as possible in preventing the war itself.

Needless to say, the adjective "neutralist" is meant in neither a complimentary nor derogatory sense. From the American point of view is should be remembered that some of the sharpest critics of present Western policy, critics whose demands and violent opposition can only be called neutralist, consider themselves to be firm friends of the United States as a country, and of the American people. They believe that their strictures against the foreign policies of Washington, as well as the new policies which they themselves demand in opposition to Washington, will be of great benefit to the United States, even if Americans do not realize it, by helping to preserve world peace as well as by substituting an effective defense against communism for one which misses the mark.

In short, an appraisal of the various points of the neutralists' position—they are frequently in disagreement among themselves—should be based on the specific merits of each demand and not only on the *a priori* assumption that they are anti-American. But the present study is not essentially concerned with an evaluation of these demands. It is concerned rather with the nature of neutralism, and particularly with the nature of its appeal; it is concerned with the factors which have made neutralism a force, or at least a potential force, in the world balance of power. To say more would be to rob the text in favor of the prologue.

CHAPTER ONE

The Nationalist Background and the Ideal of European Unity

By 1947, the increasing tension between the Communist and non-Communist worlds had reached the stage of "Cold War." In France, one of the consequences of this situation was that the alliance between the Communists and the parties of what was called the "left-center," the Socialists and the Christian-leftist *Mouvement Républicain Populaire,* was replaced by bitter hostility. This alliance already had been wearing thin after the political battle over ratification of the constitution of the Fourth Republic and, even more, over Communist excesses perpetrated under the guise of purging war-time "collaborators."[1] The Communist-led political strikes—the general strike of 1947 and the coal strike of 1948—which drove the final wedge between that party and the rest of the nation, had grown largely out of both the government's handling of the Indo-Chinese issue and internal French economic issues concerning workers' salary levels. But the extent of these strike movements and their insurrectionary character were partly a result of the developing Cold War itself.[2]

The first American reaction to the new world situation was passage of the European Recovery Program, more widely known as the Marshall Plan. Although the program was undoubtedly meant, in view of many of its supporters, to be far more than just a measure of self-defense, one of the main purposes of the plan was to prevent the Communists from taking over Western Europe. In France, it was largely the funds provided under the

Marshall Plan that made possible the modernization of the Lorraine steel industry and the coal mining industry of the Nord basin, the mechanization of agriculture in the East and the reclamation of vast areas such as the Camargue swamplands in the South. More strikingly perhaps, E.R.P. was instrumental in the vast increase of electricity production and consumption symbolized, for example, by the electrification of the railroads and by the giant hydro-electric power station of Donzère-Mondragon on the Rhône. Thus it appears that the modernization of French industry envisaged in the famous Monnet Plan for Modernization and Re-equipment, first drafted in 1947, could not have been even partially accomplished had it not been for the vast appropriations distributed by the Economic Cooperation Administration.[3]

It must be emphasized that, except for the Communists, virtually every segment of French opinion praised the principles and aims of the Marshall Plan.[4] By 1953, popular approval of American *economic* aid to France had become even more marked than at the time of the inception of the Marshall Plan.[5] But it is equally important to note that during this time, United States policy had been turning away from *economic* assistance, and that this change was producing an increasing suspicion among the French of America's foreign aid program as a whole.[6] Still, until 1953, popular opinion in France was decidedly sympathetic to the United States;[7] it is only since that date that suspicion of, and in fact hostility towards, American policy has developed into an active political force among non-Communist Frenchmen.

While the development of neutralism in France is directly related to the evolution of American policy and American attitudes, it is clear that anti-American feeling itself must be seen in the perspective of historic French tendencies towards xenophobia. In France as elsewhere, anti-foreign tendencies have been associated traditionally with certain movements of the extreme right. This xenophobia,[8] intimately connected with the other aspects of integral nationalism, particularly anti-Semitism, may have covered all things "non-French" but it focused generally on one or another nation, and particularly on Germany. It should be recalled, however, that before the present era of friendship between France and Britain, which dates back at least to 1904, there had been many centuries of bitter animosity between these two states. This feeling did not die overnight in France; it persisted particularly among elements of the extreme right, among the traditionalists who continued to relive the history of their monarchical past. The feeling expressed itself in the propaganda of the French right during the thirties and came to a head under the Vichy regime after the British navy's shelling and destruction of the French fleet at Oran.

It would seem that this strand of hostility ingrained in a significant part of the French right, and nowhere more clearly visible than in the attitude of de Gaulle towards his British hosts during the war, may well have been transferred to the other "Anglo-Saxon" nation when it in turn emerged as the world's leading power. Yet there exist many factors which might have been expected to block the growth of any significant anti-Americanism in France, beginning with a tradition of friendship which goes back, as one is so endlessly reminded, to Lafayette and Rochambeau, and includes the Statue of Liberty, General Pershing, Belleau Wood, Josephine Baker, *le jazz,* etc., etc.

Anti-Americanism did develop after the first war over the U.S.' failure to sign both the Treaty of Versailles and a mutual defense alliance with France, as well as over the dispute about war-debt payments: . . . . "Uncle Shylock." Furthermore, French Socialists and Communists, like Marxists everywhere, had come by the nineteen twenties to view America as the central pit of the capitalist hell. It should be added that during the late thirties and in the postwar era, the moderate left in France, including socialists, looked wistfully at the New Deal and regretted that their own capitalist society had been unable to reform its creaking and dilapidated yet rooted hierarchic structure.

It was after the Liberation that anti-Americanism in France became a significant factor, due partly to the contact with the unrestrained *joie de vivre* of American troops, and attributable also to resentment over the decline of France's prestige in contrast to the rise of American influence. Thus the psychological conditions for an undercurrent of anti-Americanism, or at least of disappointment with the United States,[9] consisting partly of a nationalist envy of the U.S.' power and partly of resentment of American behavior and standards, had been created.[10]

Of all the specific factors which, historically, have gone into the making of the xenophobic streak of a segment of the French population, certainly none outranks the French feeling towards Germany. If modern scholarship has shown that France did not by any means spend the forty-four years after 1870 just looking for an opportunity to take back Alsace-Lorraine,[11] it is still true that the French feel they have had in the past ample demonstration of Prussianized Germany's methods and goals.

In the period before the first World War, anti-Germanism was a sentiment that was powerful primarily within the French right. Jean Jaurès was the victim of an assassin on the very eve of the First War because nationalists considered both him and his party as "pro-German." One of the striking facts about the development of French attitudes during the inter-war period is that the development of German National-Socialism led to a reversal of this picture. The right now looked towards Germany as an exemplary state which had successfully resisted the process of "bolshevization." It overcame its traditional nationalist scruples in favor of its ideological support for an authoritarian regime. Meanwhile, the left's hatred of Hitler led it to take up a policy of diplomatic opposition to, and military preparation against, the Third Reich—a fatefully weak and vacillating policy, it should be added. Thus, although the reasons for the left's new hostility towards Germany were quite different from the old-style nationalist antagonism of the prewar right, the result of this reversal of attitudes was that the left had in effect, on the question of German policy, exchanged positions with the right.[12]

The legacy which the Second World War left in the way of French hatred of Germany is all too obvious. Defeat was bitter;

occupation was worse. In 1943, the German policy of a relative degree of correctness gave way to the full brutality of the Nazi regime and the deportation to Germany of forced labor. By the end of the war, only a small minority in France regarded the German occupant as anything but *le boche;* with the Liberation, this proportion decreased further. The massacre of Oradour-sur-Glane (in which Alsatian conscripts participated) became the symbol of Nazi terror in France. Of all the xenophobic tendencies in contemporary France, it is anti-Germanism which is by far the most important.[13]

All the dislikes of certain particular nations which have been mentioned are operative, in French opinion, as specific factors, but in addition they are merged in with a generalized, abstract suspicion of all things non-French which undoubtedly constitutes one of the underlying streaks of character in a large portion of the French population, particularly in the provinces. Thus the anti-foreign tendencies existed which could respond to the stimulus of a nationalist neutralism on the left or a neutralist nationalism on the right.

* * * * * * * *

On September 19, 1946, at Zurich, Winston Churchill gave voice to the dream of a United States of Europe.[14] The ideal of European union can be traced back to the concept of the unity of Christendom which had formed the mystique of the empires of Otto the Great and Charlemagne, or to the concept of the unity of the civilized world which had constituted the mystique of the empire of Augustus. The League of Nations had represented one aspect of this urge, as has its successor, the United Nations. But it took the agony of the Second World War to hatch anew the dream of European integration which the former and future Prime Minister was to voice again at the Congress of Europe at the Hague in May, 1948. But as it turned out, to the great disappointment of many in Europe, Churchill was not expressing the views of the government of his country.[15] In fact, it was France, against the opposition of a Britain which feared the abandonment of sovereignty involved in a European federation, that came to be the chief defender of schemes which were intended to bring about European unity,[16] or as the French express it far more vividly, to *faire l'Europe*. Indeed, the French integrationists felt their country might regain some of its lost power and prestige if it became the champion of a renovated, supra-national Europe.

This new "Europe" was to have two chief purposes. The first, of course, was the integration of the various small and medium-sized states of Europe into a more effective economic and political unit in world affairs. The second point was to bring about a reconciliation between France and Germany within the context of a "European" framework.

The integration of Europe involved many different aspects, cultural and economic, as well as political and military.[17] One of the most significant steps on this path was in the realm of political integration: the Congress of Europe, already mentioned, which brought together the various movements working for European unity and on its marquee featured such stars as Winston Churchill, Konrad Adenauer, Léon Blum, Alcide de Gasperi, Robert Schuman and Paul-Henri Spaak.[18] The outcome of the 1948 Congress was the organization in October, 1948 of various "European" groups into the European Movement, and the demand of this movement for the creation of the Council of Europe.[19]

As set up in August, 1949, the Council of Europe consisted of two organs: the Committee of Ministers, composed of the foreign ministers of the participating countries who reflect, needless to say, government views, and a Consultative Assembly which, as its name indicates, has only deliberative powers. The members of the Strasbourg Consultative Assembly are appointed, not elected, and thus the "Parliament of Europe" has been removed another step from popular interest or consciousness. On the other hand it was agreed, as a concession to the "European" point of view, that the delegates would represent various aspects of political opinion, except for the Communists, and not just official government positions.[20] Over the years, the Strasbourg Consultative Assembly has proven itself occasionally to be a valuable platform of debate, but generally, and especially in recent years, to be a little more than an ineffective forum.

In view of the way it was constituted, it could not be much else.[21] And this ineffectiveness did much to reduce the momentum of the "European" movement, at least in France.

But these hesitant steps towards the political integration of Europe were not the most important aspect of the movement towards European unification. The crucial measures were, at first, in the field of economic cooperation. In April, 1948, the Organization of European Economic Cooperation had been organized and assigned the task of acting as the European agency through which the administrators of the Marshall Plan were to channel their allocations to European countries.[22] A derivative organization for facilitating multilateral trade through the easing of currency transactions, the European Payments Union, was born two years later.[23]

The chief purpose of the economic unification of Europe was the creation of a *single European market.* On the one hand, this meant the reduction or elimination of tariff barriers and the creation of customs unions.[24] The list of proposed and actual customs unions reads like a list of items taken from an electric appliance store catalogue—or so French cynics charged: Benelux, the only significant such union (Belgium, The Netherlands and Luxembourg), Francita (France and Italy), concluded in June, 1950, Fritalux (Francita and Benelux), Finebel (France, Italy, Netherlands, Belgium and Luxembourg), Fribel (France, Italy and Belgium), and Uniscan (Britain and the Scandinavian countries), neither of the last two ever put into effect.[25]

Along with and related to, the concept of tariff reductions, the principle of a European-wide market also involved the idea of various countries pooling their resources. These "pools,"[26] which were largely the outgrowth of French initiatives, ranged from the suggested "Green Pool," or Pflimlin Plan—a proposed pool of agricultural produce which never came into being—and the abortive Petsche Plan for a European investment bank, to the pool of railway equipment—the Bonnefous Plan—the pool of atomic research and development, Euratom, and the pool for a common market which are being actively pushed today,[27] and finally the two most famous pools of all: the pool of defense forces, or European Defense Community, which will be discussed later, and the pool of coal and steel production otherwise known as the Schuman Plan.

It is these last two proposals which, more than any other suggestion or measure, came to symbolize a "European" policy.[28] The purpose of the Schuman Plan has been to coordinate the market for the coal, iron and steel industries of Germany, Belgium, Italy, France, the Netherlands and Luxembourg under the control of a single supreme authority which would have power to eliminate protective or restrictive clauses against "free competition."[29] The result was expected to be a great gain in productivity. The fear of French industrialists that the Coal and Steel Community High Authority would open a wider market to the competition of a German industrial machine which would drive French producers from the market[30] was partly offset by the modernization of Lorraine steel production, largely through Marshall Plan funds—the kind of modernization which was itself one of the very objects which the proponents of the Schuman Plan had intended to achieve through the prospect of an unprotected competitive international market. Nonetheless, the charge that the policy of the Coal and Steel Authority, headed by the Frenchman, Jean Monnet, would lead to the demise of French metallurgy was repeatedly voiced by those industrialists who, individually, did not profit from the new conditions. This attitude was to play an important role in the development of a nationalist form of French neutralism.

A second and more widespread charge against the Schuman Plan was that the supra-national authority represented in fact nothing but a cartel in disguise[31] and a coalition of the most reactionary elements of Europe's industrial plutocracy. For anticlericals, this charge was linked to the view that the Coal and Steel Community, and in fact all projects for European integration, were part of a plot hatched in the Vatican, making use of the Catholic parties of Italy, Germany, Holland, Luxembourg and France, to gain control of Europe's economy.[32] And then, for part of the French left, the Schuman Plan Authority was a dangerous "synarchy," a technocracy which would run its industrial empire along scientifically efficient lines . . . . to the complete destruction of the humanist values of European society. This attitude was to play a part in the development of left-wing neutralism. Thus France was moving from her earlier role of champion of the "European" cause to that of a reluctant prospective participant, urged on, according to the French view, by the good offices of Anglo-Saxon partners who were careful to remain outside all such schemes.

The development of the Cold War had placed all these moves towards European unification in a special light. In fact, the words "Europe," "European unification," and "Council of Europe," which have reappeared constantly in the previous pages, which are the traditionally accepted terms in this context and are part of the diplomatic vocabulary, nonetheless are misleading and quite inaccurate. Geographically, Europe runs, of course, from the Urals to the Atlantic and includes various states under Communist control. Yet as the Cold War had become intensified, the Communist countries for their part had refused to participate in international organizations which they could not control. And the non-Communist nations for their part had come to think of "Europe" as signifying in fact Western Europe. Some non-Communist European states did not participate either in one or both OEEC and the Council of Europe, for example Switzerland. And the most important unification projects of all, the Schuman Plan and the "European" Defense Community involved only a "little Europe" of six nations—as the French say *L'Europe des Six*: France, Germany, Italy, Belgium, The Netherlands and Luxembourg.[33] Britain, considered by most Frenchmen as their country's key ally in Europe or even in the world, would participate in neither. Whereas European integration had at one time been defended as an effort to strengthen Europe so as to make it more independent of American influence,[34] it looked to many sincere "Europeans" in France as though the word "Europe" and the ideal of European unification were being used to cover a regional grouping of a few powers for the purpose of a military alliance subject to the control of the State Department and Pentagon,[35] and aimed frankly *against* other European countries.

In fact, one of the striking features of developments in Europe since 1949, and one which has aroused considerable bitterness among left-wing non-Communist circles, has been precisely this increasing stress on military questions and the gradual sidetracking of economic measures in favor of military considerations. Or, to be more accurate, the increasing use of economic weapons and economic aid for military purposes, symbolized, for example, by the transmutation in January, 1952 of the Economic Cooperation Administration into the Mutual Security Agency.[36] Similarly it was charged by these same elements that the Schuman Plan was not intended to build up a vigorous European economy but to provide an arsenal for the anti-Communist coalition. Indeed, it was the moves towards the military unification of Western European which evoked the sharpest criticisms of all.

The background to this latter question goes back to 1948, the year when the governments of the Benelux countries, of Britain and of France, realizing their individual military impotence before the might of the Soviet Union and all having clearly in mind the fate that had befallen Czechoslovakia, signed the Brussels Treaty.[37] According to this treaty, the signatories were to coordinate their defense efforts and set up a combined general staff which in fact was established at Fontainebleau under the direction of Field Marshal Sir Bernard Montgomery. But these governments knew that their paper organization would make no difference in the balance of power and that their only hope of securing a defense against the threat of a Soviet invasion, which at that time—the period of the Berlin blockade—seemed to be a definite possibility if not a certainty, was to secure a guarantee of American protection. The result was the creation in April, 1949, of the North Atlantic Treaty Organization which set up a mutual defense organization combining the West European and North American powers.[38]

The creation of N.A.T.O. in 1949 accelerated the trends which have been discussed concerning the nature and aims of the moves towards "European" integration and directly gave birth to the force of neutralism.[39] At the same time it is well to recall, after the endless abuse that has been heaped upon the United States for its "imperialism" in securing bases in Europe,[40] that the presence of American troops in Europe as part of the forces of N.A.T.O., and the integration of these forces through Supreme Headquarters Allied Powers Europe under an American commander (who absorbed the functions of the Brussels Treaty Headquarters at Fontainebleau) was not the result of American initiative or demand at all but was accepted by the United States, somewhat reluctantly, at the urgent plea of the governments of these European states themselves. It is interesting to note that the despatch of American forces to Europe, considered necessary in 1949 for the safeguard of the morale of West European peoples and as a guarantee of American intervention in case of a Soviet attack, found its most serious obstacle in the opposition of the "imperialistic" American Senate.[41]

In 1950, the invasion of South Korea brought the Cold War to a new intensity and forced the United States to engage in an all-out rearmament effort. It followed naturally that the United States wished to see its allies increase their military preparations—and, from this, it followed just as naturally that the neutralists increased their protests. The most obvious way for the Western allies to reenforce their combined military strength, beyond the limits of their own defense potentialities, was to rearm the defeated ex-enemy power, a power well-known for its military capabilities and military-industrial potential.[42] But the contingency of German rearmament, which had been predicted and denounced by French opponents of N.A.T.O. in 1949, had been repudiated in advance by Foreign Minister Robert Schuman. There were certainly many Frenchmen who favored a reconciliation with Germany—the key to the "construction" of Europe—but who viewed with extreme misgiving a revival of the German army which in their minds evoked the visions of Sedan, Verdun, Panzer divisions, and Stukas. In fact, these same Frenchmen would claim that the essence of a Franco-German reconciliation was the "pacification" of the latter, and hence was quite inconsistent with its rearmament. Thus American policy calling for a German defense contribution aroused bitter opposition in France far beyond the confines of the French Communist world.[43] In order to avoid what appeared to France as the specter of a new *Wehrmacht,* the French Government, at that time, October, 1950, headed by René Pleven, put forth the proposal of an integrated European army,[44] with units taken from various nations but operating as a single and, it was hoped, homogeneous force. A new "European patriotism" would have to grow and to replace, for this army, the narrower—but more binding—incentive of national patriotism. In this way, the Pleven Plan as it was called, although in fact it too had been drawn up by Jean Monnet, would pave the way for a rearmament of Germany and would eliminate the possibility of a *national* German army launching an attack upon France. American military leaders received the suggestion for an integrated European Army with considerable skepticism concerning both its effectiveness and the time it would take to be put into operation.[45] But the United States yielded to the insistence of the French Government and accepted the principle of a European Defense Community.

With the proposal of EDC, we have reached the most dramatic and internationally the most significant of the various "pools" and of the efforts towards European, or rather West European, integration. At the same time, we have also reached the climax of the trend in accordance with which the various measures for "European" integration no longer appeared in the eyes of many Frenchmen to be aimed at the creation of a united Europe but at the erection of a military alliance directed against Communist Eastern Europe.

Those who opposed "taking sides" in the Cold war, whether for ideological reasons or out of a sense of futility, came to regard union of the six European powers as their principal target. The neutralist opposition to American policy thus expressed itself specifically in the rejection of West European integration. The European army project came to be regarded as *the* expression of American policy in Europe. Consequently opposition to EDC became the dominant characteristic of neutralism,[46] and the campaign against EDC now absorbed the main efforts of neutralist propaganda.

This development in turn brought many of the opponents of EDC, whose basic position and attitudes could not possibly be regarded as neutralist, into close *de facto* collaboration with the neutralists themselves. United in their opposition on a major point of policy, many of these anti-EDC elements, coming from opposite points of the political spectrum and originally sworn enemies—particularly the non-Communist extreme left and the nationalist right—came to share similar attitudes and to form an effective, if temporary, alliance-in-negation. Since the very object of neutralism was a negative one—the refusal of an alignment with the West—such a negative coalition, which did eventually succeed in dealing the European army project its death blow in the French National Assembly, represented itself an indirect neutralist victory.

The basic characteristic of the left in France, the thread that has linked its various and often contradictory manifestations, is the conviction that it was serving the idea of Progress. In the main, the neutralists with which this study deals developed that same conviction. Their neutralism would save France from the "reactionism" of Western policy, and a neutralist France would save the world from war. A France grown too weak to be an independent Great Power in the world could either be a spoke in the international machinery of another Great Power, or could pursue an "independent" policy asserting its distinct national individuality by acting as a bridge between the two Super Powers. In this way, it could acquire indirectly, through its status and functions, the Great Power role it could no longer assume directly by virtue of its economic and military potentialities. Thus both the social ideology of the left and the nationalism of the right could be served by a policy of neutralism. It is this convergence of conflicting ideologies and policies in France which forms the primary object of this study. And it is the significance of this convergence on the wider stage of Europe and, one may suggest, in major parts of Asia, which, it is hoped, will provide its justification.

Footnotes

1. Gordon Wright, *The Reshaping of French Democracy,* London: Methuen, 1950. François Goguel, *France Under the Fourth Republic,* Ithaca, N.Y.: Cornell University Press, 1952.

2. Ronald Matthews, *The Death of the Fourth Republic,* New York: F. A. Praeger, 1954, pp. 244-57. Herbert Luethy, *France Against Herself,* New York: F. A. Praeger, 1955, pp. 130-57. Dorothy Pickles, *French Politics, The First Years of the Fourth Republic,* London & New York: Royal Institute of International Affairs (R.I.I.A.), Oxford University Press, 1953, pp. 81-4, 101-5. Catherine Gavin, *Liberated France,* New York: St. Martin's Press, 1955, pp. 171-2.

3. U. S. Department of Commerce, Office of Business Economics, Clearing House for Foreign Transactions, *Foreign Aid by the United States Government, 1940-1951,* Washington: U. S. Government Printing Office, 1952, pp. 19, 56ff. William Adams Brown and Redvers Opie, *American Foreign Assistance,* Washington: The Brookings Institution, 1953, pp. 177-269. Warren C. Baum, "The Marshall Plan and Foreign Trade," in Edward Mead Earle, ed., *Modern France, Problems of the Third and Fourth Republics,* Princeton, N.J.: Princeton University Press, 1951. C. Gavin, *Op. cit.,* pp. 170-7, 242 n. H. Luethy, *Op. cit.,* pp. 290-8. D. Pickles, *Op. cit.,* pp. 67-8, 86, 112. Harry Bayard Price, *The Marshall Plan and Its Meaning,* Washington: Government Affairs Institute—Ithaca, N.Y.: Cornell University Press, 1955.

4. Jean B. Duroselle, Alfred Grosser and Maurice Megret, *French Opinion and the United States,* Waltham, Mass.: World Peace Foundation—Brandeis University Conference on France, June 14-18, 1956, mimeographed, p. 8.

5. *Ibid.,* p. 9.

6. Arnold M. Rose, "Anti-Americanism in France," *The Antioch Review,* Yellow Springs, Ohio, (Vol. 13, No. 4) December, 1952, pp. 471-82. C. Gavin, *Op. cit.,* pp. 175-6. Vernon Van Dyke, "The Communists and the Foreign Relations of France," in E. M. Earle, ed., *Op. cit.,* p. 249. Raymond Aron, "France and the Cold War," *The Political Quarterly,* London, (Vol. 22) January, 1951, p. 66. J. B. Duroselle, *et al, Op. cit.,* pp. 10-15 *et seq.*

7. V. Van Dyke, *Op. cit.,* p. 249. "Ce que les Français pensent de l'Amérique," *Réalités,* Paris, (No. 91) August, 1953, pp. 18-22.

8. David Thomson, *Democracy in France,* R.I.I.A., London & New York: Oxford University Press, 1946 & 1952, pp. 148-50, 157-60.

9. J. B. Duroselle, *et. al., Op. cit.,* pp. 18, 33-7.

10. A. M. Rose, *Op. cit.,* pp. 468-84.

11. Eber Malcolm Carroll, *French Public Opinion and Foreign Affairs, 1870-1914,* New York: The Century Co., 1931.

12. Charles A. Micaud, *The French Right and Nazi Germany, 1933-1939; A Sudy of Public Opinion,* Durham, N. C.: Duke University Press, 1943.

13. D. Pickles, *Op. cit.,* pp. 189-92, 195, 217-8. H. Luethy, *Op. cit.,* pp. 338-41, 415-6. R. Matthews, *Op. cit.,* p. 265. C. Gavin, *Op. cit.,* pp. 133-6, 177-8. Henry Bertram Hill, "The Reliability of France in the European System" and Fred Latimer Hadsel, "France Among the Powers," in E. M. Earle, ed., *Op. cit.,* pp. 484-6, 487-94. D. Thomson, *Op. cit.,* p. 181. Alfred Grosser, "Germany and France: A Confrontation," in: Daniel Lerner and Raymond Aron, eds., *France Defeats EDC,* New York: F. A. Praeger, 1957, Ch. IV, pp. 59-60 ff., 67-70. Jean Stoetzel, "The Evolution of French Opinion," *Loc. cit.,* Ch. V, pp. 73-6, 81-5 ff.; see especially the tables in the Appendix to Chapter V, pp. 97-101. See also André Philip, "The Interplay of Interests and Passions," *Loc. cit.,* p. 26.

14. A particularly useful collection of documents and important statements on European union, including a translation of Churchill's speech, is to be found in: Germany, Federal Republic Auswärtigen Amt [Foreign Office], *Europa, Dokumente zur Frage der europäischen Einigung,* Bonn: Bonner Universitäts-Buchdruckerei, 1953, pp. 84-5. Referred to hereafter as *Europa.*

15. Michael T. Florinski, *Integrated Europe?,* New York: The Macmillan Co., 1955, pp. 159-63.

16. D. Pickles, *Op. cit.,* p. 196. René Courtin, "French Views on European Union," *International Affairs,* London, (Vol. 25) January, 1949, pp. 8-22.

17. Several aspects of the contemporary movement for European unity have been the subject of special studies, and some general surveys of developments in this field are available. The summary discussion in the following pages has been based largely

on these sources: M. T. Florinski, *Op. cit.,* W. A. Brown and R. Opie, *Op. cit.,* pp. 270-312, D. Pickles, *Op. cit.,* Ch. XIII: "The Pursuit of Europe," C. Gavin, *Op. cit.,* Ch. X: "From Marshall Plan to N.A.T.O." and Ch. XIII: "Towards Rearmament." H. Luethy, *Op. cit.,* pp. 353-95. A particularly useful study on European unity, seen in relation to the Council of Europe at Strasbourg, is A. H. Robertson's *The Council of Europe; Its Structure, Functions and Achievements,* London Institute of World Affairs—New York: F. A. Praeger, 1956, especially Chs. VI-IX.

18. M. T. Florinski, *Op. cit.,* pp. 112-4. *Europa,* pp. 110-1.

19. M. T. Florinski, *Op. cit.,* pp. 114-25. *Europa,* pp. 197-212.

20. D. Pickles, *Op. cit.,* pp 198-9.

21. M. T. Florinski, *Op. cit.,* pp. 122-5. For another view, see A. H. Robertson, *Op. cit.,* Ch. XII.

22. *Europa,* pp. 153-67. W. A. Brown & R. Opie, *Op. cit.,* pp. 196-207, 276-8. H. B. Price, *Op. cit.,* pp. 293-304, 348-50. M. T. Florinski, *Op. cit.,* pp. 40-52.

23. *Europa,* pp. 167-74. M. T. Florinski, *Op. cit.,* pp. 52-7. Brown & Opie, *Op. cit.,* pp. 209-11, 278-94.

24. *Europa,* pp. 131-50. A. H. Robertson, *Op. cit.,* pp. 121-3.

25. M. T. Florinski, *Op. cit.,* pp. 27-40.

26. *Europa,* pp. 175-96. W. A. Brown & R. Opie, *Op. cit.,* pp. 294-300.

27. André Fontaine, "Le Comité d'Action pour les Etats-Unis d'Europe va demander la constitution d'une commission de l'énergie atomique," *Le Monde,* January 12, 1956. See also: Pierre Drouin, "Premiers contours de l'Europe atomique," Pt. I: "Le noyau; 'Euratom,'" *Loc. cit.,* November 17, 1955. "L'Euratom," *Loc. cit.,* January 20, 1956. "Le projet de pool atomique européen," *Loc. cit.,* January 20, 1956, p. 3. "Ultime discussion au Comité d'Action pour les Etats-Unis d'Europe autour du charactère exclusivement pacifique de l'Euratom," *Loc. cit.,* January 19, 1956, p. 3. Ambassade de France, Service de Presse et d'Information, *Euratom, Six Nations To Pool Atomic Research and Development,* European Affairs, No. 11, New York, June, 1957. Ambassade de France, Service de Presse et d'Information, *A New Step in Building Europe; A Common Market for 175 Million Consumers,* European Affairs, No. 10, New York, June, 1957. "French Chamber Ratifies Single Market, Atom Pacts," *The New York Times,* July 10, 1957.

28. *Europa,* pp. 301-41. M. T. Florinski, *Op. cit.,* pp. 57-76, 125-9. W. A. Brown and R. Opie, *Op. cit.,* pp. 300-11.
29. M. T. Florinski, *Op. cit.,* pp. 67-8.
30. D. Pickles, *Op. cit.,* pp. 207-8. Jaques Vernant, "European Politics Faces French Economics," in: D. Lerner and R. Aron, eds., *Op. cit.,* Ch. III.
31. M. T. Florinski, *Op. cit.,* p. 73.
32. H. Luethy, *Op. cit.,* pp. 385-91.
33. H. Luethy presents a convincing defense of the "European" policy of Adenauer and Schuman while ridiculing the charges that "little Europe" was a mystical reincarnation of the "Germanic" Carolingian Empire or the "reactionary" Hapsburg Empire, *Op. cit.,* pp. 385-90, 415-23, 424-31.
34. *Ibid.,* pp. 358, 382.
35. *Ibid.,* pp. 356-7, 359, 397, 405-8.
36. H. B. Price, *Op. cit.,* pp. 357-66. W. A. Brown and R. Opie, *Op. cit.,* pp. 471-539. M. T. Florinski, *Op. cit.,* pp. 44-6.
37. *Europa,* pp. 98-101. M. T. Florinski, *Op. cit.,* pp. 79-80.
38. M. T. Florinski, *Op. cit.,* pp. 81-96.
39. See Chapter II; also: Raymond Aron, "French Public Opinion and the Atlantic Treaty," *International Affairs,* London, (Vol. 28, No. 1) January, 1952, pp. 1-8.
40. J. B. Duroselle, *et. al., Op. cit.,* pp. 9, 18.
41. Early in 1951, at the height of the Korean conflict, the U S. administration felt it necessary to safeguard Western defense by increasing the size of the U. S. forces in Europe. This decision provoked a bitter debate in the U. S. Senate—part of the "Great Debate" on the nation's foreign policy—concerning the question of stationing American troops overseas. The debate ran, off and on, between January and August, 1951; scattered references to it can be found in the *New York Times* throughout this period, but some of the more important events, beginning with Senator Taft's attack on the administration's move, are: "Taft Opposes Troops for Europe; Calls Aid to Korea a Usurpation; Red Forces Pour South of Seoul," *The New York Times,* January 6, 1951, pp. 1, 4. "Now Taft," *Loc. cit.,* January 7, 1951 (Sunday edition), section IV, p. E. "G.O.P. in Challenge; Wherry Seeks Debate on Issue of No More Men for Europe; Resolution Offered; Jenner Asks Ultimatum by Congress to the President on War," *Loc. cit.,* January 9, 1951. "Taft Doubts Faith of U. S. in Truman on Troop Powers," *Loc. cit.,* February

11, 1951, (Sunday edition). "Hoover Expected at Troop Hearings," *Loc. cit.,* February 11, 1951, p. 12. "Debate Renewed by Hoover and Taft," *Loc. cit.,* February 11, 1951, section IV, p. E. "Taft for 20% Limit on Sending Troops," *Loc. cit.,* February 12, 1951, p. 11. "118 House Republicans' Manifesto Asks Stress on Hemisphere Defense," *Loc. cit.,* February 15, 1951. "Senate Asks Curbs on Troops to Europe; Bids Truman, 49-43, Consult Congress Before Exceeding Four Division Limit," *Loc. cit.,* April 3, 1951. "Senate Bars Curb by Law on Troops," *Loc. cit.,* April 4, 1951. "Balloting in Senate on Troop Proposals," *Loc. cit.,* April 4, 1951, p. 17. "Troops for Europe Backed by Senate; House Asked to Act," *Loc. cit.,* April 5, 1951. "Revolt in Congress Brewing on Funds, Troops for Europe," *Loc. cit.,* August 6, 1951. "Limit on Troops Mapped," in "Warning of Dim Peace Hope Speeds House Arms Debate," *Loc. cit.,* August 9, 1951. "Attack on Truman Delays Arms Bill," *Loc. cit.,* August 11, 1951.

42. C. Gavin, *Op. cit.,* pp. 181, 202-3. D. Pickles, *Op. cit.,* pp. 210-1. H. Luethy, *Op. cit.,* pp. 395-9.

43. J. B. Duroselle, *et al., Op. cit.,* pp. 9, 18. Raymond Aron, "Historical Sketch of the Great Debate," in: D. Lerner and R. Aron, eds., *Op. cit.,* pp. 3-4, 7, 10-1 ff. Alfred Grosser, "Germany and France: A Confrontation," *Loc. cit.,* pp. 66-70. Jean Stoetzel, "The Evolution of French Opinion," *Loc. cit.,* pp. 81-5.

44. M. T. Florinski, *Op. cit.,* pp. 96-103, 129-30. C. Gavin, *Op. cit.,* pp. 243-50. D. Pickles, *Op. cit.,* pp. 210-7. H. Luethy, *Op. cit.,* pp. 398-416.

45. M. T. Florinski, *Op. cit.,* p. 99.

46. Although many of the opponents of EDC, particularly those of the center Third Force parties, remained clearly distinct of the neutralist groups.

CHAPTER TWO

The Development of a Neutralist Attitude

That in 1946 Pierre Cot should have called for French neutrality in the rising tension between the Communist and non-Communist power blocs was hardly surprising.[1] After all, the former Popular Front minister had emerged from the war as a convinced Communist sympathizer and as the leader of the pro-Communist *Union Progressiste.* Under the circumstances, his opposition to the policy of a West European defense coalition intended specifically to limit further Soviet expansion—the Brussels Pact—was only to be expected. Outside the sphere of direct Communist influence, however, few important voices in France at this time opposed the formation of a West European defense system.

By 1949, international tension had reached a new level of intensity, to which the Western democracies responded with the Atlantic Pact. The possibility of another war appeared at least a step nearer, and this in turn began to have an effect upon political attitudes in France beyond the orbit of Communist influence.

> Let us suppose that the Communist peace offensive hides the darkest of strategems, let us suppose further that the Atlantic policy reflects the intentions of innocent lambs, it is still the consequences of the latter that we fear.[2]

In January, 1950, the Paris daily *Combat* published a series of articles calling for the formation of an international "Third

Force" as a mediating and pacifying factor between the American and Russian blocs. The fact that the author of these articles was a national of Sweden, a country that has traditionally stood for neutrality, was certainly not a coincidence.[3] Shortly thereafter the editor of the paper, Claude Bourdet, wrote that the organization of an armed and neutral Europe was the best way to counteract Communist propaganda in France and to avoid the provocation of the Soviet Union such as would be constituted by the presence of American armies on the European Continent.[4] Indeed, how much security would France gain from the stationing of some twenty-three American divisions in Europe as a barrier to the two hundred divisions of the Soviet Union. At best, they could provide little protection; at worst, they might be the incentive for a Russian attack.[5]

Combat and Bourdet were at this time the leading voices of the non-Communist left in France. *Combat* was born of the Resistance; Bourdet had fought in it. They embodied the socialist idealism, the mystique of social progress and of a national regeneration which had been the characteristic note of the Liberation and which had been incorporated in the outline program of the National Council of the Resistance This was the optimistic faith in a New France to be characterized by social change. Bourdet was a Marxist, but his Marxism rang with the typical fervor of the French left proclaiming the mystique of socialism as an ethical reality, not as an economic one. He accepted the Marxist version of a class struggle—in modern France, class war is not a theory—but the atmosphere of the idealism found in *Combat* was essentially that derived from the assumption of a rational perfectibility in society, which is the historic frame of reference of the French left. In short, underlying the pessimism with which *Combat* viewed the evolution of international events, and of the gradual return of France to the tensions, and to the class relations, of the Third Republic was the optimism of Progress.

It is significant that the first suspicions of the general line of Western policy developed within the French left. Partly, this is a reflection of the tradition which, since 1918, had seen any opposition to the Soviet Union as "reactionary." Besides, what would be the good for France to align herself with the United States when about one-fifth of the population, and a considerably greater proportion of the crucial male element in the factories and in the army, sympathized with the opposing camp.[6] True, a significant proportion of these might be expected to serve France with patriotism if she were attacked, but others would be likely to follow their ingrained hostility towards the capitalist United States and to translate into action what they regarded as their class ties with the Soviet Union, either in active sabotage or at least in passive resistance. Thus only a policy of neutrality for France could bring about the unity of the French nation. Such were the views of a non-Communist neutralist.[7]

The idea that Communism acted as a magnet, drawing the attention of the non-Communist left to the "Fatherland of the Proletariat," undoubtedly contains an element of truth. Yet it will appear in this study that such a factor was a relatively minor one in the evolution of non-Communist opinion in France, and that essentially the attention of the non-Communist left was focused upon Paris and Washington. At the same time, it was true that the development of a neutralist attitude was an aspect of the mystique of Movement and of social change for part of the French left. Neutralism asserted that a policy of a neutral and "independent" France would provide a *tabula rasa* upon which a socialist social policy could be built. Thus neutralists considered as intimately related their views on the role of France in the struggle between East and West and their faith in the mystique of Progress.

We have seen within the intellectual circles of the non-Communist left the germination of the idea that France should pursue a foreign policy perhaps not inimical to, but certainly quite divorced from, the line of policy of the United States.[8] As long as such an attitude remained the monopoly of a small segment of the Paris intelligentsia, it might attract a great deal of attention and comment, but it would scarcely affect French policy, or be of more than academic interest to the United States. But if this small vocal minority should strike some chord evoking a mass response, some latent sentiment that arouses the deep fears of some major element of the population, then the situation would be very different.

The first neutralist charge had been that France should not align herself with the United States in the Atlantic Pact since she could not thereby achieve national security. It was a repeated theme of neutralist propaganda that Western defense plans, assuming the probability of final American victory, could only bring about the liberation of the ashes of Europe.[9] In later years, this view was incorporated in the charge that United States defense plans really called for a "peripheral" strategy of bases,[10] and considered Western Europe as expendable. The incident of the "Fechteler Report," cited in *Le Monde* as conclusive evidence that such was the American military strategy,[11] which was proven to be apocryphal but was nonetheless considered by neutralists as representing the "real" thoughts of American military planners,[12] was an instance of the neutralists' playing upon the fear of the insecurity of France in Western defense policy. The Atlantic alliance was pictured as a division of military responsibilities in which Europe would provide the cannon fodder for the infantry while the United States, holding the cost of the war to itself at a minimum,[13] would provide weapons and the more "aristocratic" air power.[14]

Thus not only would the social and political aspects of Western policy be disastrous to the hope of social progress in France, but its military consequences[15] would threaten the actual survival of the nation. In return, however, France would have to sacrifice her national independence.[16] The equipping and financing of the French army would pass into the hands of a foreign power.[17] Collaboration between two "excessively unequal partners"[18] would force the weaker to become a mere tool of the stronger. Thus France would become dependent on the United States and French policy would be a mere tool of American interests.[19]

In this aspect of the neutralist position, one sees an expression of French nationalism. It is a striking fact about the neutralists that they appealed specifically to the national instincts of Frenchmen and moved away, in fact if not in principle, from the internationalist appeal which had constituted the proudest attribute of the pre-war left. It is again the experience of France in the war which had made its mark. Partly there had been the failure of the *classes dirigeantes*[20] to defend the country effectively, partly there had been the natural emotional reaction of a traditionally patriotic people under an enemy occupation, partly there had been the feeling that the ideological betrayal of the French right to the autocracy of the enemy had left only the left as defenders of the nation and even of bourgeois democracy, and partly there had been the hope of a new, egalitarian and "social" France. A combination of all of these factors had produced during the last years of the war a patriotic fervor within a part of the left that appeared to confirm the principle on which Jaurès had wished to base the *Armée Nouvelle*.[21] The liberation period had witnessed a kind of *Union Sacrée* of the left, something which a quarter of a century earlier would have been regarded as a contradiction in terms. During the first years of the Fourth Republic once again the left took over the symbols of an ardent national sentiment.

This was the tendency, the mood, which reappeared in the neutralist criticism of the Western alliance as a limitation of the independence of France. The nationalism of the left which was voiced by the neutralists amounted essentially to a return to the Jacobin nationalism which had characterized the left in Revolutionary France. Its essential feature is a combining of nationalism with the mystique of Progress. The implicit affirmation of the nation as a primary value in the neutralist world view was to have major consequences in subsequent years.

The developing neutralist elements constituted essentially propaganda groups. They were not a political party, nor even several political parties; they had no direct political power and any pressure they might exert on policies could be only through public opinion. It follows that the nature of the vehicles of neutralist propaganda is a particularly important consideration to the study of neutralism itself. Conversely it is also true that neutralists came to control especially important organs of communication, as a result of which their effectiveness far exceeded their numbers.

Le Monde is more than just a newspaper.[22] It is the source of news and opinion that is read by the Paris upper-middle class, by the business man, the professional man, the government official and the intelligentsia. In other words, it is the afternoon daily in Paris which is read by the *classes dirigeantes.* Its comparatively small circulation—155,000—brings it into the nerve centers of French industry and the government bureaucracy. *Le Monde* is noted for its coverage of economic and financial news, for the quality of its coverage of national events, and of the reports of its foreign correspondents. And it is noted for its militant neutralism.

The foundation of *Le Monde's* neutralism was a basic distrust of the motives of the American government that led the paper to oppose American foreign policy.[23] When the United States talked about defense, *Le Monde* saw plans of aggression and "a phantom crusade against the U.S.S.R."[24] Implicit in this attitude was the basic psychological motivation of all neutralists: the charge that the execution of American plans would not produce a *defense* system at all[25] and that there was one inevitable outcome to the trend of American policy: War.[26]

Beginning in April, 1950, *Le Monde* published a major series of articles, significant because of the position and prestige of the man who had written them.[27] Indeed, Etienne Gilson was no firebrand radical. One of France's foremost Catholic scholars, he had served after the war on the Council of the Republic as a member of the *Mouvement Républicain Populaire,* the party which has been the most steadfast advocate of close collaboration with the United States and of the policy of European integration which the United States favors. It was natural that when a man in his position called for an "independent" French foreign policy, his statement would arouse considerable feeling in Paris and also in the U. S.[28]

Having first declared that a policy of French neutrality would not be a sign of national weakness,[29] Gilson went on to say that the Soviet Union wanted and needed peace.[30] Its alleged aggressiveness was a myth, else why had it not attacked now, before the West was rearmed? The real concern of the U.S.S.R. was the success of its Socialist experiment, and Communists were convinced that war was not necessary to their eventual triumph since capitalism would fall through its own disintegration. But, while Communists felt certain that peaceful coexistence offered them an assurance of eventual success, Gilson continued, they were also convinced that the capitalist world would try to save itself by the only means left at its disposal: the unleashing of a general war. Thus they would naturally regard any Western alliance as an aggressive act.[31]

Turning his attention to the United States, Gilson paid tribute to the historic, political, economic and cultural ties that united the two countries and disclaimed any desire of belittling the great debt France owed America for this country's aid. In terms of feelings of sympathy, and in respect to moral considerations, he added, France aligned herself wholeheartedly with the United States,[32] but it was now best for his own country to follow the very precedent America had set in previous wars, and to adopt an attitude of benevolent neutrality. And, Gilson continued, this course should be followed not in the desire of opposing American plans but as a policy which would prove in the long run to be in the best interests of the U. S. as well as of France. What good to the United States, in fact, would be an ally as reluctant and divided as France? Would not an independent France, resolved upon, and united in, its own defense against any aggressor be of greater value to America?[33] Thus Gilson hoped that in the long run, a policy of benevolent French neutrality would win the encouragement and support of the United States.[34]

Indeed, *Le Monde* added that it would be in America's own interest to give a guarantee of aid to a neutral France in the event of a communist aggression.[35] Then France, and Europe, could pursue an independent foreign policy and at the same time fall back in an emergency upon a unilateral reinsurance of their security.

Here was a rare example of the urge to have one's cake and eat it. Yet it should be noted that the tone of this form of neutralism was friendly to the United States. It expressed the ideological affinity of France with American democracy and it saw in French neutrality a policy that would be beneficial to the American people.

The development of opinions just discussed is a significant aspect of the evolution of neutralism in France. Neither Gilson nor *Le Monde* can be regarded as "left." Gilson was a Christian democrat, and the social philosophy of *Le Monde* can only be termed liberal (in the American use of the term). This is a far cry from the Marxist neutralism of Bourdet. On the other hand, it is also true that it involves a basic psychological-ideological response in common with the neutralist mood reflected in *Combat*: the mystique of Movement and social progress. By no means "left" within the range of French political opinions, *Le Monde* was left-of-center in the emotions to which it appealed,[36] and this fact set it off from the right-center that was coming to resume increasing control of French political life. Though the concrete manifestations in social and economic policies are very different in the two papers, the sense of emotional dedication in the editorials of *Combat* and in many of the leading articles of *Le Monde* indicates a similar faith in the egalitarian evolution of French society and in the mystique of perfectibility that grew out of the Resistance, which in fact had been the common parent of both.

Within a few months of the publication of Gilson's articles affirming that the Communists did not think of achieving their objectives through war, the attention of the world was dramatically focused upon the Far East as Communist armies crossed the frontier of South Korea. More striking than the outbreak of hostilities were the reverses suffered by United States military forces and the great blow to America's military prestige, and at the same time the critical intensification of the U. S. rearmament program. One immediate result of the crisis in France was that some of the neutralists now rallied to America's defense. *Le Monde* published a number of articles defending the principle of collective security.[37] Jean-Jacques Servan-Schreiber, one of the paper's better-known writers and at that time a determined opponent of its neutralist editorial policy—he was subsequently to resign over the issue, and was still later converted to neutralism himself—called for an effective move by France towards an Atlantic federation.[38] Articles in *Combat,* comparing the "relative liberty" in the United States with the "total lack of liberty" in the U.S.S.R.,"[39] condemned neutralism[40] and insisted upon the necessity of an "Atlantic policy" aimed at a strong, integrated defense.[41]

But the long-term effect of the Korean campaign, especially as it dragged on inconclusively for months, was to intensify neutralist fears of the effectiveness of an alliance with the United States[42] while it simultaneously increased their apprehensions of the consequences of America's intensive rearmament,[43] and even more of the changing mood the situation was producing in American public opinion. The fear of a bellicose America provoking a new world war was greatly intensified. The editors of *Combat* again broke decisively with Western policy and reverted to an uncompromising neutralism, a neutralism directed against the new war danger from the United States.[44] Gilson, praising the pacifism of the American people, said this fact in itself would produce an irrestible temptation in the United States, when the country had reached a maximum level of militarization, to get things over with once and for all.[45]

Thus the neutralist propagandists could play both ends against the middle: American military weakness made Western policy a threat to the security of France, American military strength increased the dangers of a nuclear catastrophe which no country, and certainly not France, could survive. The decision of President Truman to go ahead with the manufacture of a hydrogen bomb was regarded as an ominous portent of the chances of European survival in a world war.

Korea seemed to offer a dramatic confirmation of the neutralist charge that Western policy would result in another cycle for France of occupation and liberation—the liberation of a wasteland. In Korea, "France had had the unexpected opportunity of witnessing a sort of dress-rehearsal of what might have happened in Europe had the Russian divisions moved West."[46] The only hope for France lay in the "peaceful coexistence of the two spheres."[47] Now the neutralists had a motto, a badge: peaceful coexistence. It had the advantage that as an ideal few people in France would disagree with it.[48]

In fact, the form of neutralism that has been described in the preceding pages was coming to an end.[49] In a sense, the years

1949 and early 1950 might be called the period of Gilsonian neutralism, of a neutralism that still inclined towards the United States. Up to this point, neutralists generally had demanded that France pursue a policy not directed against the United States, but intended rather to influence America's own policy in a different direction.[50] Gilson himself had stressed the "affinity" between the United States and France; he had expressed his appreciation of America's basic objectives, and had underlined the fact that he believed his suggestions would benefit the United States. Gilson, and the editors of *Le Monde,* had not doubted that even a policy of French neutrality must rest, in final analysis, on the military power of the United States and on the assurance of this country's aid in the remote eventuality of a Soviet attack upon Europe.[51] Such ideas represent a form of neutralism that was essentially still pro-American.[52]

The "bombing of unarmed villages," the use of napalm in Korea, these revealed the true nature of the strategy of the United States high command. Hiroshima and Korea, or Rotterdam and Guernica, were they essentially different? Why were the war criminals of only the defeated powers subject to international justice? This is "Sirius," pen name of Hubert Beuve-Méry, editor of *Le Monde,* expressing his opinion in the fall of 1950.[53] In the same period Charles Favrel, reporting from Korea, was describing American soldiers and airmen as barbarians, indifferent to atrocities they were deliberately commiting upon the civilian population.[54] A year later, Favrel, in an "Open Letter to Mr. Smith,"[55] wrote about the "saddening spectacle of an inhuman nation mercilessly seeking revenge for a humiliating loss of face," all because Americans had "determined the extermination of a people, guilty of having witnessed the G. I. in retreat." At this point, a new bitterness pervaded the statements of neutralist opinions.[56] *Le Monde* adopted an attitude vis-a-vis both the U. S. and the U.S.S.R. perhaps described as "a plague on both your houses." To be sure, this does not mean the paper became pro-Communist, either in internal or foreign policy; it does mean that *Le Monde's* position had shifted from a "pro-American neutralism" to a "neutral neutralism."[57] Thus there had now developed in

France, beyond and apart from Communist circles, an attack on the moral qualifications of the U.S.,[58] not merely an attempt to redirect the basic line of American policy from within the alliance. The existence of any ideological justification for the policy of the Western powers now was brought into question.[59]

It was again to the changed international picture after 1950 that this new situation was due. Thus, an aspect of the N.A.T.O. countries' accelerated rearmament program that was especially apt to arouse the concern of the neutralist left was the effect this situation would be likely to have on social and economic conditions in France.[60] The problem was not an academic one. The right was increasingly resuming its position of prewar power from which the Liberation had seemed to dethrone it. François Mauriac once commented that the dream of "good elections," of which the *bien-pensants* had dreamt in vain during his youth, had finally been achieved under the Fourth Republic. The marked right-wing tendency in the U.S. at this time seemed to be a parallel evolution related to the evolution of government in France. Thus the non-Communist left was convinced that an increasingly conservative American opinion would exert its considerable influence in supporting the right-wing elements, and the social status quo, in Europe.

This view tied in directly with the mystique of Progress of the neutralists of the left and of the left-center. Thus the development of Western policy and of France's relations with the United States was fitted in ever more, psychologically, with the internal *immobilisme* of the French government. The result was a composite mixture of irrational notions which lumped together the social conservatism symbolized by the Pinay government, the ethical standards in American politics of McCarthyism, and the allegedly increased tax burden for Western defense imposed upon the French worker. Right-wing Republicanism in the United States and the increasing power of the classical Party of Order in France provided apparently inter-connected targets for the economic, social, and above all the ideological hostility of the tenants of Movement, from the non-Communist left to the left-center of *Le Monde*.[61] Franco's police-state, wrote

Marcel Gimont in *Combat,* would be "the ideal Atlantic state . . . the model all of us are approaching."[62]

In this rightward evolution of American policy and its effect upon France, neutralists of the left asserted, the French worker would suffer the greatest hardships.[63] He would be forced to bear an economic burden for defense[64] which, if the differences between his standard of living and that of the American worker were given their full weight, was unjustly heavy.[65] The shift in American foreign aid from the economic basis of the European Recovery Program to the military emphasis[66] of Mutual Security, the increasing size of defense subsidies[67] all appeared to confirm the ideological fears of the French left-center and left. They also evoked the basic criticism that overemphasis on the purely military aspects of defense proceeded from an error of judgement which would have disastrous consequences upon the very democracy it was intended to save. In its emotional anti-communism, neutralists charged, the United States had failed to see that some of the most appropriate weapons against communism were in the domains of social and economic progress.[68] This neutralist criticism of Western policies was subsequently to produce echoes from points far removed from neutralist opinion, and the contention was to prove one of the most popular ideas neutralists had come up with.

As concerns the effectiveness of defense against communism, the neutralist left proclaimed that an exaggerated rearmament policy which further depressed the standard of living of European labor would be self-defeating. It would substantiate Communist propaganda attributing the lot of the French working class to America's "war policy," and it would create new frictions between the United States and the hard-pressed non-Communist labor elements of Southern Europe. In fact, such friction appeared inevitable to neutralists from the evolution of American opinion. The United States would now cast aside its mask and revert to its true role of weighting the scales in favor of capitalism and free enterprise which "in Europe permits the strong to exploit the weak."[69]

The increasing bitterness in the neutralist tone and the increasing tendency to make of America, or at least of the policy of the American government, the scapegoat for the *immobilisme* of France, and to see in American support of the Party of Order in France the major obstacle to the mystique of Progress, brought into prominence as vehicles of neutralist opinion a number of non-Communist publications that were distinctly "left." Generally, they were sympathetic to some form of socialism,[70] and they were united—despite their many differences—by their hatred of capitalist society.[71] At a time when the social conservatism of the French government, the shift towards Republicanism in the United States, and Western policies in the Cold War were seen as threads of the same cloth, organs of socialist opinion found it easy to believe that what America was defending, under the cloak of liberty, was capitalist exploitation.[72] To such groups, the scales were automatically tipped against the United States.[73]

For example, the intellectual, predominantly Catholic-socialist monthly *Esprit* which in 1951 had still reflected a "neutral neutralism,"[74] published an article some two years later which said that America's campaign against communism was an outgrowth of its frustration over the inability to "sell" the American way of life to the rest of the world.[75] Another article in the same review added the comment that "American optimism lives at the price of too many deceptions . . . and by the enslavement of too many people" to appeal to Europe.[76] As mentioned earlier, one of the marks of neutralism now came to be the questioning of the moral qualifications of the United States.

From the left's characterization of American policy as concerned only with the defense of the capitalist system against social revolution, it followed that present world tension was interpreted as the result of an attempt of the American imperialist bloc at world domination.[77] Thus the United States, having reached economic maturity, was described as having little room for internal expansion[78] and was consequently engaged, according to classical capitalist procedure, in economic imperialism[79]—for example in Guatemala.[80]

Cited as a primary instance of the economic imperialism of the United States was this country's opposition to East-West trade, and particularly the restrictions imposed by the Battle Act.[81]

The United States was pictured as preventing normal economic exchange which would have provided some additional revenue for the strained economy of France[82] and which even might lead to a *détente* in East-West relations.[83] Furthermore, the United States was seen as consciously intensifying the economic dependence of West European nations upon America[84] in an effort to control their markets[85] In this way, American imperialism was making the countries of Western Europe into mere satellites,[86] first economically and militarily, then politically and culturally.[87] It was the expansive nature of American imperialism that was now leading the United States to seek world domination.

The economy of the U.S.S.R., on the contrary, was expanding within the Soviet Union's own borders. The Communist world was creating an integrated planned economy on a vast international scale while the West was still at the level of "free enterprise" or of economic planning limited to a national framework. While it was France's duty to try to break down the system of two competing world blocs, it was also her duty to align herself generally with "the camp of socialism."[88]

In this form, neutralism has come so far from its original position that far from being "benevolent neutralism" towards the United States, or even "neutral neutralism," it had emerged as anti-American neutralism.[89] It was the United States which was now regarded as the *primary* threat to world peace.[90]

More typical of the non-Communist left than the Christian socialism which dominated *Esprit* was the attitude of the new weekly *L'Observateur* (currently *France-Observateur*). The very fact of the appearance of this magazine was in itself a landmark in the history of French neutralism. In 1950, as a consequence of a disagreement with Henry Smadja, the owner of *Combat,* Claude Bourdet had been forced to resign his editorship of the paper. A few months later, he was editor of the new weekly of strongly Marxist tendencies, the program of which could be summed up in one word: neutralism.

While the group of *Esprit* had sought, in the main, to weld together a Marxian analysis and a Christian sense of charity, *L'Observateur* expressed the mystique of revolution in a more traditional pattern for the French left as a materialist pseudo-rationalism. It has already been observed that the assumption underlying this attitude was the idea of perfectibility, the mystique of Progress. As viewed from the perspective of *L'Observateur,* the interconnection between the defense policy of Western nations and all those things which a Marxist conception of progress assailed had become an unbreakable tie;[91] thus it would be possible to achieve the latter only by a complete break with the former.

Indeed in the version of *L'Observateur,* the neutralist interpretation of world events would lean towards the Communists' view.[92] Significantly, various articles called for the formation of a Popular Front, based on a neutralist program.[93]

Gradually, the tone of *L'Observateur* came to be scarcely distinguishable from the bitter anti-Americanism of Jean-Paul Sartre's famous literary monthly, *Les Temps Modernes.* From 1952 until the crisis in Hungary, Sartre aligned himself unequivocally with the Communist bloc.[94] Neutralism for him was the antechamber of the Communist party. We are now in the world of the *Progressistes* and the various movements rotating in the powerful gravitational pull of communism. We have come back to our point of departure: the neutralism of Cot.

Passing from one form of neutralism to another, we have seen that a chain of individual ideological links exists connecting the "bourgeois neutralism" of *Le Monde,* which had itself become increasingly bitter and increasingly "left," to the Socialist neutralism of *Combat,* connecting the left-Catholic neutralism of *Esprit* to the extreme socialist neutralism of *L'Observateur* and on, through Sartre and *Les Temps Modernes,* to the openly pro-Communist neutralism of the *Progressistes.*

This is a convenient place to pause for a moment in the consideration of neutralism and to turn to the Communist attitude towards these developments.[95] The French Communist party approached the question of neutralism on two different levels and with two radically different attitudes. From the point of view of doctrine, the party naturally attacked a movement that claimed to be neutral. How could one be neutral towards crime; how could one be neutral on the issue of war and peace?[96]

Pierre Courtade declared that the neutralist program represented the "minimum demands" of active aggression formulated by Washington, but that neutralists nonetheless were part of the war camp itself.[97] This aspect of the Communist reaction to neutralism was undoubtedly motivated by the party's fear of a French Titoism and by its desire to keep Communists from associating with movements that not only felt free to criticize the policy of the Soviet Union,[98] but also could not be controlled easily by the party itself.

On the other hand, the anti-American tone of much of neutralist propaganda, the fact that the neutralists and Communists campaigned on the same side against American influence in France, against the war in Indochina, against American policy in the Far East and against EDC all induced a certain Communist sympathy for neutralism. But since the party could not voice such an opinion officially, it left the expression of similar views to its affiliated organizations and allies, for example the *Union Progressiste* and the *Combattants de la Paix*. It is here that we find the link between left-wing neutralism and the Communist party.[99] Thus while the party officially castigated all those, including neutralists, who were not actually within the Communist orbit, it also regarded the neutralism of its allies like Pierre Cot and Jean Paul Sartre as an idea that might appeal to the unenlightened and bring them closer to the "peace camp."[100] With the development of the Soviet Union's peace platform and the French Communist party's campaign for a Popular Front, this second aspect of the Communists' attitude became by far the predominant one.

While it cannot be denied that the anti-American campaign of the French Communist party played its part over the years in influencing the development of neutralism, the general impression is that neutralist opinions evolved essentially in response to developments in the United States, to the evolution of American foreign policy, and to the latter's effect on France and on the chances of world peace.[101] In other words, except perhaps in the case of Sartre, there seems to have been very little conscious attraction towards communism among French neutralist circles; it was essentially an evolution against the United States[102] and what this country seemed to represent.[103] Simplifying to the very limit, it might be said that intellectual left-wing neutralism in France responded to the evolution of the United States by becoming synonymous with anti-Americanism.

The evolution of American political attitudes which was regarded by the neutralists of the left and left-center as such a threat to their faith in social progress was nowhere more sharply drawn than in the Rosenberg case. Opinions varied from those who considered the punishment excessive to those who considered the verdict a crime:[104] "The Rosenbergs are innocent."[105]

While the Rosenberg case permitted the moral indignation of the neutralists, and their questioning of the moral fitness of the United States to lead Western nations, to reach at a moment of great emotional intensity a wider and more sympathetic audience than they had on any previous issue, in the long run it was still the effect of the temper in America upon the United States' foreign policies which was the matter of lasting concern among neutralists. One of the characteristics of the neutralism of the left and left-center, as an expression of the mystique of Progress, was to see various manifestations of the right in the world as fitting a general pattern. Thus the moral criticism of the United States, inherent in the attitude on the Rosenberg case, was part of a pattern in the neutralist world view into which McCarthyism fitted perfectly—was it not plausible to believe that the McCarthyite hysteria[106] had produced a miscarriage of justice?—and this in turn fitted in with American foreign policy, with N.A.T.O. and frantic rearmament, and with the evolution of France. The danger of McCarthyism in Washington[107] or New York was the danger of McCarthyism in Paris.[108]

In the various aspects of what neutralists considered to be a general phenomenon, it was the reactionary nature of American foreign policy which posed the greatest danger to France because its logical outcome could only be war. Commenting on the famous issue of *Collier's* magazine of October 27, 1951 entitled "Preview of the War We Do Not Want," one neutralist wrote:

> Thus it is no longer necessary for the potential enemy to attack in order to precipitate war, it is sufficient that he refuse to change his views and policies! . . .
>
> In the last analysis, the twenty-three Americans who have revealed to us their dreams and have concocted this special issue of *Collier's,* have rendered a singular service to the men of our Continent. Those of us who had forgotten that a gulf separated American and European ways of thought suddenly realize that this gulf has only widened in recent years. Those who saw only the power of the United States suddenly discover its weakness. And those of us who had the greatest confidence in its peaceful intentions are seized by an irresistible urge to shout to these sleep-walkers that it is time for them to wake up and forget their terrible dreams.[109]

In two areas particularly did the neutralists consider the dangers to peace inherent in American foreign policy to be critical; those were Germany and the Far East.[110] It was in the Far East that the charges of American provocation to war were confirmed for neutralists[111] and appeared even to many non-neutralists to have acquired a foundation in fact. The name of MacArthur became identified with the worst apprehensions as to the intentions of American policy,[112] just as McCarthy soon after came to stand as the symbol for their worst fears about American opinion—an analogy that was all the more convenient for the French who did not grasp the different spellings of "Mac."

American support of Syngman Rhee,[113] ominous suggestions in American newspapers about the bombing of Manchuria, talk of American support for an invasion of the Chinese mainland by Chiang Kai-shek pointed towards the gravest danger: the launching by the United States of a preventive war.[114] American generals in the Far East must be restrained,[115] and Americans at home must be brought back to their senses.[116]

In this view of things,[117] it was the United States and not the Soviet Union which was opposed to any compromise,[118] which stood in the way of peace;[119] it was the hypnotic power of the American's dream of a "roll-back" of communism[120] that, unless the Americans were to be held back by their European allies,[121] made war inevitable.[122]

> If some day things take a turn for the worse, will not France, in the terrible over-simplification of total war, find herself reduced to fighting side by side with Syngman Rhee, Chiang Kai-shek or Franco . . . and some other war criminal overlooked at Nurenberg or Tokyo. All this, of course, in the name of Christ or of Liberty . . .[123]

While American policy in the Far East seemed to neutralists to be fanning the fires of international conflict, it was the United States' policy toward Germany which was seen as threatening France with a whole series of dire consequences, from economic vassalage to war itself. It was American policy toward Germany which was seen as affecting most directly the daily life of the Frenchman, his prosperity and his security, and as touching many Frenchmen's most sensitive nerve.[124]

As viewed from the perspective of French neutralists, United States policy toward Germany consisted in making of the former enemy power the pivot of America's alliance with Europe, or even one end of a Washington-Bonn axis.[125] This policy implied the return of German industry to its prewar dominance and American support of Adenauer's conservative ideology against any social-democratic movements in Europe. Above all, it implied German rearmament.[126]

From one point of view, the European Coal and Steel Community and the European Defense Community were steps towards the unification of Europe, an ideal for which there existed wide sympathy in France. But in the context of the international situation they appeared more like, and in fact they were, military measures of the Atlantic powers against the Communist bloc, or for a "little Europe,"[127] mere fragment of the real one. In this context, they were regarded by neutralists as a positive bar to real unification,[128] or at least a distortion of it for the benefit of American military strategy. The United States considers the integration of Europe only as "a merger of uniforms" complained Marcel Gimont.[129] France must not participate in what would be essentially a military coalition against the Soviet Union.[130] What these projects could not disguise was that they would place France at the mercy of Germany.[131]

Then came the release of Krupp by the American authorities —the munitions king released from jail and given back his private fortune! It seemed to symbolize American support of those who had supported Hitler.[132] Seen in the perspective of the French left, once more all the pieces of the puzzle fell into place: the rightest evolution of American opinion and the support of reactionary elements abroad, American military strategy and the support of German militarists, German hegemony in EDC and American support of key industrial figures in the Third Reich. Thus, as the lines of different objects in a picture converge upon a single point of perspective, so the various elements of American policy in Europe were pictured as converging upon the rearmament of Germany.

> We shall see to what extent it is possible to create [a united] Europe with a rearmed Germany, the Germany of Adenauer, of the Vatican and the Wehrmacht, studded with former Nazi officials.[133]

In its most direct sense, the fear of an armed Germany was the fear of a new invasion of France.[134] But this was only one of many dangers, and one of many hated implications. The thought of French *poilus* serving under former Nazi officers,[135] perhaps the very ones that had occupied France, was obviously galling to any French patriot. With the military training of German youths the militant character of old Germany, never far below the surface,[136] would be reawakened.[137] With a powerful war industry and a new army, only thinly disguised by EDC,[138] the specter of pan-Germanism would reappear.[139] This would be the critical moment for Europe and the world:[140] either Germany would try to reconquer her Eastern provinces,[141] thus provoking a new world war, or, finding that the other side now had more to offer, she would take herself and her new army into the other camp.[142] In either case, for France and for Europe it would be the end.

All the reasons advanced for opposing EDC were reasons for opposing the policy of the foreign government most vigorously urging the project.[143]

In the various arguments advanced against EDC, one can observe that the neutralists' ideological opposition to American policy was compounded by a different but equally powerful mystique, derived from different roots and appealing to a different set of emotions, which was now superimposed on their existing motives of antagonism: national sentiment.[144] The result was a combination of psychological factors of explosive intensity. To the neutralist, sentimentally linked to the Resistance—and virtually all of them were—the implications of an armed Germany in any form aroused passions which virtually eliminated any possibility of rational argument. For many on the right and on the left, the international circumstances meant that anti-German sentiment was translated into a more bitter hostility toward the United States.

The result of the convergence of left-wing ideological opposition and opposition born of national sentiment was a kind of Jacobin nationalism which considered the fight for Progress and for national "independence" as synonymous. The significance of this transition should become clear when we consider the transformation of neutralism from a set of policies ardently defended by small circles of left-wing intellectuals, and assuming world-wide importance only in the narcissistic columns they wrote for each other's benefit (*Le Monde* is a major exception to this generalization) into ideas and emotions which had appeal to at least a potential mass audience.

* * * * * * * *

Esprit, Temps Modernes or *L'Observateur,* these were publications that reached small circles of intellectuals. Even *Le Monde* with its 155,000 readers was not a mass-circulation paper like *Le Figaro,* and *L'Aurore* with almost 500,000 readers each,[145] and most of the readers of *Le Monde* were not neutralists.[146] In other words, neutralism began as an attitude, as a frame of mind, limited to certain elements of the Paris intelligentsia. As long as it remained a movement of this type, it might make a lot of noise, but it would have little significance.

When the national elections of June, 1951 were coming up, a lot of attention was focused on the neutralists. They had been proclaiming their doctrines loudly for two years—had they struck any response among large audiences? Did they speak for a mass following?

For the electoral campaign, the neutralists of the left had elected to give battle only in a terrain favorable to themselves: Paris. A number of splinter groups of left-wing Socialist tendencies, Christian leftists such as Paul Boulet, Charles d'Aragon and Jacques Madaule, and the Abbé Pierre Grouès, better known today as the Abbé Pierre of the Communities of Emmaus,[147] Marxists of the *Union Progressiste* variety,[148] assorted Trotskyites and other leftists had formed the *Centre d'Action des Gauches Indépendantes*.[149] The C.A.G.I. platform included socialist economic reforms but its primary emphasis, and the tie that held its various factions together, was neutralism.[150] Here was the New Left, not tied to Moscow yet opposed to the war policy of Washington. No C.A.G.I. candidate was elected.[151]

In 1951 it seemed that neutralism had passed by the political life of France without leaving so much as a scar. The question, therefore, arises: would the neutralists eventually be able to effectuate a meeting with a mass segment of public opinion, with some latent feeling on the part of a significant proportion of the population?

In the summer of 1953, a poll on French attitudes toward the U.S. by the French Institute of Public Opinion was published.[152] It indicated widespread sympathy among Frenchmen not only for the United States and for Americans, but for most of the aims of American policy as well. Nonetheless, while 60% were reported to be in favor of maintaining the alliance with the U.S.—though with the reservation that France enjoy greater freedom—ten percent favored an alliance with the U.S.S.R. and thirty percent advocated a policy of complete neutrality. When asked whether they approved of the alliance in its present form, twenty-eight percent were hesitant, thirty-six percent listed themselves as in favor, and thirty-six percent as opposed.[153]

Thus the sentiment for French neutrality in principle could not be considered negligible.[154] While much of this support undoubtedly came from Communist sympathizers—it is interesting that even a majority of these did not favor an alliance with the U.S.S.R.[155]—the proportion of the opposition indicated that it went considerably beyond that element of the population.[156] By 1953, it could be said that there existed a considerable undercurrent of neutralist sentiment.

It is in this context that the issue of EDC assumed major importance for the status of neutralism.[157] We have seen that the proposal of a European army which would mean the limitation of French sovereignty in favor of an integrated community[158] that, it was widely believed, would be dominated by Germany, touched many a Frenchman on the very sensitive issue of his anti-German prejudice.[159] Here the ideological opposition of neutralists to the policy of the United States was supplemented by the appeal to a fundamental French reflex: nationalism.[160]

Thus it is not surprising to find neutralists making contact on the issue of opposition to EDC with various other political tendencies in France. When Edouard Herriot, for example, openly advocated some of the most cherished goals of the neutralists,[161] the least that can be said is that neutralism had become politically "respectable." Putting the situation another way, it has been seen that the general movement of neutralist groups had been towards the left. Now, on the issue of EDC, the neutralists also made contact with the main body of opinion on their right.

An illustration of this development was the appearance of a new weekly periodical which was definitely left-of-center, but considerably to the right of Bourdet and his group. In fact, *L'Express*[162] manifested a form of neutralism that takes one back to Gilson and to *Le Monde* of 1950 for its mood and attitudes.[163] Bevan's neutralist program, which at one time had come to France via the columns of *L'Observateur,* now came in through the pages of *L'Express.*[164] Jean-Jacques Servan-Schreiber completed his wanderings in and out of neutralism by contributing neutralist opinions to the new periodical of which he was one of the chief editors. François Mauriac split his personality between editorial duties to the conservative *Figaro* and a frequently bristling page in the new leftist weekly. Above all, it was the dynamism, the intense mystique of Progress and Movement, which for a time came to be associated with the New Left around Pierre Mendès-France, that found its most ardent support in *L'Express*. The fact that this new political coalition also received, in the spring of 1954, the endorsement of *Le Monde* and *Combat* completes the circle.

At the same time, the moderate neutralism of *L'Express* went back to Gilsonist neutralism in the sense that it was not fundamentally hostile to the U.S. It was even prepared to support Western policy provided that certain fundamental changes in it in the direction of neutralist demands were to be made, particularly the undertaking of serious negotiations toward a peaceful settlement with Moscow. Peaceful co-existence was a phrase that frequently appeared in the pages of *L'Express*.

In yet another sense was *L'Express* a symbol of a new synthesis of the old neutralists of the left and various elements on their right: it presented the opinions of some of the leading followers of General de Gaulle. In the next chapter, we shall see how after the collapse of the RPF, the rump of the Gaullists evolved to a point where they had merged with their nationalism demands for social and economic change and a new political spirit which brought them closer to the moderate elements among the neutralists. We have already seen that the neutralists for their part had combined their ideological opposition to Western policy with a keener national sentiment of their own.[165] The result was a striking rapprochement between these two previously hostile groups,[166] a rapprochement symbolized by the contributions of Gaullists like Jacques Soustelle and Gaston Palewski to *L'Express*.

The neutralists of the left had thus come to effectuate a junction with the nationalists of the right. Moreover, the question of EDC had given the neutralists an opportunity of playing upon certain emotions which at last struck a responsive chord in a mass segment of the population. A junction between the militant, professional neutralists of the intellectual circles and a powerful, latent current of popular opinion now was possible.

The spring and summer of 1954 formed a critical period for France. It saw the climax of two conflicts in which the neutralists had been most violently opposed to American policy: that over central Europe and that over the Far East. Of all the various issues neutralists had raised, it was their conflict with American policies in these two areas that they had regarded as most critical and as involving the most basic of their complaints. It was over these conflicts that they had exerted their most intensive propaganda efforts. And consequently it was in these two cases that the outcome, by proving them indirectly to have been "right" or "wrong," would constitute a major victory or a major defeat.

In Indo-China, the military disaster which the neutralists had long predicted[167] became a fact and the negotiations they had long demanded became a necessity. However, such negotiations could be undertaken only in a definite break with the Far Eastern policy of the United States which the neutralists had so violently attacked as a provocation to general war. For months, neutralists, who had always opposed the Indo-China conflict on ideological grounds, had found in American opposition to a negotiated peace with the Communists another case of American war-mongering in line with the old, hated policy of General MacArthur. They demanded that the French government go ahead with negotiations with Ho Chi Minh despite the opposition of the United States.[168] When the break finally came at Geneva,[169] neutralists added that although the United States had set the example of a negotiated peace in Korea,[170] now that others were engaged in the fighting, it wanted the war to continue.[171]

The position defended by the neutralists won out: an agreement with the Vietminh was accepted, not because the neutralists had demanded it but because there existed no other workable alternative for France. Yet the fact remained: the government of Mendès-France had followed a policy in direct conflict on a major issue with that of the United States.[172]

On this issue, events had proven the neutralists right; a new government had felt itself obliged to act in accordance with the neutralist position. The neutralists found themselves moving with the mainstream of the new political current. *They had found a mass-audience.*

It appears as a coincidence of history that after years of delay, two of the main issues of foreign policy confronting the French were decided within the space of a few weeks. In fact, the Premier of a government which was seeking a "new" direction[173] wished, having seen "one abscess cleared," for good or bad, to see the same of the other one. In mid-August, the French National Assembly took up the final debate on the ratification of EDC. Few, if any of the actors involved underestimated the importance of the occasion. A negative decision would commit France to rejection of one of the main objectives of American strategy, indeed of Western policy. This would be no mere academic opposition; it would be an overt act which, everyone knew, could not fail to produce a violent shock on the U.S. government. For months both sides had explained that this decision would be the crucial one for the future of France; there could be no minimizing of the results now.

For a few days the Palais Bourbon, as in an earlier epoch, was the center of international attention; the tenor of the debate was followed with anxiety by American diplomats, although it was not really believed the treaty could be rejected. One by one, the leading opponents of a European army went to the rostrum: nationalist generals of the right, Gaullists, heroes of the Resistance, anti-Germans, Communists, neutralists, the Chairman of the Committee on Foreign Affairs, Edouard Herriot.[174] Procedural matters came up, and the debate shifted from principles to points of order.[175] But the atmosphere grew more somber. Meanwhile, the President of the Council, Mendès-France sat at his bench in a neutral silence which thinly disguised his contempt.[176] The vote came on August 30th. On a point of order, the National Assembly buried EDC.[177]

* * * * * * * *

An extraordinary set of circumstances had produced an extraordinary result. Among the deputies who voted for the

Aumeran resolution,[178] which had killed the European army before it was born, a significant proportion were not inclined to neutralism in any of its forms, quite apart from the Communists who had contributed a decisive share of the negative votes. As for public opinion, it contained a plurality that favored the defeated project.[179]

Thus, this was not a "neutralist victory"; but it was a victory for neutralists. They had made EDC the central point of their criticisms; EDC had been defeated. They had taken a major part in the campaign, they must share in the credit and the blame. Many of the basic criticisms of Western policy which initially had been stated and defended by the neutralists and which had formed the substance of their propaganda were now repeated in the views of political groups that were not neutralist.[180] In other words, the neutralists had influenced the general atmosphere of French life, the climate in which attitudes on international questions were formed. They had succeeded in spreading a note of distrust about Western aims, an undercurrent of criticism of the motives of American policy in Europe, and a desire for an understanding with the Soviet Union, that went far beyond the relatively restricted confines of the neutralist groups themselves.[181] Where once these ideas had left neutralists isolated among the non-Communist elements in France, they now provided the links which put them in contact with various political forces. In this far more than in particular decisions did neutralism have a major influence upon France.[182]

Above all, the defeat of EDC had marked, within the general coalescence of oppositions,[183] the convergence of the two most important elements of a neutralist attitude and psychology: the ideology of Progress of the left, the mystique of Nationalism of the right.

The continuation of this story belongs in the next chapter. It is sufficient to say here that the combination proved to be highly unstable—that too is inherent in its nature. At this stage, the significant fact is that the combination had been achieved, that it could be achieved. It had left its mark in the history of France. But France, after all, is only our test case.

Footnotes

1. I. William Zartman, *De la Résistance à la Révolution: Postwar French Neutralism,* Yale University thesis, 1956, p. ii. Mr. Zartman's thorough and interesting discussion of French neutralism is the most important study available on this subject. It will be seen that on a number of points, his analysis differs from the present writer's treatment. In this volume, all citations of Mr. Zartman's work refer of necessity to the manuscript version.

2. Claude Bourdet, "Beaucoup de colombes," *Combat,* (Paris) April 20, 1949, p. 3.

3. Bertil Svahnstrom, "La neutralité suédoise: refuge égoiste ou première pierre de l'Europe," *Combat,* January 17, 1949, p. 3. B. Svahnstrom, "On ne peut à la fois créer une Fédération Européenne et adherer au Pacte Atlantique," *Loc. cit.,* January 18, 1949, p. 3. B. Svahnstrom, "La France détient la clé des problèmes allemand et européen," *Loc. cit.,* January 19, 1949, p. 3.

4. Claude Bourdet, "Les constatations de M. Thorez," *Combat,* February 24, 1949, p. 3.

5. Etienne Gilson, "Querelle de mots," *Le Monde,* (Paris) August 23, 1950.

6. See also: Jean-William Lapierre, "La neutralité française: utopie ou solution," *Esprit,* (Paris) March, 1951, pp. 375-92 [383-4]. Jean-Baptiste Duroselle, Alfred Grosser and Maurice Megret, *French Opinion and the United States,* pp. 28-9, states that it is among the younger age groups in France that the highest proportion of negative comments about the United States and the greatest resentment of American influence are to be found.

7. Etienne Gilson, "Le labyrinthe," *Le Monde,* August 24, 1950. Sirius, "Les chemins de la paix," *Loc. cit.,* April 4, 1951. Claude Bourdet, "Les constatations de M. Thorez," *Combat,* February 24, 1949, p. 3. "Un double danger" (signed "Combat"), *Loc. cit.,* September 10, 1951.

8. Claude Bourdet, "Beaucoup de colombes," *Combat,* April 20, 1949, p. 3. Maurice Duverger, "Pax Europeana," *Le Monde,* December 13, 1950.

9. "De la guerre froide à la vraie guerre," *Le Monde,* February 10, 1950. "Esquisses d'une politique," Pt. IV: "La paix sans communisme," *Loc. cit.,* June 12, 1951.

10. Jean Fabiani, "Mendicité ou indépendance," *Combat,* October 12, 1952. Marcel Gimont, " La défense de l'Europe," *Loc. cit.,* February 27, 1951. Jean-Jacques Servan-Schreiber, "Les plans des Américains," *Le Monde,* November 5, 1953.

11. "Un rapport de l'Amiral Fechteler au National Security Council," *Le Monde,* May 10, 1952, p. 3. See also: "La Méditerranée, enjeu de la rivalité Anglo-Américaine," *Combat,* May 12, 1952.

12. "Le Rapport Fechteler n'a rien 'révélé,'" *Les Temps Modernes,* (Paris) July, 1952, pp. 164-9. Gilles Martinet, "Le Rapport Fechteler," *L'Observateur politique, économique et littéraire,* (Paris) May 15, 1952, p. 10. This publication appeared later for a short time under the title *L'Observateur d'Aujourd'hui,* and is currently published as *France-Observateur.* Henceforth, it will referred to in this work simply as *L'Observateur.*

13. Bertil Svahnstrom, "Le Pacte Atlantique vise-t-il à déplacer en Europe une guerre que les U.S.A. ne veulent pas mener en Alaska?," *Combat,* March 23, 1949, p. 3.

14. Jean Fabiani, "Solutions 'réalistes,'" *Combat,* October 18, 1950. J. Fabiani, "Mendicité ou indépendance," *Loc. cit.,* October 12, 1952. For a similar concept applied to Asia, see *L'Express'* report of: General Van Fleet, "Comment vaincre le communisme," *L'Express* (Paris), May 2, 1954, p. 6.

15. H. de Galard, "Le réarmement des Etats-Unis n'est pas celui de l'Europe," *L'Observateur,* August 14, 1952, pp. 6-8.

16. "Un double danger" (signed "Combat"), *Combat,* September 10, 1951.

17. "Double danger" (signed "Combat"), *Combat,* September 14, 1951.

18. Sirius, "Une oeuvre virile," *Le Monde,* January 31, 1951. Thomas Balogh, "L'Europe sous la menace d'une crise aux Etats-Unis," *L'Observateur,* October 8, 1953, pp. 12-3.

19. Claude Bourdet, "Fin de l'Europe," *L'Observateur,* April 20, 1950, p. 2. H. de Galard, "Aux vents de l'Atlantique," *L'Observateur,* April 13, 1950. H. de Galard, "1950, Année de l'Extrême Orient," *Loc. cit.,* December 28, 1950, pp. 4-5. Louis Martin-Chauffier, "Les Etats-Unis et la politique française," in "Tableau politique de la France (1951)," *La Nef,* (Paris) special issue, April-May, 1951, pp. 185-9.

20. Léon Blum, *A l'Echelle Humaine,* Paris: Gallimard, 1946, especially chs. III and IV. For a different view of the same

question, see the address of Maurice Thorez to the National Conference of the French Communist party at Ivry, cited in *L'Humanité,* June 8, 1954.

21. Jean Jaurès, *L'Organisation Socialiste; L'Armée Nouvelle,* Paris: J. Rouff, 1911. Harold Weinstein, *Jean Jaurès; A Study of Patriotism in the French Socialist Movement,* New York: Columbia University Press, 1936.

22. However, the allusion sometimes made to *Le Temps,* and the inference that *Le Monde* had inherited the semi-official status of that staunchly rightist prewar paper, has no justification.

23. Robert Borel, "Retour à la réalité," *Le Monde,* October 12, 1951. "Il est temps encore" (signed "Esprit"), *Esprit,* March, 1952, pp. 329-36. Louis Martin-Chauffier, "Les Etats-Unis et la politique française," in "Tableau politique de la France (1951)," *La Nef,* special issue April-May, 1951, pp. 184-9.

24. Maurice Duverger, "Pax Europeana," *Le Monde,* December 18, 1950.

25. Jean Fabiani, "Washington et les deux ans," *Combat,* August 18, 1952. Marcel Gimont, "Derrière la façade," *Loc. cit.,* January 12, 1951. A. Fontaine, "Vers la nouvelle Wehrmacht," *Le Monde,* November 21, 1951.

26. Roger Stéphane, "Les Equivoques du neutralisme," in: "Tableau politique de la France (1951)," special issue of *La Nef,* April-May, 1951, pp. 200-4. Jean Lacroix, "Faire la paix," *Esprit,* March, 1951, pp. 326-32. "Un double danger" (signed "Combat"), *Combat,* September 10, 1951.

27. Etienne Gilson, "Défaitisme et neutralisme," *Le Monde,* April 23, 1950. E. Gilson, "La neutralité vers l'Est," *Loc. cit.,* April 29, 1950. E. Gilson, "La neutralitè vers l'Ouest," *Loc. cit.,* April 30—May 2, 1950. See also E. Gilson, "Au pays de Descartes," *Loc. cit.,* July 21, 1950. E. Gilson, "Dans l'étau des faits," *Loc. cit.,* August 6 & 7, 1950.

28. "L'Affaire Gilson" (signed A.B.) in "Journal à plusieurs voix," *Esprit,* April, 1951, pp. 590-3. "Une lettre de M. Etienne Gilson," *Le Monde,* February 28, 1951. Hubert Beuve-Méry, "L'Affaire Gilson," *Loc. cit.,* March 10, 1951.

29. Etienne Gilson, "Défaitisme et neutralisme," *Le Monde,* April 28, 1950.

30. E. Gilson, "La neutralité vers l'Est," *Le Monde,* April 29, 1950.

31. *Ibid.*
32. E. Gilson, "L'Ombre et la servitude," *Le Monde,* January 12, 1950.
33. E. Gilson, "Le labyrinthe," *Le Monde,* August 24, 1950. For a similar line of reasoning but in a different context, see also: "Rapport du Sénat Américain sur le communisme mondial," *L'Express,* November 21, 1953, pp. 6-7.
34. E. Gilson, "La neutralité vers l'Ouest," *Le Monde,* April 30-May 2, 1950.
35. "Esquisses d'une politique," Pt. IV: "La paix sans communisme," *Le Monde,* June 12, 1952.
36. Sirius, "Une oeuvre virile," *Le Monde,* January 31, 1951.
37. Jean-Jacques Servan-Schreiber, "Que vaut la puissance américaine," *Le Monde,* July 27, 1950. J. J. S. Schreiber, "Que peut faire l'Europe," *Loc. cit.,* August 1, 1950. Paul-Henri Spaak, "Une Armée Européenne," *Loc. cit.,* November 23, 1950. J. J. S. Schreiber, "L'Amérique a choisi," *Loc. cit.,* January 25, 1951. André Fontaine, "Le Pacte Atlantique a deux ans," *Loc. cit.,* April 6, 1951.
38. J. J. S. Schreiber, "Que peut faire l'Europe," *Le Monde,* August 1, 1950. For an example of Schreiber's subsequent views, see his article: "Avec qui et contre qui," *Loc. cit.,* January 23, 1953. See also the articles in *Le Monde* favorable to European integration: Paul-Henri Spaak, "Europe unie: premier bilan," *Le Monde,* May 13, 1950. G. Scelle, "Européanisme et mondialisme," *Loc. cit.,* June 18-19, 1950. G. Scelle, "Fédéralisme et neutralisme," *Loc. cit.,* July 16-17, 1950. André Fontaine, "Le Pacte Atlantique a deux ans," *Loc. cit.,* April 6, 1951.
39. Louis Pauwels, "Lettre ouverte aux camarades d''Esprit,'" *Combat,* September 9-10, 1950.
40. "Les révolutionnaires de gauche refusent le neutralisme," *Combat,* September 12, 1950.
41. Louis Pauwels, "Nous autres cannibales . . .," *Combat,* October 7-8, 1950. René Dany, "Deutschland Erwache!," *Loc. cit.,* September 15, 1950.
42. Etienne Gilson, "Le temps de la décision," *Le Monde,* July 13, 1950. Maurice Duverger, "Sodome et Gomorrhe," *Loc. cit.,* July 14, 1950.
43. Marcel Gimont, "Virage dangereux," *Combat,* November 6, 1950. Jean Fabiani, "Solutions 'réalistes,'" *Loc. cit.,* October 18, 1950. Jean Duvignaud, "Du devoir de vigilance," *Loc. cit.,*

September 11, 1951. See also Jean José Marchand, "A Tableau of the French Press," in: D. Lerner and R. Aron, eds., *Op. cit.*, pp. 105-7.

44. Editorials signed "Combat": L'échéance 1952, *Combat,* August 28, 1951. "Idéologies et réalités," *Loc. cit.,* September 6, 1951; "Un double danger," *Loc. cit.,* September 10, 1951; "Double danger," *Loc. cit.,* September 14, 1951.

45. J. M. Domenach and Paul Fraisse, "De la peur à la coéxistence," *Esprit,* March, 1951, pp. 333-343 [341]. Etienne Gilson, "Epilogue," *Le Monde,* September 29, 1950.

46. Sirius, "C'est la foi qui manque le plus," *Le Monde,* July 20, 1950. Sirius, "Combats en retraite," *Loc. cit.,* December 13, 1950. Charles Favrel, "Pitié pour les Coréens," *Loc. cit.,* February 11-12, 1951.

47. Maurice Duverger, "Pax Europeana," *Le Monde,* December 18, 1950. M. Duverger, "Le dernier tournant," *Loc. cit.,* January 11, 1951. See also: Jean Fabiani, "Risque calculé," *Combat,* December 18, 1950. Jules Isaac, "Guerre atomique ou coéxistence?," *La Revue Socialiste,* (Paris), July, 1954, pp. 113-28.

48. "La propagande politique," *Sondages,* 16th year, 1954, No. 1, pp. 15-6, *et seq.* "Le gouvernement Mendès-France et l'Opinion, Juin '54—Fevrier '55," *Loc. cit.,* 17th year, 1955, No. 1. p. 25.

49. E. Gilson, "Un échec," *Le Monde,* September 7, 1950.

50. Jean-Jacques Servan-Schreiber, "L'Avenir de la coalition Atlantique," *Le Monde,* April 5, 1950. J. J. S. Schreiber, "La troisième étape," *Loc. cit.,* April 15, 1950. Etienne Gilson "Un appel américain," *Loc. cit.,* August 17, 1950. Maurice Duverger, "Formose n'est pas la Corée," *Loc. cit.,* August 9, 1950. M. Duverger, "Europe ou Asie," *Loc. cit.,* December 3 & 4, 1950.

51. E. Gilson, "L'ombre et la servitude," *Le Monde,* January 12, 1950. "De la guerre froide à la vraie guerre," *Loc. cit.,* February 10, 1950.

52. Sirius, "C'est la foi qui manque le plus," *Le Monde,* July 20, 1950. Jean Lacouture, "Des frigidaires dans l'honneur et dans la dignité" ("Les illusions perdues," Pt. III), *Combat,* September 2-3, 1950. For an excellent summary of the situation of French neutralism as of mid-1951, see: Raymond Aron, "French Public Opinion and the Atlantic Treaty," *International Affairs,* January 1952, pp. 1-8.

53. Sirius, "Crimes de guerre," *Le Monde,* November 22, 1950.

54. Charles Favrel, "Premiers aspects de la guerre des Nations

Unies," *Le Monde,* August 8, 1950. Also by the same author and in *Le Monde*: "Comment les renforts furent jetés dans la bataille," August 15, 1950: "En attendant l'heure," August 20-21, 1950; "Comment on 'progresse vers Chinju,'" August 22, 1950; "La grande caravane," January 21-22, 1951; "Pitié pour les Coréens," February 11-12, 1951, *et. seq.* Most bitter of all Favrel's articles in *Le Monde*: "Le civil est-il un objectif militaire?," January 30, 1951; and "L'oeil de la vérité," February 7, 1951.

55. Charles Favrel, "Lettre à Mister Smith," *Esprit,* November 1951, pp. 629-47.

56. Sirius, "Une oeuvre virile," *Le Monde,* January 31, 1951.

57. *Le Monde* did still publish occasional editorials which reaffirmed the necessity, as well as the drawbacks, of tacit American support for an "independent" French policy ("Esquisses d'une politique," Pt. IV: "La paix sans communisme," June 12, 1951; Sirius, "L'espoir renait," April 9, 1953). But the great majority of the paper's editorials and articles came to reflect a far more militantly "neutral" view: Sirius, "Situations impossibles," February 20, 1952.

58. Jean-William Lapierre, "La neutralité française, utopie ou solution," *Esprit,* March, 1951, pp. 375-92 [p. 378]. Albert Béguin, "Réflexions sur l'Amérique, l'Europe et la neutralité et quelques autres sujets de préoccupation," *Loc. cit.,* June, 1951. Henri Pierre, "Le Public américain applaudit à la mort des traîtres . . .," *Le Monde,* June 21-22, 1953. "Forces spirituelles et insomnies," in "Journal à plusieurs voix," *Esprit,* October, 1952, pp. 515-6. "Affaire Dreyfus—Affaire Rosenberg" (signed J. B. M.) in "Journal à plusieurs voix," *Loc. cit.,* August, 1953, pp. 217-23 [223].

59. Maurice Duverger, "Les mains propres," *Le Monde,* August 30, 1950. Sirius, "Une oeuvre virile," *Loc. cit.,* January 31, 1951. Sirius, "Vers la troisième? . . .," *Loc. cit.,* June 11, 1952.

60. Jean Fabiani, "Le prix du réarmement," *Combat,* January 1, 1951. Georges Altschuler, "Dangereux tournant pour la France et L'Europe," *Loc. cit.,* September 22-23, 1951.

61. Sirius, "Une oeuvre virile," *Le Monde,* January 31, 1951. See also Louis Martin-Chauffier, "Les Etats-Unis et la politique française," *La Nef,* April-May, 1951, pp. 184-9.

62. Marcel Gimont, "Propos de généraux," *Combat,* December 11, 1941, p. 3.

63. Marcel Gimont, "Le point," *Combat,* November 9, 1952.

Robert Borel, "La révision des conceptions atlantiques s'impose," *Le Monde,* Pt. I: August 30, 1951; Pt. II: August 31, 1951.

64. Jean Fabiani, "Le prix du réarmement," *Combat,* January 1, 1951. Georges Altschuler, "Dangereux tournant pour la France et l'Europe," *Loc. cit.,* September 22-23, 1951.

65. R. Borel, "La révision des conceptions atlantiques s'impose," *Le Monde,* August 30-31, 1951. See also: Thomas Balogh, "L'Europe sous la menace d'une crise aux Etats-Unis," *L'Observateur,* October 8, 1953, pp. 12-3.

66. "Le rapport Hillman sur l'aide américaine fait le procès de la France," *L'Express,* July 25, 1953, pp. 6-7.

67. Georges Altschuler, "Dangereux tournant pour la France et l'Europe," *Combat,* September 22-23, 1951. R. Borel, "Communauté Atlantique ou 'End Day,'" *Le Monde,* September 9-10, 1951.

68. Jacques Armel, "L'Occident craint-il la coéxistence?," *L'Observateur,* March 12, 1953, pp. 12-3. Jean-Jacques Servan-Schreiber, "La proposition de la France," *Le Monde,* April 19, 1950. André Fontaine, "La maladie infantile de l'atlantisme," *Loc. cit.,* June 7, 1951. R. Borel, "La révision des conceptions atlantiques s'impose," *Loc. cit.,* Pt. I: August 30, 1951; Pt. II: August 31, 1951. Paul Ricoeur, "Pour la coéxistence des civilisations," *Esprit,* March, 1951, pp. 408-19. See also: Maurice Duverger, "Défendre Hanoï ou Défendre Paris?," *La Nef,* April-May, 1951: "Tableau politique de la France, 1951," pp. 177-83.

69. "Un double danger" (signed "Combat"), *Combat,* September 10, 1951.

70. Gilles Martinet, "La gauche non-conformiste," in "Tableau politique de la France (1951)," special issue of *La Nef,* April-May, 1951, pp. 46-56.

71. See for example the views of that old revolutionary Socialist militant Marceau Pivert, "Vingt ans après . . . Irons-nous vers la paix ou la guerre," *La Revue Socialiste,* Pt. I: March, 1954, pp. 275-85; Pt. II: April, 1954, pp. 396-410. M. Pivert, "Les communistes, les socialistes et la paix," *Loc. cit.,* November, 1954, pp. 337-55. The extent to which a leftward political orientation, outside and even against the Communists, came to be associated with a basic suspicion of American policy is indicated by a poll reported in *Sondages* in 1952. It revealed that the left-Socialist paper *Franc-Tireur,* which at that time had a well-established editorial line in support of Western policy

and Atlantic defense, and which was bitterly critical of the Soviet Union, had a higher proportion of readers who blamed the U.S., as opposed to the U.S.S.R., for the war tension than did any other paper except *L'Humanité* (*Sondages,* 14th year, 1952, No. 1, pp. 25-9).

72. Pierre Naville, "Etats Unis et contradictions capitalistes," *Les Temps Modernes,* December, 1952, pp. 899-914.

73. Henri Bartoli, "Deux systèmes économiques," *Esprit,* March, 1951, pp. 357-74 [373-4].

74. "La paix possible," special issue of *Esprit,* March, 1951.

75. Jean Marie Domenach & Paul Fraisse, "De la peur à la co-éxistence," *Esprit,* March, 1951, pp. 333-43 [341].

76. Albert Béguin, "Réflexions sur l'Amérique, l'Europe, la neutralité et quelques autres sujets de préoccupation," *Esprit,* June, 1951, pp. 869-90 [890]. For the expression in *Esprit* of a contrasting opinion, see: Mario Einaudi, "Lettre à *Esprit,*" *Loc. cit.,* June 1951. In this connection, see also: Joseph Hours, "Les Catholiques Français face aux projets d'Europe," *La Nef,* January, 1954, pp. 59-68.

77. "Idéologies et réalités" (signed "Combat"), *Combat,* September 6, 1951. For a measure of popular opinion on this question, see J. B. Duroselle *et al., Op. cit.,* pp. 11, 13. For a breakdown of the figures according to political parties, see *Ibid.,* p. 32.

78. Paul Baran, "L'économie américaine malade de la paix," *L'Observateur,* February 25, 1954, pp. 12-4.

79. "Les hommes d'affaires américains ont prévu le partage du monde," *L'Express,* December 5, 1953, pp. 6-7. "Le rapport Hillman sur l'aide américaine fait le procès de la France," *Loc. cit.,* July 25, 1953, pp. 6-7.

80. Armand Gatti, "La libération du Guatémala," *Esprit,* November, 1954, pp. 572-88. Elena de la Souchère, "La Hispanidad sous la loi du 'gros baton,'" *Les Temps Modernes,* August, 1954, p. 340-67. Jacques Soustelle, "La 'libération' du Guatémala," *L'Express,* June 26, 1954, p. 6. Paul Rivet, "Néo-colonialisme," *Le Monde,* June 23, 1954, p. 3.

81. "M. Battle doit-il encore dicter les réponses de la France aux propositions commerciales de l'Est?," *Le Monde,* June 16, 1953.

82. Elie Gabey, "L'appel de l'Est," *L'Observateur,* May 4, 1950, p. 5. Jacques Armel, "Ce que j'ai vu à la Conférence de Mos-

cou," *Loc. cit.,* April 17, 1952, pp. 12-3. Robert Lacoste, "La reconnaissance de la République populaire chinoise serait un acte de paix," *Loc. cit.,* June 17, 1954, p. 3.

83. "Ce que peut rapporter le commerce avec les Soviets," *L'Express,* January 30, 1954, pp. 6-7. R. Lacoste, "La reconnaissance de la République populaire chinoise serait un acte de paix," *L'Observateur,* June 17, 1954, p. 3.

84. J. Gordon, "L'économie européenne face à la paix," *L'Observateur,* April 23, 1953. J. B. Duroselle *et. al., Op. cit.,* pp. 11, 14.

85. "Les hommes d'affaires américains ont prévu le partage du monde," *L'Express,* December 5, 1953, pp. 6-7.

86. Thomas Balogh, "L'Europe sous la menace d'une crise aux Etats-Unis," *L'Observateur,* October 8, 1953, pp. 12-3.

87. H. de Galard, "1950, Année de l'Extrême Orient," *L'Observateur,* December 28, 1950, pp. 4-5.

88. Henri Bartoli, "Deux systèmes économiques," *Esprit,* March, 1951, pp. 357-74.

89. "L'éxécution des Rosenberg" (signed J. M. D.), and "Chronique du salaud" (signed B. A.), in "Journal à plusieurs voix," *Esprit,* July, 1953, pp. 59-63. Jean-Marie Domenach, "Une politique extèrieure," *Loc. cit.,* January, 1954, pp. 10-9. Michel François, "Americanisme 54," *Loc. cit.,* May, 1954, pp. 679-84, [693]. "Il est temps encore" (signed "Esprit"), *Loc. cit.,* March, 1952, pp. 329-36.

90. Jean-William Lapierre, "La neutralité française: utopie ou solution?," *Esprit,* March, 1951, pp. 375-92, [383].

91. Claude Estier, "Le Parti Socialiste pour ou contre l'Armée Européenne," *L'Observateur,* January 25, 1954.

92. Pierre Gousset, "Ce qui c'est passé réellement en Allemagne orientale," *L'Observateur,* June 25, 1953, pp. 11-4.

93. Gilles Martinet, "Les problèmes du Front Populaire," *L'Observateur,* July 2, 1953, pp. 6-8. G. Martinet, "Front unique et peur du communisme," *Loc. cit.,* July 16, 1953, pp. 12-3, 24. G. Martinet, "Il faudra bien faire le Front Populaire," *Loc. cit.,* September 10, 1953, pp. 5-6. Claude Bourdet, "La gauche, les communistes et les autres," *Loc. cit.,* November 5, 1953, pp. 5-7. "Socialistes et communistes ont multiplié les votes communs depuis deux ans," *Loc. cit.,* August 13, 1953, p. 10.

94. Jean Paul Sartre, "Les communistes et la paix," *Les Temps*

Modernes, Pt. I: July, 1952, pp. 1-50; Pt. II: October-November, 1952, pp. 693-763.

95. For a detailed discussion of the relations between neutralists and Communists, see I. Zartman, *Op. cit.,* pp. 115-41.

96. Pierre Courtade, "C'est le parti de la guerre qu'il faut 'neutraliser,'" *L'Humanité,* (Paris) February 13, 1950, p. 3.

97. *Ibid.*

98. Roger Stéphane, "Le problème des camps de travail en U.R.S.S.," *L'Observateur,* November 30, 1950, pp. 12-3. Claude Bourdet, "Les aveux de Prague," *Loc. cit.,* November 27, 1952, pp. 5-6.

99. Abbé Jean Boulier, "La neutralité? Discutons en," *Action,* (Paris) September 11-17, 1950.

100. Waldeck Rochet, "La classe ouvrière, les neutralistes, et l'union pour la paix," *Cahiers du Communisme,* (Paris) February, 1951, pp. 161-72.

101. Jean-Jacques Servan-Schreiber, "La guerre contre les Slavons," *Le Monde,* February 18, 1953.

102. Claude Bourdet, "Lettre aux Américains," *L'Observateur,* July 12, 1952, pp. 5-6.

103. Stetson and Kay Kennedy, "Le travail forcé aux Etats-Unis," *Les Temps Modernes,* Pt. I: March, 1953, pp. 1369-405; Pt. II: May 1953, pp. 1736-74. "The American way of death" (signed "T. M.," i.e., "Temps Modernes"), *Loc. cit.,* July, 1953, pp. 1-5. Albert Béguin, "Réflexions sur l'Amérique, l'Europe, la neutralité et quelques autres sujets de préoccupation," *Esprit,* June, 1951, pp. 869-90.

104. Henri Pierre, "L'affaire Rosenberg vue par la presse française et étrangère," *Le Monde,* January 17, 1953. Sirius, "Une victoire de Staline," *Loc. cit.,* February 23, 1953. "Marchandage sur la mort," *Loc. cit.,* June 5, 1953. Sirius, "Justice est faite," *Loc. cit.,* June 21-22, 1953. Henri Pierre, "Le public amércain applaudit à la mort des traîtres . . .," *Loc. cit.,* June 21-22, 1953, p. 3. Claude Bourdet, "Les Rosenberg: Trois mondes," *L'Observateur,* February 19, 1953, pp. 5-6. "Les Rosenberg," *Loc. cit.,* June 18, 1953, pp. 3-4. "Les Rosenberg condamnés sans preuves," *Loc. cit.,* June 18, 1953, p. 6. Claude Bourdet, "Rosenberg, Rhee, Berlin et la paix," *Loc. cit.,* June 25, 1953, pp. 5-6. Paul Rivet, "Après l'éxécution des Rosenberg–l'Aveu," *Loc. cit.,* June 25, 1953, p. 10. "Un contre-procès Rosenberg," *Loc. cit.,* July 2, 1953, p. 3. "L'éxécution des Rosenberg" (signed

J. M. D.), and "chronique du salaud" (signed B. A.), in "Journal à plusieurs voix," *Esprit,* July, 1953, pp. 58-63. "Affaire Dreyfus —Affaire Rosenberg" (signed J. B. M.), in "Journal à plusieurs voix," *Loc. cit.,* August, 1953, pp. 217-23.

105. René Guyonnet, "L'affaire Rosenberg," *Les Temps Modernes,* December, 1953, pp. 1018-38. R. Guyonnet, "Nouveaux développements de l'affaire Rosenberg," *Loc. cit.,* June, 1953, pp. 2002-8. "American way of death" (signed "T. M.," i.e., "Temps Modernes"), *Loc. cit.,* July, 1953, pp. 1-5.

106. "L'inquisition télévisée," *Esprit,* May, 1954, includes: Michel François, "Américanisme 54," pp. 679-94; Jacques Evens, "Les appuis du Sénateur," pp. 703-10; François Fejto, "Mac Carthyisme et Fascisme," pp. 711-26; Lucien Martin, "L'affaire Alger Hiss," pp. 727-48. Other sources include: René Guyonnet, "La chasse aux sorcières aux Etats Unis," *Les Temps Modernes,* October-November, 1952, pp. 693-763. H. de Galard, "Avènement du Mac Carthyisme," *Loc. cit.,* February, 1954, pp. 1432-66. Rhoda Miller da Silva, "U. S. Go Home," *Loc. cit.,* June, 1954, pp. 2194-206. Henri Pierre, "Le Sénateur Mac Carthy pèse d'un poids chaque jour plus grand sur la vie publique américaine," *Le Monde,* April 25, 1953. Marcelle Henry, "Qu'est-ce-que le Maccarthyisme," *Loc. cit.,* November 13, 14, 15-16, 1953. George Tavas, "Le régime de l'inquisition," *L'Observateur,* January 1, 1953, pp. 12-3. H. de Galard, "McCarthy, le dentiste, et le Président des Etats Unis, *Loc. cit.,* March 11, 1954, pp. 12-3. "Silence sur l'Amérique," *L'Express,* June 27, 1953, p. 6. Theodore S. Kaghan, "Comment j'ai été 'Mac Carthysé,'" *Loc. cit.,* June 27, 1953, p. 7.

107. Sanford Gottlieb, "Le phénomène Maccarthy est-il en regression," *L'Observateur,* August 6, 1953, pp. 6-7.

108. "Mac Carthy à Paris," *L'Observateur,* June 18, 1953, p. 4.

109. Gilles Martinet, "Psychanalyse de Collier's. Vingt trois Américains rèvent à haute voix," *L'Observateur,* November 8, 1951, pp. 11-4.

110. Jean Fabiani, "Un risque calculé," *Combat,* December 18, 1950. J. Fabiani, "Une motion pour rien," *Loc. cit.,* February 18, 1952. J. Fabiani, "De Berlin à Pan Mun Jom," *Loc. cit.,* May 17-18, 1952. "Le rapport américain sur l'Asie," *L'Express,* April 17, 1954, pp. 8-9.

111. Marcel Gimont, "Quand MacArthur propose la paix," *Combat,* March 26, 1951. Jean Fabiani, "Halte à l'aventure,"

Loc. cit., April 9, 1951. M. Gimont, "La leçon d'une disgrâce," *Loc. cit.,* April 12, 1951. Jean Duvignaud, "Du devoir de vigilance," *Loc. cit.,* September 14, 1951.
112. H. de Galard, "La dinde Mac Arthur," *L'Observateur,* November 30, 1950, pp. 3-4. André Fontaine, "Ceux qui veulent la paix . . . et celui qui veut la guerre," *Le Monde,* April 8-9, 1951. Maurice Duverger, "L'Europe et la sécurité américaine," *Loc. cit.,* May 4, 1951.
113. "Croisade contre la Chine communiste," *L'Express,* June 27, 1953, p. 3. Claude Bourdet, "Rosenberg, Rhee, Berlin et la paix," *L'Observateur,* June 25, 1953, pp. 5-6. Sirius, "Vers la troisième? . . .," *Le Monde,* June 11, 1952.
114. Sanford Gottlieb, "La politique des Etats Unis en Extrême Orient," *L'Observateur,* August 27, 1953, p. 16. Jean-Jacques Servan-Schreiber, "Nos buts de guerre en Asie," *Le Monde,* March 14, 1953. Claude Bourdet, "La paix et la guerre autour d'Eisenhower," *L'Observateur,* March 29, 1953, pp. 5-6. "Washington ne croit pas à la négociation," *Loc. cit.,* December 7, 1950, p. 3.
115. "Croisade contre la Chine communiste," *L'Express,* June 27, 1953, p. 3.
116. Marcel Gimont, "Derrière la façade," *Combat,* January 12, 1951. "L'échéance 1952" (signed "Combat"), *Loc. cit.,* August 28, 1952. M. Gimont, "Un Bilan," *Loc. cit.,* September 15-16, 1951.
117. "Idéologies et réalités" (signed "Combat"), *Combat,* September 6, 1951.
118. J. Fabiani, "Washington et les deux ans," *Combat,* August 18, 1952. "L'échéance 1952" (signed "Combat"), *Combat,* August 28, 1951.
119. "Un double danger" (signed "Combat"), *Combat,* September 10, 1951.
120. "Rapport du Sénat Américain sur le communisme mondial," *L'Express,* November 21, 1953, pp. 6-7. See also: J. B. Duroselle, *et al., Op. cit.,* p. 14.
121. E. N. Dzelepy, "La leçon de Corée," *Les Temps Modernes,* May, 1952, pp. 1982-2002. E. N. Dzelepy, "L'Amérique à l'heure européenne ou la nouvelle 'leçon de Corée,'" *Loc. cit.,* June, 1953, pp. 1901-46.
122. E. N. Dzelepy, "La leçon de Corée," *Les Temps Modernes,* May, 1952, pp. 1982-2002.

123. Sirius, "Une oeuvre virile," *Le Monde,* January 31, 1951.
124. Edgar S. Furniss, "French Attitudes Towards Western European Unity," *International Organization,* Boston, (Vol. 7) May, 1953, pp. 199-212. J. B. Duroselle *et. al., Op. cit.,* p. 18.
125 Maurice Duverger, "Alliance ou protectorat," *Le Monde,* February 6, 1953, p. 2.
126. Jean Fabiani, "Un malentendu à dissiper," *Combat,* November 3, 1952. Robert Borel, "Un danger majeur: le réarmement allemand," *Le Monde,* July 12, 1951. Maurice Duverger, "Vers la Wehrmacht?," *Loc. cit.,* January 11-12, 1953. H. de Galard, "L'Armée Européenne contre l'Europe," *L'Observateur,* Pt. I: January 22, 1953, pp. 12-4; Pt. II: January 29, 1953, pp. 10-2. André Fontaine, "Les deux coéxistences," *Le Monde,* Pt. II: "France-Allemagne," October 4-5, 1953. Maurice Duverger, "La Communauté allemande de Défense," *Loc. cit.,* November 18, 1953. Also see: Bernard Lavergne, "Le projet de traité instituant l'Armée dite Européenne." *Le Monde,* January 22, 1953. Marcel Gimont, "Virage dangereux," *Combat,* November 6, 1950. Maurice Ferro, "Réalités, illusions et dangers d'une politique," *Le Monde,* October 5, 1950. H. de Galard, "Aux vents de l'Atlantique," *L'Observateur,* April 13, 1950. Elie Gabey, "Unité allemande ou 'intégration,'" *Loc. cit.,* April 20, 1950, p. 6. For a collection of all the arguments against the line of Western policy towards Germany, see the issue of *La Nef* (New series, No. 1) December, 1952: "Le Problème allemand." See also Jacques Vernant, "European Politics Faces French Economics," in: D. Lerner and R. Aron, eds., *Op. cit.,* pp. 45-53.
127. Pierre Rungis, "M. Monnet, pélerin de la 'petite Europe,'" *L'Observateur,* May 28, 1953, p. 16. Gilles Martinet, "Front unique et peur du communisme," *Loc. cit.,* July 16, 1953, pp. 12-3, 24.
128. André Fontaine. "L'Armée européenne contre l'Europe," *Le Monde,* Pt. I: March 7, 1953, Pt. II: March 10, 1953. Marcel Gimont, "La 'résolution' socialiste," *Combat,* December 4, 1952. See also: Alfred Sauvy, "Il faut faire une Europe," *L'Express,* February 6, 1954, p. 12.
129. Marcel Gimont, "La défense de L'Europe," *Combat,* December 1, 1949, p. 3.
130. Many French political figures who were definitely not neutralist agreed in principle with this criticism. See, for example, statements by: René Billères, *Journal Officiel de la*

République Française. Débats Parlementaires, Assemblée Nationale (henceforth this source will be referred to as *J.O.*), 1st session of November 24, 1953, pp. 5480-2; Jules Moch, rapporteur de la Commision des Affaires étrangères, *Loc. cit.,* 1st session of August 28, 1954, pp. 4379-86; Max Lejeune, président de la Commission de la Défense nationale, *Loc. cit.,* 2nd ssesion of August 28, 1954, pp. 4398-4401. Comments by Jules Moch, *Loc. cit.,* 3rd session of August 29, 1954, pp. 4446-7. Statements by: Edouard Herriot, *Loc. cit.,* session of August 30, 1954, pp. 4463-70; Vincent Badie, *Loc. cit.,* 2nd session of December 20, 1954, pp. 6656-8; Jules Moch, *Loc. cit.,* 1st session of December 22, 1954, pp. 6737-42; Edouard Daladier, *Loc. cit.,* 1st session of December 22, 1954, pp. 6761-5; Edouard Bonnefous, *Loc. cit.,* 3rd session of December 23, 1954, p. 6834. See also: Edouard Daladier, "Europe After the Ratification of the London and Paris Agreements," *Yale French Studies,* New Haven, No. 15 (Winter, 1955), issue on: "Social and Political France," pp. 38-41.

131. "Le plan allemand pour le conquête de l'Europe," *L'Express,* November 14, 1953, pp. 6-7.

132. "Le retour de l'"I. G. Farben,'" *L'Express,* November 21, 1953, p. 11. "Krupp Forever" (signed J. M. D.), in "Journal à plusieurs voix," *Esprit,* April, 1951, pp. 587-8.

133. Roger Quillot, "La grande désespérance du peuple français," *La Revue Socialiste,* Pt. I: March, 1954, pp. 286-98.

134. Julien Benda, "Le danger est allemand," *L'Express,* January 23, 1954, p. 12.

135. Claude Bourdet, "Non, pas dans cette armée," *L'Observateur,* March 5, 1953, pp. 5-6.

136. *Ibid.* Georges Penchenier, "L'Allemagne et L'Europe," Pt. II: "Sur les chemins de Walhalla," *Le Monde,* October 11, 1951, p. 3. "Le rôle de l'Armée allemande en politique" (Based on John Wheeler-Bennett's *The Nemesis of Power; The German Army in Politics, 1918-1945*), *L'Express,* February 13, 1954, pp. 6-7.

137. Georges Penchenier, "L'Allemagne et l'Europe," Pt. I: "Bilan de deux occupations," *Le Monde,* October 10, 1951. César Santelli, "Réarmer le jeunesse de Bonn, n'est-ce-pas souffler sur un brasier qui allait s'éteindre?," *Loc. cit.,* February 12, 1952, p. 3. C. Santelli, "Faut-il réarmer la jeunesse de Bonn?," *Loc. cit.,* February 13, 1952. Joseph Rovan, "La France a-t-elle une politique allemande?," *La Nef,* April-May, 1951, pp. 165-6.

138. Marcel Gimont, "La 'résolution' socialiste," *Combat,* December 4, 1951.
139. E. N. Dzelepy, "Le grand tournant," *Les Temps Modernes,* July, 1952, pp. 144-63.
140. Julien Benda, "Le danger est allemand," *L'Express,* January 23, 1954, p. 12. See also J. Stoetzel, "The Evolution of French Opinion," in: D. Lerner and R. Aron, eds., *Op. cit.* pp. 81-5, 97-101.
141. H. de Galard, "Armée européenne ou Conférence à Quatre," *L'Observateur,* September, 10, 1953, pp. 7-8.
142. Roger Stéphane, "Le 'problème allemand' est celui des frontières orientales," *Les Temps Modernes,* October-November, 1952, pp. 818-31. Claude Bourdet, "De Munich à Rapallo," *L'Observateur,* April 30, 1952, pp. 5-6. H. de Galard, "L'U.R.S.S. n'est pas prête à capituler," *Loc. cit.,* October 1, 1953, pp. 8-9.
143. In a study by the *Institut Français d'Opinion Publique* in 1951 it appeared that those elements which opposed a European army (26% as against 42% in favor and 32% with no opinion at that time) were essentially the same ones as those who felt that the primary danger of war came from the U.S. (*Sondages,* 1951, No. 3, pp. 19 *et. seq.*). See also: Alfred Grosser, "Les Anglo-Américains et l'Allemagne," *La Nef,* December, 1952: "Le Problème allemand," pp. 102-3.
144. Albert Duquet, "La Constitution française autorise-t-elle la disparition de la France," *Le Monde,* March 22-23, 1953. Claude Bourdet, "Lettre aux Américains," *L'Observateur,* July 12, 1952, pp. 5-6. See also: Daniel Lerner, "Reflections on France in the World Arena," in D. Lerner and R. Aron, *Op. cit.,* pp. 208-9 ff.
145. As of 1957: Walter H. Mallory, ed., *Political Handbook of the World, 1957,* New York: Council on Foreign Relations, 1957, pp. 74-5.
146. While not a direct comment on this point, a survey by the *Institut Français d'Opinion Publique* on the breakdown of opinion concerning the causes of international tension revealed that in 1952 a definite plurality of the readers of *Le Monde* held the U.S.S.R. responsible, although the proportion was not comparably as large as among readers of *Le Figaro* (*Sondages,* 14th year, 1952, No. 1 p. 29).
147. "La Nouvelle Gauche," *Documents et Informations Parlementaires. Etudes et Documents,* (Paris: mimeographed), November 12, 1955, pp. C544-6.

148. Raymond Barillon, "Desseins et destin de la Nouvelle Gauche." Pt. I: "Pourquoi cette expression nouvelle d'un permanent désir de renouveau?," *Le Monde,* April 22, 1955.
149. The C.A.G.I. was subsequently merged into the "New Left." This is not to be confused with another movement of the same name which grew up in 1954 around Pierre Mendès-France and the remnants of the Gaullists, and which will be the subject of a more detailed discussion in a subsequent chapter.
150. R. Barillon, "Desseins et Destin de la Nouvelle Gauche," Pt. III: "Doit-on et peut-on dialoguer avec le Parti communiste?," *Le Monde,* April 24, 1955. R. Barillon, "Desseins et Destin de la Nouvelle Gauche," Pt. II: "Des beautés du programme aux difficultés de la fédération," *Loc. cit.,* April 23, 1955, especially the sub-section "Echec électoral." "Les élections anticipées; La 'Nouvelle Gauche' entend promouvoir l'Union pour le Front populaire," *Loc. cit.,* November 15, 1955, p. 5; and: "Réunie en Congrès à Paris, la Nouvelle Gauche fait de sérieuses réserves sur l'action de M. Mendès-France," *Loc. cit.,* November 13-14, 1955, p. 8.
151. R. Barillon, "Des beautés du programme aux difficultés de la fédération," *Le Monde,* April 23, 1955.
152. "Les Etats-Unis, les Américains et la France, 1945-1953," *Sondages,* 1953, No. 2. The most pertinent elements of this material were also published in the monthly *Réalités* under the title: "Ce que les Français pensent de l'Amérique," (August, 1953, pp. 18-22).
153. See also: J. B. Duroselle *et. al., Op. cit.,* pp. 10-20, *passim*; and Jean Stoetzel, "The Evolution of French Opinion," in D. Lerner and R. Aron, eds., *Op. cit.,* pp. 76-8.
154. "La propagande politique," *Sondages,* 16th year, 1954, No. 1, pp. 15-6 *et. seq.*
155. *Ibid.,* p. 15.
156. *Ibid.,* pp. 15-6. A poll taken by the *Institut Français d'Opinion Publique* in 1955 gives the following breakdown on opinion at that time on the relative dangers to France from the U.S. and from the Soviet Union (question paraphrased):

	Country most dangerous to France		Country least dangerous to France	
U.S.S.R.	35%	(c)	7%	(a)
U.S.S.R. and U.S.	10	(b)	—	
U.S.	10	(a)	24	
Germany	12		1	
Britain	1		14	

(*Sondages,* 17th year, 1955, No. 1, p. 24)

It is worth indicating that, apart from the usual small margin of error allowed for scientific polls, a straight comparison of these figures would still give a misleading impression of what may roughly be viewed as Communist (a) and neutralist (b) opinions. It is a well-known fact that in France a considerable portion of the most anti-Communist elements (c) are taken from among the middle-aged and older portions of the population. On the other hand, Communist strength lies largely with the young elements in the factories and among the farmers of the south-west. The neutralist appeal has been largely aimed at the younger groups among middle class intellectuals, including university circles. This situation suggests that an estimate of the relative significance of these various attitudes calls for a detailed breakdown of the over-all figures.

157. Gilles Martinet, "La classe ouvrière et la question européenne," *L'Observateur,* January 8, 1953.

158. Albert Duquet, "La Constitution Française autorise-t-elle la disparition de la France?," *Le Monde,* March 22-33, 1953.

159. J. B. Duroselle *et. al., Op. cit.,* p. 18.

160. Edgar S. Furniss, "French Attitudes Towards Western European Unity," *International Organization,* Boston, May 1953, pp. 199-212. Jean Stoetzel, "The Evolution of French Opinion," in: D. Lerner and R. Aron, eds., *Op. cit.,* Ch. V. I. Zartman (*De la Résistance à la Révolution*) distinguishes between the opposition to EDC of the neutralists, motivated by hostility not to the Germans as a people but only to German militarism, and that of other anti-EDC elements who reacted on the basis of a violent prejudice against Germany *per se.* The latter, he explains, view Germany as a permanent menace whereas the

former express hope in the emergence of a pacific German nation:

> The neutralists in general were those who hoped for something better out of Germany and were therefore sorely disappointed to see conditions evolve in such a way as to favor the development of undersirable elements; the anti-Germans were those who could only fear for something worse. The former placed a premium on conditions, the latter on the nature of the people.

(*Ibid.*, p. 105)

A similar distinction is made by Stanley Hoffman, "The Post-mortems," in D. Lerner and R. Aron, eds., *Op. cit.*, p. 193. This distinction is a useful one. At the same time, it should be noted that many neutralists of the left had developed an emotional anti-German bias during the Resistance. On the other hand, even de Gaulle, who aproached this issue from a particularly nationalist point of view, had repeatedly affirmed that a Franco-German rapprochement was the key to peace, and he did not relegate Germany to the role of an incurably aggressive nation. All opponents of EDC, neutralist or not, agreed that hope for the development of a peaceful neighbor hung by a very thin thread, one which the slightest boost to German militarism would snap. In other words, they placed a premium on the nature of the German people under certain conditions.

One must conclude that, in practice, virtually all French opponents of EDC were convinced that the security of France depended upon not reproducing in Germany conditions under which a militarist psychology might thrive. Thus, whether they believed in theory that Germans would be good if one did not give them a gun or that Germans would never be good but at least without a gun could do no damage, they could all agree upon opposition to EDC and to an American policy predicated on the rearmament of Germany.

161. Edouard Herriot statement, *J.O.*, session of August 30, 1954, pp. 4463-70.

162. I. Zartman, (*Op. cit.*, pp. 35-6) does not consider this type of opinion neutralist at all. For a further discussion of this point, see Introduction.

163. "La clef de l'indépendance française," *L'Express,* December 26, 1953, pp. 6-7.
164. Edouard Depreux, "Bevanisme anglais et français," *L'Observateur,* January 1, 1953, pp. 7-8. Andrew Roth, "Bevan, Nehru et Tito," *Loc. cit.,* February 19, 1953, pp. 5-6.
165. Claude Bourdet, "Lettre aux Américains," *L'Observateur,* July 12, 1952, pp. 5-6.
166. Jean Fabiani, "De Gaulle reste," *Combat,* October 21, 1954.
167. There exists a vast documentation concerning the demand of French neutralists for an end to the war in Indo-China. This particular reference has been selected because of the specially detailed way in which it gives the extreme neutralist point of view: *Les Temps Modernes,* August-September, 1953; the entire issue on: "Viet-Nam." See also: Maurice Duverger, "Défendre Hanoï ou défendre Paris," *La Nef,* April-May, 1951, pp. 177-83.
168. Claude Bourdet, "Les Français ont assez de cette guerre," *L'Observateur,* October 29, 1953. Jean-Jacques Servan-Schreiber, "L'impasse à l'Armée européenne par l'Indochine," *Le Monde,* Pt. I: January 31, 1953; Pt. II: February 1-2, 1953, p. 2. J. J. S. Schreiber, "N'y a-t-il plus personne?," Pts. I & II: *Loc. cit.,* April 28-29, 1954.
169. "Avec ou sans Dulles, la paix" (signed "France-Observateur"), *L'Observateur,* July 15, 1954, p. 6.
170. Statement of Jacques Soustelle, *L'Express,* May 2, 1954, p. 7.
171. Jean Rous, "De huit ans d'occasions manquées à la Conférence de Genève," *Les Temps Modernes,* July, 1954, pp. 126-37. "Comment Nixon voit l'Indochine" (based on Joseph Alsop articles), *L'Express,* November 28, 1953, p. 12.
172. Sirius, "L'heure de la vérité," *Le Monde,* September 1, 1954. Maurice Duverger, "Après le déluge," *Loc. cit.,* Pts. I & II: September 8-9, 1954.
173. Pierre Mendès-France, "Equilibre Economique et Progrès Social," *La Nef,* (New Series, X, 3) June, 1953, special issue on "Le Franc, Mythe et Réalité," pp. 209-40. Pierre Rimbert, "Mendès-France: Espoir ou Illusion," *La Revue Socialiste,* July, 1953, pp. 157-67. P. Rimbert, "La doctrine économique de Mendès-France," *Loc. cit.,* December, 1954, pp. 449-56. P. Mendès-France, "L'union pour que cela change," *Loc. cit.,* February, 1954 (Part of a special series of issues titled: "Pour une nouvelle orientation politique"), pp. 127-30. See also: Jean Fabiani, "L'expérience Mendès-France va commencer," *Combat,* October 27,

1954. J. Fabiani, "Sur le chemin de la paix," *Loc. cit.,* October 19, 1954. Roger Stéphane, "Un tournant de la législature," *L'Observateur,* June 11, 1953, pp. 7-8. Claude Estier, "La majorité 'rassurée,'" *Loc. cit.,* June 11, 1953, p. 8. See also: Claude Bourdet, "L'étape Mendès-France," *Loc. cit.,* June 4, 1953, pp. 6-7, for a left-Socialist opinion of Mendès-France at the time of his first attempt to form a cabinet.

174. Statements by: Jules Moch, rapporteur de la Commission des Affaires étrangères, *J.O.,* 1st session of August 28, 1954, pp. 4379-86; Max Lejeune, président de la Commission de la Défense nationale, *Loc. cit.,* 2nd session of August 28, 1954, pp. 4398-4401; Pierre-Olivier Lapie, *Loc. cit.,* 1st session of August 29, 1954, pp. 4416-9; Daniel Mayer, président de la Commission des Affaires étrangères, *Loc. cit.,* 3rd session of August 29, 1954, pp. 4441-2; Jules Moch, *Loc. cit.,* 3rd session of August 29, 1954, pp. 4446-7. Jules Isaac, "Guerre atomique ou coéxistence," *La Revue Socialiste,* July, 1954, pp. 113-28.

175. One of the points made by supporters of EDC against the vote of August 30 was that after a succession of speakers attacking the project only two were heard in its defense: statements by René Mayer, *J.O.,* 3rd session of August 30, 1954, pp. 4445-9, and Alfred Coste-Floret, *Loc. cit.,* pp. 4449-51.

176. Speech by Pierre Mendès-France, Président du Conseil, *J.O.,* 2nd session of August 29, 1954, pp. 4422-9; see also: *Loc. cit.,* 3rd session of August 29, 1954, p. 4443. Mendès-France subsequently pushed through the National Assembly, against considerable opposition, the London and Paris agreements which constitute the diplomatic basis for a German defense contribution: *J.O.,* 3rd session of December 23, 1954, p. 6840; *Loc. cit.,* 2nd session of December 29, 1954, pp. 6941, 6959-60. A result was consternation among many of his neutralist supporters: Claude Bourdet, "La capitulation inutile," *L'Observateur,* January 6, 1955, pp. 6-7. Sirius, "Quel est le pire?," *Le Monde,* December 24, 1954, "Sic vos . . .," *Loc. cit.,* December 26-27, 1954. "Sans nous," *Loc. cit.,* December 28, 1954. Léo Hamon, "Il ne faut pas jouer la détente sur un pari," *Loc. cit.,* December 28, 1954, p. 3. Maurice Duverger, "L'impasse," *Loc. cit.,* January 4, 1955. Jacques Kayser, "Derrière la menace la réalité," *Loc. cit.,* October 19-20, 1954. Bernard Lavergne, "M. Pierre Mendès-France, parain d'une nouvelle Wehrmacht?," *La Tribune des Nations,* (Paris) October 8, 1954. André Ulmann "Fixe-t-on à

Londres les conditions de la guerre Franco-Allemande?," *Loc. cit.,* October 8, 1954. B. Lavergne, "M. Mendès-France, disciple de M. Robert Schuman, ou le réarmement massif de l'Allemagne," *Loc. cit.,* November 5, 1954. Statement by André Denis, *J.O.,* 2nd session of February 4, 1955, pp. 763-4. Statement by Pierre Cot, *Loc. cit.,* session of October 12, 1954, pp. 4666-8. Gilles Martinet, "*L'Express,* Mendès-France et le neutralisme," *L'Observateur,* August 26, 1954, pp. 6-7. But Mendès-France made it clear that his purpose in doing so was different from that of American policy, that he envisaged this step not as a prelude to the rearming of Germany and to further emphasis on the military strengthening of the West but rather as a bargaining weapon to be used in negotiations towards a peaceful settlement in Europe with the U.S.S.R.: Statements of Jules Moch, *J.O.,* 1st session of December 22, 1954, pp. 6737-42; of Edouard Bonnefous, *Loc. cit.,* 3rd session of December 23, 1954, p. 6843, and the replies of Mendès-France: *Loc. cit.,* 1st session of December 22, 1954, pp. 6743-4; *Loc. cit.,* 2nd session of December 23, 1954, pp. 6811-22; *Loc. cit.,* 2nd session of December 29, 1954, pp. 6937-9. See especially statement by Mendès-France, *Loc. cit.,* 2nd session of October 8, 1954, pp. 4646-55, 4653. See: "Deux discours," *Combat,* December 6, 1954. David Schoenbrun, *As France Goes,* New York: Harper & Bros., 1957, pp. 312-3. For further comments, see: Stanley Hoffman, "The Postmortems," in: D. Lerner and R. Aron, eds., *Op. cit.,* Ch. VIII, pp. 172-3, 183-4. Raymond Aron, "Historical Sketch of the Great Debate," *Loc. cit.,* pp. 18-9. Jacques Fauvet, "Birth and Death of a Treaty," *Loc. cit.,* pp. 156-63.

177. *J.O.,* session of August 30, 1954, pp. 4471, 4473-4 (breakdown of the vote, 319-264).

178. Jacques Fauvet, "Birth and Death of a Treaty," in D. Lerner and R. Aron, eds., *Op. cit.,* Ch. VII, pp. 155-6. See the breakdown on the vote on the *question préalable* moved by General Aumeran which ended EDC: *J.O.,* session of August 30, 1954, pp. 4443-4. See also the statements of various Socialist speakers and chairmen of committees of the National Assembly, above, ft. note 174. Pierre-Olivier Lapie, "Pour une communauté européenne de l'armement," *La Revue Socialiste,* October, 1953.

179. In a major poll on attitudes concerning EDC undertaken by the *Institut Français d'Opinion Publique* in November, 1953,

the following revealing results were obtained (the questions have been paraphrased, the figures have been quoted):

Europe could best be defended by:

each country having its own army	20%
a European Army	39
a combination of both	15
don't know	26

("Résultats d'ensemble d'une enquête sur la Communauté Européenne de Défense," *Sondages,* 1953, No. 2, Supplement, p. 1)

Europe could be defended better:

with the participation of German troops	50%
without the participation of German troops	25
No opinion	25

(*Ibid.,* p. 4.)

Would the existence of German troops constitute a danger for France:

yes	57
no	25
don't know	18

(*Ibid.,* p. 4.)

The danger from German troops would be greater in the form of:

a German army	61
a European army	8
other answers	8
don't know	23

(*Ibid.,* p. 4.)

One of the principle questions was how the individual himself would vote in a referendum on EDC consisting of the six nations actually concerned (France, Germany, Italy, Belgium, Holland and Luxemburg):

for	46
against	22
would not vote	13
don't know	19

(*Ibid.,* p. 4.)

Thus on one of the most direct questions, opinion was more than two to one in favor of the European army project (for a summary of the reasons advanced by those polled, see *Ibid.,* pp. 5-8). Quite significantly, when the question was asked how the person would vote in a referendum on the treaty in the form in which it was before the National Assembly, the answers were:

for	30
against	21
would not vote	13
don't know	36

A footnote in the article explains that since the poll had been taken, new conditions in agreement with the interests of France had been incorporated in the text.

(*Ibid.,* p. 9)

The discrepancy between the answers to this question and the virtually identical one previously cited is noteworthy. Of all the questions in the poll, the last one cited is the one which comes closest to an even division of opinion. It indicates that as of November, 1953, there existed in France popular opinion of a minimum of about three to two in support of EDC among those who had any opinion at all on the matter. See also: Maurice Duverger, "L' Affaire du sondage," *L'Express,* November 21, 1953, p. 12; and see: Jean Stoetzel, "The Evolution of French Opinion," in D. Lerner and R. Aron, eds., *Op. cit.,* Ch. V.
180. Statements by: Edouard Bonnefous, *J.O.,* session of November 18, 1953, pp. 5242-8; Edouard Daladier, *Loc. cit.,* 2nd session of November 19, 1953, pp. 5295-8; Jules Moch, *Loc. cit.,* 1st session of August 28, 1954, pp. 4379-86; Moro-Giafferi, *Loc. cit.,* 2nd session of August 28, 1954, pp. 4404-5; Pierre-Olivier Lapie, *Loc. cit.,* 1st session of August 29, 1954, pp. 4416-9. Daniel Mayer, président de la Commission des Affaires étrangères, *Loc. cit.,* 3rd session of August 29, 1954, pp. 4441-2; Edouard Daladier, *Loc. cit.,* 2nd session of December 22, 1954, pp. 6761-5.
181. R. Quillot, "La grande désespérance du peuple français," *La Revue Socialiste,* Pt. I: March, 1954, pp. 286-98, Pt. II: April, 1954, pp. 411-25. Jules Isaac, "Guerre atomique ou coéxistence," *Loc. cit.,* July, 1954, pp. 113-28. Statement by Edouard Bonnefous, *J.O.,* session of November 18, 1953, pp. 5242-8.
182. In the conclusion to his study, Mr. Zartman (*Op. cit.*)

states that neutralists have not been able to exert any direct influence over the French Government or over official policies (*Ibid.*, pp. 214-5). This view is consistent with Mr. Zartman's contention that the attitude of *L'Express* has not been in any sense a manifestation of neutralism and that the defeat of EDC was largely a non-neutralist phenomenon (ft. note 167). We are back once more to the question of definitions and particularly of the meaning of the word "neutralism." Suffice it to say here that policies were adopted, in the spring and summer of 1954, by a strongly anti-Communist French premier which, concerning the vital questions of Indo-China and EDC, were nonetheless in *fundamental* opposition to the basic policy of the United States.

As for the influence of neutralists on public opinion, Mr. Zartman continues, that too, measured by their success at the polls, has been negative (*Ibid.*, p. 216). The evidence on this point would appear to be conclusive—for the spring of 1951. What then can be said of the significance of neutralism in France? Mr. Zartman answers that one must distinguish between the positive program of the neutralists, which had no prospects of success, on the one hand, and their negative program on the other; neutralism is essentially a protest movement. But even in its aspect as a protest movement, Mr. Zartman believes that the significance of neutralism has been quite limited (*Ibid.*, pp. 217-9). It has at times contributed to make France "drag her feet"; it has contributed to the defeat of single items of policy, but only, he notes, with the help of other, more powerful, political forces. The final impression from Mr. Zartman's work remains that neutralism has exerted only an incidental influence on French political life.

In considering these points, it should first be remarked that when any group stands for a policy of non-involvement, or as Mr. Zartman puts it, non-alignment and refusal to choose (*Ibid.*, pp. 192-6, 210-11, 217-9), a negative victory is in itself a real success. Defeat of a course of positive action, by its very nature, amounts to "non-choice." Thus any negative victory over a proposed policy for the Western alliance becomes a positive victory for the principle of non-entanglement. But it is in the realm of opinion, admittedly somewhat intangible, rather than in the questions of the effect of neutralism upon official Franch policies, or even the lack of success of a particular neutralist group at the polls, that the main issue concerning the development of neutralism in France appears. It is, indeed, in the realm of the psychological effect of neutralist propaganda in developing a climate of French opinion suspicious of America's motives and leadership, and indirectly in contributing to the growth of a similar streak in the larger fabric of European attitudes—which in turn have played some part in the subsequent orientation of American policies—that the most interesting conclusions about neutralism in France can be found.

183. J. B. Duroselle, *et al., Op. cit.,* pp. 33-52. "Le problème allemand," issue of *La Nef,* December, 1952.

CHAPTER THREE

Gaullism: The Development of Nationalist Neutralism

In postwar France, anti-Communism has been a characteristic shared by virtually all political parties, except the *Progressistes*. But it is the names of Charles de Gaulle and the *Rassemblement du Peuple Français* which symbolize, during the early years of the Cold War, the most violent hostility towards the Communist party, or towards those whom de Gaulle himself had dubbed the "separatists."[1] As for the Communists, they in turn ranked *le grand Charlie* first in their catalog of assorted French fascists.[2]

It is also true that the idea of French nationalism in the postwar period automatically brings to mind the same names of the RPF and de Gaulle. Especially in its early stage, the *Rassemblement* was constituted by a very heterodox coalition drawing together conservative industrialists and old-guard officers on one side, a sprinkling of former left-wing intellectuals and a number of workers on the other, plus a mass-following of conservative petty bourgeois and *bien pensants* in the middle. About the only bonds that held this motley alliance together were these twin factors of anti-Communism and of nationalism—nationalism in the sense of a belief that de Gaulle himself *was* the grandeur of France.

Under the circumstances, there was no question as to where the RPF stood prior to 1951, not only on the matter of its alignment in the East-West conflict[3]—de Gaulle specifically referred to the ties of friendship between France and the United States.[4]—but also on the particular policies that followed from the division of the world into two blocs. For many years, de Gaulle had argued that France should have the military power and equipment consistent with the prestige of a great nation.[5] Thus the RPF was in agreement upon the urgent need for French rearmament[6] as advocated also by N.A.T.O. council meetings. In fact, a large-scale French rearmament program would satisfy both the RPF's hostility to communism, and its call for the reassertion of France's national grandeur.[7]

At the same time, the Gaullists were uncompromising in their denunciation of neutralism.[8] One of their charges against the governments of the Third Force was that these governments were actually motivated by secret neutralist tendencies.[9] Not only were most neutralists attacked as dangerous and unconscious, or more often conscious, agents[10] of the Communists, but their position was denounced as a retreat, a cowardly national abnegation[11] wholly at variance with the tradition of French courage and virility, as symbolized by General de Gaulle. Actually, the idea of the "impotence" of neutralists contrasted to the "virility" of pro-N.A.T.O. Frenchmen had been stressed first by Pierre Brisson, editor of the right-wing but non-Gaullist *Le Figaro*.[12] The same view was shared, however, by *Le Rassemblement,* the official RPF weekly.[13]

What accounts for the fact that within three years, Gaullists were not only campaigning side by side with neutralists on a crucial issue, and voting with them in the National Assembly, but that de Gaulle talked of the historic friendship of France and Russia while the members of the old RPF cooperated with neutralists in the creation of various new left-wing movements? What were the larger implications of this striking reversal? These are the questions with which the following pages deal. An explanation of the change requires a look at the history of Gaullism, which will relate the changing outlook of the RPF to events in France, as well as provide the background that explains the particular direction of the change. The reversal can then be understood in the perspective of two closely connected questions: 1) a change in the nature of Gaullist nationalism, and 2) a changed attitude toward American policies which implied a significant shift in values.

The role of champion of the most uncompromising hostility not only to communism but toward any appeasement by pussy-footed neutralists came naturally to the party of the French right, the party of militant nationalism. The purpose of the RPF was to achieve the unity of Frenchmen in the service of France. The myth of a unitary nation, *L'Union sacrée,* which at one time had been the prerogative of the Jacobins, in modern times passed to the right. It is hardly surprising that in a country with an old nationalist tradition and with a streak of chauvinism embedded even in its most individual anarchists—witness Péguy—the appeal to national pride should find a responsive audience. There exists in France a nucleus of nationalist elements which under favorable circumstances becomes the core of a powerful mass-movement, particularly if *patriotisme* and *incivisme*[14] can be combined into a single attitude of chauvinism and contempt for the government. The consequences of this combination is a hybrid, abstract, national sentiment which feels itself under no obligation to meet civic responsibilities that are identified not with the nation but with the regime.

Thus the sense of dedication and patriotism which had marked the Resistance provided a good platform for the new representative of the Party of Order which held in contempt the ministers of the state.[15] In 1947 perhaps more than ever before conservative nationalists in France felt a desperate need for organization and resistance to a climate of opinion as well as a program of government that was confusedly but definitely left: the rise of the RPF[16] from 1947 to 1949 was meteoric.[17]

Ostensibly, the *Rassemblement* was not a political party; it was the national conscience; it was France.[18] Such a catholic movement could have little internal cohesiveness. In fact, the RPF was a hodge-podge of various social components, of conflicting ideologies, divergent political backgrounds and of opposite economic interests. That, of course, was precisely what the supra-party *Ralliement* had set out to be. The Gaullists were convinced that the mystique of nationalism and the personal mystique of their leader would forge out of this mass of conflicts a unified force which could regenerate France, somewhat as the Resistance had done.

For the alchemy of nationalism to work and to transmute such a motley following into a constructive force, obedience to the *mots d'ordre* of the chief was essential. The authoritarianism with which the headquarters in the *Rue de Solférino* were charged[19] was nothing but the inevitable attribute of a supra-party rally whose leader could be only a "fascist dictator" or the "savior of France."[20] The result of this centralization, however, was the further accentuation of the centrifugal tendencies in the RPF. Resignations followed; the trend now was downward. It is an axiom of politics that a movement whose appeal lies largely in its emotional fervor, a movement which has no local tradition to fall back upon, no cadres of militants with a vested interest in carrying out the inevitable political chores, but which does have a highly volatile clientele, such a movement cannot lose its momentum and still survive. The Radicals or Socialists, for example, benefiting from the reflexive "second thoughts" of the voter, can stage a come-back; short of a *deus ex machina,* a movement like the RPF cannot.

If the internal dynamics of Gaullism spelled the decline of the RPF, it was the external situation that brought about its fall. The point would be of purely academic interest were it not for the fact that in the process the movement was transformed into something new, something with a new concept of French nationalism, which was to have a short-lived but noteworthy impact upon the evolution of contemporary France. Yet more significant than the effect of the new Gaullism upon France—a transitory phenomenon—was its character of an embodiment of a particular state of mind and scale of values that have international scope and for which France serves here as a case study. In other countries as in the Fourth Republic, the ensuing compound of values and forces has proven very unstable; but it suggests in these countries, as it has demonstrated in France, that when circumstances do bring it about, it can have major repercussions on international relations and vital meaning for the United States.

It has been observed that while the *Rassemblement* presented itself as a movement of social regeneration, vaguely defined in its master plan, the "capital-labor associations,"[21] the supporters of the movement came largely from that class in society which had a vested interest in the preservation of the economic status quo.[22] When in the spring of 1952 Antoine Pinay became Premier of France, there seemed to exist no reason for the conservative *classes dirigeantes* to continue supporting a political movement which had little prospect of achieving power in the foreseeable future. Besides, the right-wing radicalism of some of the general's schemes undoubtedly frightened many of those who had felt obliged to support him when the only alternative had been the nationalizations and social legislation of a Third Force which included Marxists, not to mention the still darker threat of the unfathomable extreme left.[23] Now the latter danger had receded—internally—and the former danger was rapidly disintegrating before an invigorated right-center. Elementary prudence dictated the support of a conservative cabinet.

But such support would constitute a direct denial of the goal of the RPF which consisted not only of the restoration of the government to the forces of Order but also of the use of authority to bring about a new sense of national solidarity which incidentally might threaten the stability of the existing social hierarchy. Pinay and de Gaulle might conceivably agree on many points of a government program; yet the former stood for the expedient replastering of a regime which his success might prolong, the latter could see the national good emerging only from the washing away of the original sin that damned the regime itself. It is ironic to find here on the issue of strong government and national unity a reappearance of the old quarrel between the orthodox and revisionist wings of the Socialist International concerning the advantages of participating in and transforming the bourgeois national state versus those of an uncompromising hostility that would hasten the inevitable day of internationalist victory. Like the orthodox Marxists who considered themselves the embodiment of the international spirit of the proletariat, a General who regarded himself as the personification of the national soul could not compromise without denying his mission.

To the RPF, the Constitution of the Republic must reflect the life of the French nation. Thus constitutional reform and nationalism were inextricably interwoven; what France required was not a government which could make the instrument function for a while, de Gaulle believed, it was a new expression of national consciousness. The only alternative was a perpetuation of the atomization of France and the triumph of forty million egoisms.

In the thirteenth year of the Fourth Republic, few persons are likely to disagree with de Gaulle's diagnosis even if they reject the cures he prescribed and his notion that out of constitutional change would emerge new national mores. But like most nationalists, de Gaulle, in his concentration on the notion of the state, naturally has tended to think in primarily political terms. Furthermore, it seems far from implausible to maintain that the institution of effective government capable of ending the paralytic stability imposed upon the country by its governing bureaucracy might have produced just such a sense of national purpose as the General dreamed of achieving.

It appears that if Gaullism and the government of Antoine Pinay were compatible in their interest in a return to Order, they were incompatible on the question of nationalism. To the General, the second point was the real issue; to most of his conservative supporters the first point was the primary objective. Some of them proclaimed pointedly that they could no longer reconcile a policy of belligerent anti-communism with a practice which resolved itself in the mixing of RPF votes with those of the separatists. This joint opposition, in principle, to the government, this meeting of two extremes against the middle, constituted a negative alliance indicative of a future community of interests. The stage had been set for August, 1954.

It was Pinay who broke the RPF. For many of its erstwhile supporters his right-center government had deprived Gaullism of all reason for existence—or at least of reason sufficiently powerful to justify sacrificing the reality of power and the prestige of ministerial portfolios. As a political movement, Gaullism was doomed. Even among those of its adherents who remained with the General there were many who leaned strongly to the policy of the rebels.[24] After various vicissitudes, the rump of his followers reorganized themselves into the *Union*

Républicaine d'Action Socialiste and, after further schisms, the rump of the rump formed the *Républicains Sociaux*. They too participated in the political games of the Assembly and thus threatened to deprive de Gaulle's nationalism of its chief attribute: purity from partisan politics. He had no choice but to disassociate himself from his remaining loyal followers and to release the former RPF deputies.[25] Gaullism without de Gaulle —the whole thing was preposterous.

Clearly, it was the dissidents who had correctly gauged the inclination of the old RPF electors.[26] The voters of the *Rassemblement* had been after stability in government, a strong executive, and resistance to Marxism—even the Christian Marxism of the MRP! They had only a secondary interest in the purity of which de Gaulle spoke, but they had a very direct concern in the political by-play which might affect government subsidy of beets. The increasingly powerful right-center[27] of MM. Pinay, Billotte and Barrachin provided them with a congenial and natural habitat.[28]

Gaullism was wrecked. Yet in a sense the Gaullist remnant had been purged. Many of those who had joined the RPF out of opportunism, or because they saw in the General an instrument for political change but a bulwark against the mobility of the social hierarchy, had now quit the movement. Among the remnant, a significantly larger proportion had come originally from the left. They combined with their nationalism a search for a new *élan vital* in a basically egalitarian reform of the economic structure contrasting strikingly with the social philosophy of the dissidents.

The new atmosphere was reminiscent of the idealism and élan of 1944. The very remoteness in the France of 1953 of the enthusiasm and sense of purpose that had characterized the end of the occupation accentuated the nostalgia with which the idealist followers of de Gaulle looked back upon the mystique of Gaullism as it had stood at the close of the war.

With the RPF, and its reduced successors, disintegrating as a political force, Gaullism was transformed increasingly back again into a mystique. In fact, Gaullist leaders successfully compensated for the political defeats of more recent times by consciously re-evoking the memories of the old Gaullism.[29]

And this, in turn, involved a return to the nebulous but definitely leftist program of the National Council of the Resistance, to the mystique of Progress which has characterized the great moments in French history. The irony of the situation was that in the form of a mystique Gaullism could capitalize on the basically emotional nature of its appeal, and thus achieved a greater, if less tangible, influence than it had as a political movement. Political failure thus "freed" Gaullism from the reality of politics and from the attacks of its old political enemies on the left. The wider appeal of Gaullism which followed from its debacle as a Rally[30] itself compensated for that very failure. From a partisan movement, Gaullism had been transformed into a state of mind.[31] *Que la République était belle sous l'Empire!*

We have come to the fulfillment of the evolution of political Gaullism. This is what the story is about, and the vicissitudes of the RPF that have figured in these pages are of concern to us only because they provide the "how" and the "why" of this conclusion. And this conclusion, in turn, will appear in its full meaning when it is considered as the specific expression of a general attitude, or of certain psychological and sociological factors, which have a critical bearing on the conflict between the Communist and non-Communist worlds.

The search for a "new solution" by the Gaullist left did not imply just any change but meant specifically movement in a "social" direction. To be sure, Hitlerism in its early stages had represented similar tendencies, and the parallel was too apparent to escape the notice of the critics of this revived "social fascism." Nonetheless, the new nationalism was essentially an ideology of dynamism—born just at the time, and largely as a result of, the practical weakness of the movement—very different from the static nationalism of the classical French right. Some of the former RPF members who had remained "faithful" to de Gaulle took this idea to its logical conclusion and arrived at a conception of the Permanent Revolution which placed them squarely in the extreme left. Thus the splinter group of the

Union Démocratique du Travail had come back full circle to its proletarian leanings. René Capitant, Louis Vallon, Manuel Bridier and Mme. de Lipkowski took their personal allegiance to de Gaulle with them into the militant leftist *Centre d'Action des Gauches Indépendantes,* headed by Claude Bourdet and Gilles Martinet.[32] At a time when some of its left-wing Marxist allies were still held back[33] by the unpleasant memories of August 23, 1939,[34] the UDT was calling for a new Popular Front.[35] Consequently, if a comparison between the remnants of Gaullism and National Socialism naturally springs to mind, it would be fully as appropriate to draw an analogy with the old radical nationalism of the Jacobins. This new Gaullism shared with the Jacobin tradition not only its idealist authoritarianism but also its concept of *la patrie* as a mystique of permanent revolution rather than of permanent stability. Implicit in the nature of this new Gaullism was a nationalism that was essentially left. The point is vital; we shall return to it in a moment.

With the succession of schisms and resignations Gaullism lost not only the major portion of its followers but most of its press support as well. This may be an appropriate place to open a parenthesis in the narrative. It has probably not escaped the reader that whereas the discussion of neutralism was primarily concerned with the expression of various opinions in response to American policies, the pages of this chapter are taken up mostly with an analysis of events. The distinction is one that is inherent in the nature of the available evidence, and this, in turn, is a reflection of the two different types of movement that are involved. The core of the neutralists was a highly vocal group of intellectuals for whom the development of an abstract position in an article was second nature and who consequently spelled out detailed programs for every contingency. All shades of opinion were carefully scrutinized by the neutralist press, which itself was of many hues. Gaullism on the other hand, had little program beyond a general sketch, and its enemies claimed it had none at all. While its propaganda consequently had less variety and interest, the fact that the movement had been a powerful political force actively intervening in political affairs about which the neutralists of the left could only write indignant articles means that the description of historical events has a far greater significance in this case. Thus, the difference in the character of these two chapters is itself a reflection of the difference in the kind of influence left-wing neutralism and Gaullist nationalism had upon French politics.

It would certainly be an error to conclude from the above that Gaullism in its hey-day did not have an active propaganda machine, or did not enjoy some powerful support from the organs of the nation's press.[36] Extremely friendly to de Gaulle were such widely known and quoted voices of opinion as the Paris daily *L'Aurore* and the political-literary weekly *Carrefour* —not to mention the official publications of the movement. We had reached the point in our account where these two organs, which had represented the extreme rightism of the RPF were moving away from Gaullism as the latter developed along new political lines. Hidden in this divorce was a very significant divergence. Indeed, *L'Aurore* and *Carrefour* represented a concept of nationalism identified with *immobilisme* in France, with the status quo in foreign relations—and especially France's status as an imperial power.[37] The changing Gaullism, on the other hand, saw in France a transcendental, yet absolute, reality which was not identified with any particular social pattern. If the latter had to be sacrificed in favor of Eternal France as an idea above any particular France—or above what Luethy calls the France of M. Gingembre[38]—so be it. The transcendency of this ideal of a pure ethos of France, separate from any of the characteristics of a given period and behind each of its infinite manifestations, that idea is contained in the final mystique of Gaullism. That idea is the real significance of the radical nationalism of most of the Gaullist "ultras." Were it not for this important feature, the decline of the RPF would be a dull story indeed. Was it unnatural that that attitude should generate a radically different view of the world around France?

* * * * * * * * *

By definition, the concept of nationalism calls for opposition to any supra-national federation[39] or to any abandonment of national sovereignty.[40] The conservative nationalism of the old RPF had been opposed to any economic oragnization which might imperil the protected structure of France industry and tear down the tariff walls behind which an inferiority-minded entrepreneurial group felt secure. Indeed, many industrialist had a stake in preserving the status quo of the French production system, and they consequently opposed any supra-national integration of the economy. They found a natural ally in the nationalism of the RPF and URAS. Those industrialists who feared the competition of a European market supported the RPF's attack on the European Coal and Steel Community—misnamed the Schuman Plan. Thus Gaullist national ideology and capitalist profits in certain industries[41] found a common target in one of the foremost "Europeans," the "instigator" as de Gaulle once referred to Jean Monnet in a violent denunciation.[42] Above all, the fear of the European Coal and Steel Community was, on the part of the Gaullists, the classical French rightist fear of Germany—the eventual fear of German arms[43] but more pressingly the fear that Germany's huge productive machine would benefit from European integration[44] at the expense of French industry.[45] In this form, *the psychology of nationalism was definitely rightist,* even though it came to the same conclusion as the ideological opposition to the Cold War integration of Western Europe expressed by the left-wing neutralists.

The question of the Schuman Plan was a sideline affair, or rather a preliminary bout. The real issue was EDC. As tension between the East and West developed, the question of German rearmament had become an ever-more pressing issue. The solution adopted, at the specific request of the French Government which feared the reappearance of a national German army, was the principle of a coalition-army embodied in the European Defense Community. It should be added that in the eyes of many of its French supporters the EDC plan was contingent upon certain conditions[46] which nationalists considered as the absolute minimum guarantees for France, namely German acceptance of both the permanent "Europeanization" of the Saar and the economic integration of the area with France,[47] British participation in the Community, an official American pledge concerning the maintenance of United States troops in Europe,[48] and the assurance that aid to the former Axis powers would never talk precedence over aid to former Allies. These guarantees, some of the Plan's supporters felt—and all of its enemies proclaimed—had never been adequately implemented.

At first, the opposition of the RPF to EDC stemmed from the same psychological attitudes and values as had its opposition to the Coal and Steel Authority. It was the opposition of generals[49] concerned with the traditions of their regiments, of industrialists who had equal forebodings of a supply system for a European army as they did for a common coal and steel authority. De Gaulle saw in EDC essentially a dangerous surrender of French sovereignty, a weakening or severing of the ties of the French Union,[50] and an abandonment of the French Army.[51] Similar opinions were expressed by numerous French generals who, as a group, were generally sympathetic to the RPF. It is not surprising that to a major proportion of the French officer class, reared in the tradition of historic French military valor, the concept of the submersion of the French army into a countryless European force that would include German soldiers, seemed beyond the realm of reason.[52] How could EDC inspire the patriotism of its troops as could *la patrie* and *la Marseillaise*?[53] What was an army without patriotism?[54] However, if French officers, such as Marshal Juin and General Koenig,[55] did not regard EDC as the logical answer to the logic of several hundred Russian divisions, their opposition did not necessarily imply hostility to the general line of N.A.T.O. policy.[56] While this opposition was no less effective for being a matter of self-interest, it was not an opposition of ideology. At a time when neutralists already opposed EDC *because* it signified German rearmament, de Gaulle was still proclaiming that he opposed the formation and the militarization of a new Reich[57] but that German participation in Western defense was necessary and inevitable.[58]

Meanwhile French industrialists who feared the economic consequences of a common market with its competition of foreign producers were making use of the classical nationalism expressed by the RPF to join in the opposition to EDC. Thus certain industries which are largely dependent upon military procurement for their survival are reported to have contributed heavily to the campaign against the European army in the fear that such an army could fulfill its mass requirements in equipment elsewhere at lesser cost.[59] The specific nature and extent of such activities is difficult to determine,[60] but there is no doubt that they played a part. Other industrialists, engaged in trade with Eastern Europe or Communist China,[61] found a different but no less compelling motive[62] for supporting a campaign against a project which their customers particularly opposed.[63]

Perhaps it was a coincidence that EDC became the dominant issue in France at approximately the time that the profound changes in the nature of Gaullism which have been described were taking effect. In any event, the old RPF hostility to the European army was subtly changed, or rather was supplemented by a new and more violent form of opposition—more violent because it involved an added ideological conflict. And EDC itself sharpened the ideological differences. Thus, while the opposition to EDC derived, in principle, from the old nationalism of the RPF and was in a way the logical continuation of the opposition of the right to all schemes of supra-national sovereignty already expounded in the opposition to the Schuman Plan, it also went considerably beyond this position. For the first time, Gaullists found themselves campaigning on the same side of an issue with left-wing neutralists like Jean Fabiani of *Combat* and Claude Bourdet.

The intensity of the anti-EDC sentiment of the URAS and the *Républicains Sociaux* had its emotional roots in the mood of the Occupation and Resistance. Whereas in 1951, the Gaullists had opposed EDC because of the *way* it would bring about a German defense contribution,[64] in 1953 they attacked it for the *fact* that it did so.[65] The European Defense Community, de Gaulle stated in 1954, would "deprive France of self-determination for fifty years, that is to say forever, take her own army away from her, forbid her all access to nuclear weapons, transfer to the American commander-in-chief the sole right to decide how she should be defended and even whether she should be,"[66] and "dissolved her by mixing her with vanquished Germany."[67] The Gaullist leader, Jacques Soustelle, opposed the recreation in Germany of a permanent "instrument of aggression"; the Germans, he continued, had not renounced their imperialism.[68] A remilitarized Germany, the Gaullists now proclaimed, would sooner or later try to reconquer its Eastern provinces,[69] either by changing sides[70] or by provoking World War III.[71] Cartoons[72] and reports[73] in the Gaullist press about Germany's character and about the *Wehrmacht* yielded nothing in bitterness to similar items appearing at the time in neutralist papers.[74] When a trip of various French parliamentarians to Poland was organized as part of the campaign against the remilitarization of Germany, it was the Gaullist deputies André Lebon and Jacques Soustelle who led the group.[75] A Gaullist spokesman even declared that a crisis in N.A.T.O.—which he believed would be reparable—would be preferable to France's condoning of German rearmament.[76] There was, of course, nothing new in nationalist French opposition to Germany.[77] But the important point is that the hierarchy of national threats and international dangers had changed radically. The prime enemy was no longer, as it once had been, the Soviet Union,[78] it was now Germany, and a potentially rearmed Germany.[79]

Anti-German, the tone of Gaullist opposition was also that of the Liberation with its implicit ideal of a New France. We see here the effect of the transformation that was described earlier upon the attitude of Gaullists on foreign affairs: *psychologically, the opposition to EDC manifested a nationalism of the left.*

As an instance of this, it is interesting to note one of the new charges developed against West European integration as part of the Gaullist campaign, the charge of a synarchical or pseudo-fascist capitalism[80] which had so often been levelled against the RPF itself. The fear was voiced that a supra-national authority with extensive powers would inevitably generate a bureaucratic technocracy which, not being responsible to any parliament[81] or other agent of the popular will,[82] would develop into an international managerial dictatorship.[83] Jean

Monnet again[84] was the individual who was portrayed as the typical technocrat or "synarchist," seeing Europe's problems only in terms of economics and productivity.[85] An international, largely independent authority modelled on such men and ideas, would lead to the eventual mechanization, the complete dehumanization, of European life. It would think nothing of depriving entire regions in France of their essential industry[86] in order to concentrate production in more efficient areas,[87] regardless of the sacrifice in human terms.[88] Efficiency yes, a Gaullist added, but a policy of increased productivity which left the worker at the mercy of a technocracy would be pure reaction.[89] This fear of a technocracy fitted in perfectly with the fear that in a supra-national community the Germans would soon emerge as masters. Indeed, what nation in Europe seemed the best example of a technocracy if not Germany, and particularly postwar Germany? But more strikingly, the fear of a synarchy also fitted in with the left's ideological picture of an inhuman capitalist system, personified by the United States, which sacrifices human values to economic profit.

A new nationalism had been superimposed upon the old, and the change had occurred without anyone fully realizing it. But while the position of the Gaullists on EDC remained essentially an expression of nationalism, the parallelism of this attitude with the ideological neutralism of the left had become increasingly evident. While neutralists were in opposition to American policies in the Cold War, and as a result came to oppose West European integration which they considered an aspect of those policies, Gaullists opposed West European supranational federation in principle, and as a result came to oppose American policies in the Cold War. Thus, having started from opposite poles neutralist and nationalist forces were converging first in joint opposition to certain policies, secondly in similar propaganda campaigns, thirdly in similar slogans and traditions —for example, the evocation of the Occupation—and finally in attitudes. Thus the nationalism of the URAS and *Républicains Sociaux,* not to mention the UDT, took on many of the ideological characteristics of the neutralists themselves. Jacques Soustelle,[90] attacking the European Army treaty in the National

Assembly, was not simply an old-line nationalist; Louis Vallon and Mme. de Lipkowski in the same function[91] were voicing one of the dreams of an earlier decade, a dream of French national consciousness synonymous with a consciousness of Movement and Progress which takes one back to Péguy. Positions on issues of international affairs and the atmosphere of Gaullism were inextricably tied together.

It was mentioned earlier that over the years EDC, in which the U.S. was not to participate, had come to be so intimately associated with the policy of the U.S. in Europe that they came to appear as two faces of the same coin. Thus opposition to EDC and to West European integration slid easily into denunciation of American policy in general, and eventually of American intentions. As an indication of this shift in attitude one can compare two items that appeared in *Le Rassemblement* at different periods. Early in 1952, this Gaullist organ had praised the *New York Herald Tribune* writer, George Slocombe,[92] who had "denounced the fable" of Gaullist anti-Americanism.[93] About two years later, when another article in the same paper began with a statement from *Le Monde* to the effect that the U.S. State Department was "dissatisfied to say the least, with General de Gaulle,"[94] *Le Rassemblement* commented that this foreign opinion proved who best could speak in the name of France.[95]

The anti-Anglo-Saxon streak which had developed out of de Gaulle's wartime relations[96] with the Allies[97] and had been buried in the anti-Communist period, came to the surface again in the new anti-American period. Neither "the dictatorship of Moscow nor the protectorate of Washington," de Gaulle had once remarked,[98] and Louis Terrenoire, General Secretary of the RPF had echoed the phrase: "Neither in the pockets of the U.S. nor under the yoke of the U.S.S.R."[99]

Whereas in 1951 de Gaulle had endorsed the Marshall Plan,[100] and defended close collaboration in foreign policy with the United States,[101] by 1953, *Le Rassemblement* was not only criticizing American policy toward France and Germany,[102] but also engaging in the favorite French pastime of denouncing the United States in terms of culture and ideology—with particular reference to McCarthyism.[103] A few years earlier, there were many in France who would have called this a case of the pot calling the kettle black! And what could be said when in 1954 Jacques Soustelle, as a leader of the movement which had most insistently proclaimed France's permanent "presence" in her overseas territories,[104] denounced as a moral wrong the economic imperialism of the United States in Guatemala.[105] The irony of the situation is that even on the question of imperial relations the Gaullists and the neutralists of the left, who had stood as far apart as any two groups can, were coming together[106] in a denunciation of American imperialism in the world generally, and in French possessions particularly. Thus the suspicions of the classical right of any American "intervention" in the French Union[107] facilitated the transition from a *de facto* to a *de jure* anti-Americanism of the Gaullists at a time when colonial questions in the Far East and North Africa were coming to dominate French political life.[108]

The intensity of the feeling revealed itself in the bitterness of the criticism. A biting attack on the United States was made by Gaston Palewski who charged that this country had concluded peace in Korea where its own troops were involved but that in Indo-China where its forces were not engaged it wanted the fighting to continue.[109] Meanwhile, de Gaulle himself had come to demand peace in Indo-China[110] in opposition to the policy of Washington—a striking reversal[111] for the great imperialist,[112] explained by the fact that he had become convinced that a continuation of the campaign might be to the advantage of the United States but not of France.[113]

> Having lately gone so far as to make an expedition to Korea, she [the U.S.] took care to limit the struggle and then to end it when she had the chance. Finding it very good that the French are fighting the battle in Indo-China, she contributes to keep it going with material and money, she intervenes in the way the battle is run, she seems ready to push into it yellow and white contingents furnished by allies in Asia and Australasia, and even to engage her own long-range weapons in it, but she does not dream of sending her battalions there. Preparing for a world war, she develops

> great efforts to arm all the countries which would be capable of fighting hand to hand with the Communist armies, and she takes care to assign to herself the command of their forces, but she has chosen for herself a peripheral strategy which would engage as few as possible of her sons on the battlefield . . .[114]

In view of these attitudes, it is hardly surprising to find de Gaulle himself referring in condescending terms to "our American friends" and to the vacillations of American foreign policy. To be sure, he said, he understood that Secretary Dulles was forced to deal with the fickle American public, but he regretted that the "Americans have bet on a bad horse [EDC] and, noticing that for two years it has been running in circles without ever reaching the post, insist on renewing their bet."[115]

Why, the General asked, among all the nations not participating in EDC—first of all, Britain, but also the Scandinavian countries, Ireland and others, not to mention the United States which would never envisage such an infringement of its sovereignty—why was it specifically France that had been singled out for admonishments and threats by Secretary of State Dulles? "That is only too easily explained since the aim of the operation is precisely to dissolve France, and, moreover, it is considered in Washington since 1946 that French officials will conform to instructions given them even if they take the form of a timetable."[116]

This newly violent anti-Americanism showed itself in the Gaullists' voicing of an idea which hitherto had been the prerogative of neutralists and Communists, namely that American policies were threatening the world with a new war. In 1951, one of the commentators writing in *Le Rassemblement* had unequivocally defended MacArthur's policy in Korea[117] and berated those timid politicians and pacifists who, by forcing the American commander to limit his field of operations and by eventually obtaining his removal had given the Communists a critical psychological victory in the Far East.[118] The Gaullist weekly *Carrefour* not only had castigated the "cowardly surrender" in Asia advocated by British Laborites[119] but even had criticized President Truman's attitude towards the American Commander.[120] In 1953, Gaullists referred to the dangers of war inherent in America's foreign policy[121]—what had happened to the detestable neutralists of 1951? No longer was it only the neutralists of the left who asserted that America's way of opposing communism would lead to a Communist victory,[122] and it was now also de Gaulle who proclaimed France's position for preserving world peace by working out a compromise between East and West.[123] Now it was Gaullists as well as neutralists who were declaring that the real danger of communism was not the threat of Soviet armies with which the U.S. was obsessively concerned, but of the social injustice and the disreputable conditions of existence inflicted upon so many people in France.[124]

Even N.A.T.O., the most basic of Western policies, was not spared the Gaullist attack.[125] The nationalist concept of an independent France, which in the early postwar years had meant resistance to communism, then opposition to Germany, now came to mean acting as a bridge between Washington and Moscow,[126] or as the mediator between the two great blocs.[127] The words "peaceful coexistence," which could have served as the *devise* of the neutralists now found their way into the speeches of Gaullists,[128] and General de Gaulle prescribed a new mission for France:

> A truly French policy would take as its first objective to bring about this easement between the two opposing blocs . . . . From the moment that the possibility of organizing co-existence between Moscow and Washington appears to offer itself, it is we whom it behoves to do everything to do so . . . . it is humanity that the atomic peril threatens. The mission of France, therefore, consists of doing everything to prevent the two halves of the world hurling themselves to death together . . . . At the same time, without ceasing to be members of the Atlantic alliance, let us organize Europe along lines which do not prevent such easement [sic] and do not tear us apart. Above all, let us remain France, sovereign, independent and free![129]

Such a role of mediation could not be played by a weak nation, he said. On the contrary, French efforts to reconcile the two blocs had nothing whatever to do with pacifist nonviolence. These efforts would require France to abandon her "congenital inferiority complex" in foreign affairs and to cease to provide "auxiliaries" for the leader of the Western bloc. France must make an effort "on her own account, for the same price that we are paying for a system that makes us subordinates."[130]

The first step in such a mission was to promote negotiations with the Communists,[131] and an agreement on arms limitation.[132] The Communist demand for a Four-Power conference, which had been staunchly defended in the neutralist press, was taken up with great vigor by Gaullist deputies. While the Communists praised the evolution of their erstwhile enemies, a Gaullist commentator writing in *Le Rassemblement* explained that if the Communists, in their opposition to EDC, happened to be on the right side, this was no reason for the RPF, because it opposed communism, to go over to the wrong side. It was now particularly important, he continued, not to let the French Communists present themselves as the only group that, ironically, had the true interests of the French nation at heart.[133] If the outcome was a sort of *de facto* collaboration,[134] well–. After all, the Communists were defending Russia; the RPF was defending France. This would not be the first time the interests of the two countries had coincided.[135]

> From the refusal of the Popular Front, it does not follow that we should spurn all contact with the Communists. We are well aware that there can be no joint labor union action without the CGT. We know that the participation of Communists in the fight against EDC may be decisive. Thus we must reject any overture to organic unity, but we must not fear to meet Communist militants and show them who we are and what we can do.[136]

Louis Terrenoire, Secretary of the RPF, set the record straight by repudiating soon afterwards any active collaboration with the Communists, even on a temporary basis.[137] The very fact that such a *mise au point* had been necessary, or even conceivable, would have seemed preposterous two years earlier.

From nationalism to opposition to EDC, from opposition to EDC to opposition to American policy in Europe and the Far East, from opposition to American policy to opposition to the United States itself, from opposition to the United States to the assertion that the U.S. and the U.S.S.R. were equal dangers to peace, from the equating of these dangers to the assertion that France must act as a bridge between the two blocs, such was the long road travelled by the General and his companions.

The Communists, who had lately discovered Joan of Arc[138] as the symbol of French anti-Anglo-Saxon pride, could well understand a nationalism[139] that stepped from the campaign against EDC and German rearmament to the call for a France "independent" of the United States.[140]

The neutralists, who during the early years of the RPF had regarded de Gaulle with scarcely less animosity than did the separatists, now changed their tune. *Combat* adopted a sympathetic attitude; Jean Fabiani wrote "De Gaulle Remains" and concluded: "The man who saved this country's honor in 1940 continues to represent our national conscience in its purest form."[141] The columns of *L'Express* featured regular contributions from Jacques Soustelle, Jean and Gaston Palewski, and André Malraux.

As for Gaullism, looking back nostalgically to the more glorious days of liberated France,[142] it was looking back also to those days when a triumphant leader of free France had signed a mutual assistance pact with the Soviet Union[143] and had called M. Thorez into the government. Perhaps the new Popular Front would consist after all of Thorez, Cot and de Gaulle! Anyway, the junction of neutralism and nationalism had been achieved.[144] It was consumated in the vote of August 30th, 1954.

* * * * * * * *

It is one of the small ironies of history that at the moment when the political power of the Gaullists had sunk to its lowest point, one of the movement's basic demands was achieved:

EDC was rejected. We have already seen that the very decline of Gaullism as a political force—and a political threat—enhanced its influence as a mystique and also broke down the political isolationism in which Gaullism had found itself in the last years of the RPF. Yet the fact remains that political Gaullism had been moribund for months. In the spring and fall of 1954 it seemed to come to life again for a moment as Gaullists took a leading part in the creation of the new coalition around Mendès-France.[145] The new leftist nationalism of de Gaulle's remaining "companions" seemed to have achieved some positive result in contributing to the enthusiasm which surrounded the New Left.[146] Yet all this was the last spurt of energy of the dying. The combination of nationalism and Jacobin revolutionism is usually explosive; but it is also unstable. The new coalition did not last beyond the normal tour of a premiership; and the Gaullists were among the first to break it up.

For some of them, the old habits of a rightist nationalism were too hard to break, at least when the issue of overseas territories came up and could no longer be side-stepped by the simple expedient of joint opposition to American interference. For others, the new demands of a leftist nationalism went beyond the limits of possibility of government action: Mendès-France *had to* stand by the London and Paris agreements on Germany; Soustelle[147] and Palewski[148] did not. Unity against EDC was one thing; unity for something else was another.[149]

Even the remnants of the RPF did not survive the elections of 1956 as a recognizable political element. How could they have; how could the Gaullists who had gone over to Mendès-France receive the votes of their electors who had stayed where they always had been, near M. Pinay . . . or who went over to Pierre Poujade?[150]

As a national tradition,[151] Gaullism exercises an unsuspected influence. As a factor in parliamentary life, the RPF is merely an episode of French history.[152] Grown essentially out of the right, Gaullism could not live as a movement of the left. In making the attempt, it had been instrumental in the creation of a new political force, a new dynamic element in France:

Mendèsisme. Parliamentary Gaullism did not survive 1955; political *Mendèsisme* did not survive 1956.

In history, it is often failure which is the most successful lesson. We have seen develop in France a combination of neutralism and nationalism, of extreme right and non-Communist left, in opposition to American policy. The compound proved to be very unstable, yet while it lasted, it showed itself to be powerful. Policies or situations which normally would arouse the hostility of either one of these elements—for instance, American anti-colonialism and the hostility of the right; McCarthyism and the hostility of the left—in fact aroused the joint hostility of both. Opposition became contagious.

We saw that neutralism of the left was essentially a response to American policies; on the other hand, the critical change in the nature of Gaullism occurred as a result primarily of developments in France. There is no easy answer to the question, what causes nationalist neutralism and no single policy that will "meet" neutralism's varied aspects. However, one will go further towards an understanding if one remembers that it is primarily a mood, an attitude of values, and only secondarily a policy, or set of policies. Thus, impressions given are as influential as decisions made. While it is true that the instability of the merger leaves little danger of a long-term positively neutralist policy being evolved in France, the negative effect can be of serious threat to American policies in Western Europe and for this, if for no other reason, merits our attention. And if it is true that no particular Western policies can affect all the political and psychological factors, internal as well as external, that go into the neutralist-nationalist combination, it is also true that the U.S. has a primary interest in avoiding cumulative reaction to its position such as to bring about the union of opposites and the sharing of private animosities towards Western policy.

That at least is the conclusion to which leads an examination of neutralism and nationalism in France. How much greater will its significance be if it should appear that in other nations similar situations exist.

Footnotes

1. "Les saboteurs et les criminels communistes n'ont jamais été vraiment inquiétés,, *Carrefour,* (Paris & Montreal; the references until September, 1951, are to the Montreal edition) March 6, 1951. "Jacques Duclos ne craint qu'un homme en France," *Loc. cit.,* May 15, 1951. "La cinquième colonne communiste paralysera la défense nationale si le régime continue," *Le Rassemblement,* Paris: R.P.F., July 29, 1950. "Le régime laisse les séparatistes se préparer à la guerre," *Loc. cit.,* August 12, 1950. "La soi-distant unité syndicale prépare la nouvelle Kollaboration," *Loc. cit.,* January 5-11, 1951, p. 3. "Pour vaincre les communistes," *Loc. cit.,* June 8-14, 1951.

2. "Importante déclaration de Jacques Duclos: 'Nous ne tolérerons pas la montée de de Gaulle au pouvoir,' " *L'Humanité,* Paris, May 8, 1951, p. 1; continued under heading: "Le fascisme ne passera pas," *Loc. cit.,* p. 3.

3. De Gaulle interview, *Le Rassemblement,* June 29—July 5, 1951, pp. 8-9. "Pour la France, pour la République: de Gaulle," *Loc. cit.,* April, 13-19, 1951, p. 5. For the RPF's attitude towards the United States prior to 1952, see also: Robert de St. Jean, "Truman devant les sphinx de 1951: U.R.S.S., Chine, Commonwealth, etc. sans oublier MacArthur et Taft," *Carrefour,* January 16, 1951, p. 5. "'Cinq griefs de Joe Smith contre la France. Cinq reproches de Jean Dupont aux U.S.A.," *Loc. cit.,* January 16, 1951.

4. Le Rassemblement du Peuple Français, *La France sera la France, Ce que veut Charles de Gaulle,* Paris: R.P.F., 1951, p. 225: excerpts of de Gaulle speech at Strasbourg, April 6, 1947, and p. 227: excerpts of de Gaulle speech April 27, 1947. Henceforth this source, consisting predominantly of extracts from the speeches of de Gaulle, will be referred to simply as: *La France sera la France.* See also: "Avec des faibles: guerre et catastrophe. Avec des forts: la vie et la paix. Discours prononcé par le général de Gaulle le 7 Janvier à Nîmes," *Le Rassemblement,* January 12-18, 1951, p. 3.

5. *La France sera la France,* pp. 212-42, especially pp. 221 ff.: speech of de Gaulle at Marseilles, April 16, 1948.

6. Robert de St. Jean, "Une interview exclusive du général Koenig, candidat à Strasbourg, 'J'ai quitté la "Grande Muette" pour dire la vérité au pays: Une France mal-défendue appelle

l'invasion . . .,'" *Carrefour,* May 29, 1951, p. 1; same article continued under heading: "'Il faut réarmer sans délai pour que la France ne soit ni "Coréanisé" ni "soviétisée,"'" p. 5. R. de St. Jean, "Si Eisenhower comprehend que la France veut vivre, l'Occident sera sauvé," *Loc. cit.,* January 9, 1951, p. 5.

7. "Avec des faibles: guerre et catastrophe. Avec des forts: la vie et la paix. Discours prononcé par le général de Gaulle le 7 Janvier à Nîmes," *Le Rassemblement,* January 12-18 1951, p. 3. "Les falsifications du réarmement," *Loc. cit.,* January 19-25, 1951.

8. Jean Nocher, "Le mépris du Monde," *Le Rassemblement,* May 16-22, 1952, p. 2.

9. "Le neutralisme le plus dangereux . . . . Celui que cache . . . mais pratique le cabinet Pleven," *Le Rassemblement,* January 26—February 1, 1951, pp. 8-9. "Retarder le réarmement de l'Europe pour ne pas déplaire à l'U.R.S.S., voilà la vraie 'politique' Moch-Pleven," *Loc. cit.,* November 4, 1950. "M. Pleven se tourne vers Moscou qui compte sur un autre Munich pour affaiblir l'Occident," *Loc. cit.,* November 11, 1950. Claude Couband, "L'U.R.S.S. veut neutraliser l'Europe," *Loc. cit.,* March 9-15, 1951, p. 5. André Desmond, "Tandis que nos soldats tombent en Extrême Orient, le gouvernement livre de l'acier à Mao Tse Tung," *Carrefour,* January 9, 1951.

10. "Communistes et neutralistes," *Le Rassemblement,* March 2-8, 1951, p. 14. Claude Couband, "L'U.R.S.S. veut neutraliser l'Europe," *Loc. cit.,* March 9-15, 1951, p. 5. Jules Monnerot, "La politique d'isolement qui n'ose dire son nom," *Loc. cit.,* January 5-11, 1951, p. 3.

11. Pierre Louis Berthaud, "Le professeur Pasteur Vallery-Radot, de l'Académie française, commente la fuite d'un de ses collègues: 'L'Académie devrait exclure M. Gilson!,'" *Carrefour,* February 20, 1951. Jules Monnerot, "La politique d'isolement qui n'ose dire son nom," *Le Rassemblement,* January 5-11, 1951, p. 3. Jean Nocher, "Le mépris du Monde," *Loc. cit.,* May 16-22, 1952, p. 2.

12. Pierre Brisson, "Les insexués," *Le Figaro,* (Paris) January 8, 1951.

13. Jules Monnerot, "La politique d'isolement qui n'ose dire son nom," *Le Rassemblement,* January 5-11, 1951, p. 3.

14. For a penetrating analysis of the *incivisme* and political degeneration of the French middle class, see: E. Drexel Godfrey,

"France: Collapse of a Class," *The Antioch Review,* Yellow Springs, Ohio (Vol. 14) Summer, 1954, pp. 131-48.

15. "Le grand dessein du régime: laisser à de Gaulle une terre brulée," *Carrefour,* April 3, 1951.

16. Launched by de Gaulle's famous address at Strasbourg on April 7, 1947, which had followed his dramatic re-entry into politics at Bruneval on February 27.

17. In the elections to the National Assembly of June, 1951, the RPF, campaigning in isolation against the heavy odds of a weighted electorial law, still polled 20.84% of the ballot. See also François Goguel, *Géographie des élections françaises de 1870 à 1951,* Cahiers de la Fondation nationale des Sciences politiques, no. 27, Paris: Librairie Armand Colin, 1951, pp. 139-42.

18. For a defense of Gaullism at this time, see: *The Case for de Gaulle, A Dialogue Between André Malraux and James Burnham,* New York: Random House, 1948. Excerpts of these texts also appeared, under the title "Thorez n'est pas la Gauche, Blum n'est pas le Centre, de Gaulle n'est pas la Droite," in *Carrefour,* April 13, 1948. Roy Pierce, "De Gaulle and the R.P.F.–A Post-mortem," *The Journal of Politics,* Gainesville, Florida, (Vol. 16) February, 1954, p. 91.

19. H. Stuart Hughes, "Gaullism," in Edward Mead Earle, ed., *Modern France, Problems of the Third and Fourth Republics,* Princeton: Princeton University Press, 1951. R. Pierce *Op. cit.,* p. 107.

20. David Thomson, *Two Frenchmen: Pierre Laval and Charles de Gaulle,* London: Cresset Press, 1951. Emile Henri Désiré Muselier, *De Gaulle contre le Gaullisme,* Paris: Editions du Chêne, 1946. William L. Langer, *Our Vichy Gamble,* New York: Alfred Knopf, 1947. When de Gaulle, having defended in 1954 Marchal Juin's right to oppose EDC in public and having condoned the Marshal's refusal to respond to a convocation from his government, was asked if he (de Gaulle) would have tolerated such action from an officer while he was head of the state, he replied: "I was France, the State, the Government. I spoke in the name of France. I was the independence and sovereignty of France. And this is why, without hesitation, everyone obeyed me." See: "'Le traité de C.E.D. porte gravement atteinte à notre soverainetė et à notre indépendance' affirme

le général de Gaulle," *Le Monde,* April 9, 1954, p. 4; and the introductory note of Raymond Barillon.

21. Assemblée Nationale, Deuxième Législature, Session de 1952, Annexe au Procès-Verbal du 2 Décembre, *Proposition de loi tendant à l'établissement de contrats d'association capital-travail, présentée par M. Louis Vallon et les membres du groupe du Rassemblement du peuple français.*

22. For an exceptionally illuminating analysis of the stratification of French society and its effect upon French life, see: Herbert Luethy, *France Against Herself,* New York: F. A. Praeger, 1955, especially Pt. I: "The National Structure," and Pt. II: "Back to the Third Republic."

23. For a discussion of the political mentality of the contemporary *classes dirigeantes,* see: E. Drexel Godfrey, "France: Collapse of a Class," *The Antioch Review,* Summer 1954, pp. 131-48. H. Luethy, *Op. cit.,* Pts. I & II as cited, and Pt. IV: "The Fulcrum."

24. Who took the name of *Action Républicaine et Sociale,* until they merged with the *Indépendants.* Their leaders were General Billotte and Edmond Barrachin.

25. On May 7, 1953, de Gaulle officially withdrew the RPF from an active role in French politics. See also R. Pierce, *Op. cit.,* pp. 115 ff.

26. Jacques Fauvet, "Les cinq caractéristiques du scrutin," *Le Monde,* January 4, 1956. J. Fauvet, "La géographie des partis après les élections," Pt. IV: "Des voix R.P.F. de 1951 se sont portées aussi bien sur le poujadisme que sur les listes mendèsistes," *Le Monde,* January 13, 1956, p. 5. See especially *Sondages,* 14th year, 1952, No. 3, pp. 32-7, particularly p. 34.

27. Based on the *Indépendants* and *Paysans.*

28. Illustrated by the fact that the ARS and the *Indépendants* since then have merged.

29. *Jours de France,* June 16-23, 1955, pp. 45-8.

30. "Les gaullistes déchirés," in: "L'Assemblée retarde de vingt-quatre heures le scrutin définitif sur les accords de Paris," *Le Monde,* December 31, 1954, pp. 2-3. "A l'occasion d'une journée nationale, le général de Gaulle dissoudra le Rassemblement crée en 1947; les élus R.P.F. se regrouperont librement," *Loc. cit.,* October 27, 1954.

31. Raymond Barillon, "Le général de Gaulle laisse ses chances à Mendès-France," *Le Monde,* December 5-6, 1954, p. 3. R. Pierce,

Op. cit., p. 119. Henry Giniger, "De Gaulle Waits and Watches," *The New York Times Magazine,* December 1, 1957, pp. 116, 118-9.

32. "La Nouvelle Gauche," *Documents et Informations Parlementaires: Etudes et Documents,* November 12, 1955, pp. C544-6. Raymond Barillon, "Desseins et destin de la Nouvelle Gauche," Pt. I: "Pourquoi cette expression nouvelle d'un désir permanent de renouveau," *Le Monde,* April 22, 1955.

33. R. Barillon, "Desseins et destin de la Nouvelle Gauche," Pt. II: "Des beautés du programme aux difficultés de la fédération," *Le Monde,* April 23, 1955.

34. The day of the signature of the Ribbentrop-Molotov agreement and of the most dramatic of all the Communist reversals.

35. I. W. Zartman, *De la Résistance à la Révolution,* pp. 36-9. R. Barillon, "Desseins et destin de la Nouvelle Gauche," Pt. III: "Doit-on et peut-on dialoguer avec le Parti communiste?," *Le Monde,* April 24, 1955.

36. Besides the official weekly, *Le Rassemblement,* which was the chief source of Gaullist opinion, the RPF had published at one time or another various organs aimed at special groups and concerned primarily with internal matters, such as *L'Etincelle* for the rural population and another weekly, *Le Rassemblement Ouvrier,* for the Gaullist worker. In 1955, the Gaullists launched a small weekly to replace the defunct *Rassemblement,* entitled *Courrier d'Information* (Paris)—see special issue of July, 1955.

Among the papers and periodicals which at one time had supported the RPF, besides numerous right-wing dailies in the provinces, the ultra-nationalist sensationalist *L'Aurore* and the weekly *Carrefour* were featured prominently. The right-wing Paris dailies, *Le Parisien Libéré,* directed at conservative financial circles, and *L'Epoque,* favored the RPF as did the sensationalist, popular afternoon paper *Paris-Presse-L'Intransigeant.* The popular illustrated weekly, *Le Rouge et le Noir*—it seems indeed that most of the Gaullist and pro-Gaullist press belonged in this category, in contrast to the intellectual organs of the neutralist left—voiced Gaullist sympathies, and since 1955 the new weekly, *Jours de France* has interspersed its pictures with nationalist, pro-Gaullist captions and text (see, for example, the issue of June 16-23, 1955). Among provincial sources, André Stibio's comments in *La Voix du Nord* were widely cited as expressions of the RPF's position.

37. Bernard Simiot, "La vérité sur le Maroc," *Carrefour,* January 16, 1951. "Le gouvernement prépare-t-il son repli en Afrique du Nord?," *Loc. cit.,* February 20, 1951. R. de St. Jean, "Qui abdiquera au Maroc, le Sultan ou la France?," *Loc. cit.,* April 10, 1951, p. 5. R. de St. Jean, "Le Maroc dont va discuter l'O.N.U. n'a qu'un tort: il n'éxiste pas," *Loc. cit.,* November 26, 1952, p. 5. "Est-ce la curée sur ce que fut l'Empire français?," *Loc. cit.,* December 10, 1952, pp. 1, 6.

38. *France Against Herself,* pp. 187, 301, etc.

39. J. B. Duroselle, "The Crisis in French Foreign Policy," *The Review of Politics,* (Vol. 16) October, 1954, pp. 429-30. See: Edgar S. Furniss, Jr., "French Attitudes Towards Western European Unity," *International Organization,* Boston, May, 1953, pp. 199-212. Mr. Furniss describes the decrease in the momentum of the Schuman policy, and the general rise in France of opposition to the idea of European integration, particularly the fear of being "boxed in" with Germany.
See also Jacques Fauvet, "Birth and Death of a Treaty," in D. Lerner and R. Aron, eds., *Op. cit.,* pp. 128-30 ff., 141-2, and especially 146-8.

40. The Gaullists proclaimed themselves to be in favor of European unity but by a gradual or organic process; they likened their attitude to the position of the British Government. They claimed that they were only against a process of "superimposed federation," especially of what could be at best a "shadow Europe." What the RPF apparently advocated was a sort of Concert of European Powers, or a confederation of sovereign states: Assemblée Nationale, Deuxième Législature, Session de 1951, No. 2283, Annexe au Procès verbal du 29 Décembre 1951, *Proposition de résolution sur l'organisation d'une Confédération européenne.* Assemblée Nationale, Deuxième Législature, Session de 1951, No. 2284, Annexe au Procès verbal du 29 Décembre 1951, *Proposition de résolution présentée par M. Billotte et les membres du groupe du Rassemblemente du peuple français tendant à inviter le Gouvernement à présenter et soutenir devant les instances internationales un projet de communauté militaire européenne dans un cadre confédéral.* Général Koenig, "Pour rendre efficace la défense de l'Occident, donnons à l'Europe son statut politique," *Carrefour,* October 22, 1952. "Pour une communauté politique et militaire européenne," *Le Rassemblement,* June 4-10, 1952, pp. 6-7. Albert

Ollivier, "Confédération ou Fédération de l'Europe," *Loc. cit.,* October 1-7, 1953, p. 5. De Gaulle declaration and press conference of April 7, 1954; the citations used here are taken from the official English translation of the full text published by the RPF itself under the title: *Press Conference of General de Gaulle held in Paris, 7th of April 1954,* Paris: Imprimerie Ed. Dauer (1954). For major extracts from the speech see: "'Il appartient à la France de faire une réalité de la détente Est-Ouest', déclare le général de Gaulle," *Le Monde,* April 9, 1954, p. 4. Général de Monsabert, "Novembre 1951; Alerte à la France," *France-Illustration,* November 10, 1951, pp. 495-6. Général de Gaulle, "Faisons d'abord l'alliance des Etats libres d'Europe," *Le Rassemblement,* February 26—March 4, 1953, p. 6. "Nous ne laisserons pas vendre la France. Michel Debré au Conseil de la République: 'Parceque nous voulons l'association de toutes les Nations d'Europe pour leur défense, nous refusons la C.E.D. qui divise l'Armée et l'Union française en armant l'Allemagne pour la reconquête de l'Est.,'" *Loc. cit.,* November 5-11, 1953. "A l'approche du débat de politique extèrieure, le général de Gaulle préconise la participation de l'Allemagne à une 'grande alliance' des armées de l'Europe libre," *Le Monde,* November 13, 1953, p. 1. "La déclaration du général de Gaulle," *Loc. cit.,* p. 5. Joseph de Goislard de Monsabert (général de Monsabert) statement, *J.O.,* session of January 6, 1954, pp. 12-3. Félix Garas, "Le Plan Schuman devant l'opinion publique," *Carrefour,* April 24, 1951, p. 3. ("Chronique internationale"). *La France sera la France,* pp. 294-5; extracts from de Gaulle speech of November 14, 1949. Jacques Soustelle, "France and Europe," *Foreign Affairs,* New York, (Vol. 30) July, 1952, pp. 545-53.

41. "Comment on devient milliardaire—Les Gros: Tome II," *Le Crapouillot,* new series No. 23, pp. 31-2, 50-1.

42. "Après la conférence de presse du général de Gaulle, le groupe 'R.P.F.' demande que la France ne s'engage ni à la Haye ni aux Bermudes," *Le Monde,* November 14, 1953. "'La France doit rechercher s'il est possible d'obtenir ou non un arrangement avec le monde soviétique' déclare le général de Gaulle," *Loc. cit.,* p. 5. De Gaulle's remark also cited in: "Il faut organiser l'Europe," *Le Rassemblement,* November 19-25, 1953, p. 4; and in: *Le Crapouillot,* new series No. 27: "Scandales de la IVe République," p. 74 (*Le Crapouillot* itself violently attacks Jean Monnet). For another Gaullist criticism of Monnet,

see: "Le proconsul Jean Monnet a des ennuis," *Le Rassemblement,* March 17-23, 1953.

43. Claude Estier, "La C.E.D. bouleverse l'échiquier politique," *L'Observateur,* November 5, 1953, p. 8. See also Daniel Lerner, "Reflexions on France in the World Arena," in D. Lerner and R. Aron, eds., *Op. cit.,* pp. 213-5, 219-20.

44. Jacques Soustelle statement, *J.O.,* 2nd session of December 21, 1954, pp. 6696-702. Félix Garas, "La politique étrangère de la troisième force," *Carrefour,* June 5, 1951, p. 3.

45. Louis Vallon statement, *J.O.,* session of March 24, 1953, pp. 2262-3. "La concurrence écrasante de l'industrie lourde allemande," *Le Rassemblement,* February 9-15, 1951, p. 7. Gaston Palewski, "Le Plan Schuman et les réalités européennes," *Loc. cit.,* April 6-12, 1951, p. 3. "La vérité sur le pool charbon-acier. Pour l'Allemagne ce sont des avantages, mais pour la France c'est un danger," *Loc. cit.,* December 14-20, 1951, p. 12. "L'économie et les travailleurs gravement menacés," *Loc. cit.,* December 14-20, 1951, p. 12. "La France va-t-elle laisser à l'Allemagne la direction de l'Europe?," *Loc. cit.,* February 8-14, 1952, p. 3. Jacques Soustelle, "Le régime des féodalités perd la France," *Loc. cit.,* October 29—November 4, 1953.

46. Guy Mollet, "Nos trois conditions seront-elles remplies?," *La Revue Socialiste,* June 1953, pp. 1-9. Oreste Rosenfeld, "Les lignes générales de la politique internationale du socialisme," *Loc. cit.,* April, 1954, pp. 326-7. See also: G. Mollet, "Les Socialistes et l'Armée européenne," *Loc. cit.,* January, 1952, pp. 1-8. Gérard Jacquet. "Pour une Armée européenne véritable," *Loc. cit.,* March, 1952, pp. 225-32.

47. For a Gaullist view of the Saar question, see Michel Debré, "Coup d'essai allemand sur la Sarre," *Carrefour,* February 6, 1952. For a Gaullist view of the connection between the Saar issue and the Schuman Plan, see: Félix Garas, "Le Plan Schuman devant l'opinion publique," *Loc. cit.,* April 24, 1951, p. 3. See also: *La France sera la France,* pp. 296-7: excerpts from de Gaulle speech of March 16, 1950. Jacques Vendroux, "Un Allemand de la Sarre favoriserait le nouveau Reich souhaité par M. Staline," *Le Rassemblement,* March 28—April 3, 1952, p. 1.

48. Joseph de Monsabert statement, *J.O.,* session of January 6, 1954, pp. 12-3. See also: J. B. Duroselle, "The Crisis in French Foreign Policy," *The Review of Politics,* October, 1954, p. 424.

See also: Guy Mollet, "France and the Defense of Europe; A French Socialist View," *Foreign Affairs,* (Vol. 32), April, 1954, pp. 365-73.

49. See, for example, the attitude of General Billotte: "MM. Daladier, Lapie, Billotte, Denais, Barrès s'élèvent contre le traité," *Le Monde,* November 14, 1953, p. 4. See also Jacques Fauvet, "Birth and Death of a Treaty," in: D. Lerner and R. Aron, eds., *Op. cit.,* pp. 135-6 ff., 158.

50. "La France est en péril. C.E.D.=hégémonie allemande et rupture de l'Union française," *Le Rassemblement,* October 1-7, 1953.

51. Michel Debré, "A une nécessité, le projet d'armée européenne répond par des erreurs," *Le Rassemblement,* July 4-10, 1952.

52. Général (Joseph) de Monsabert, "Novembre 1951: Alerte à la France," *France-Illustration,* November 10, 1951, pp. 495-6.

53. Général (Joseph) de Monsabert, "Le réarmement moral," *France-Illustration,* January 6, 1951, p. 5. Général de Monsabert, "Armée française ou Armée européenne," *Loc. cit.,* March 17, 1951, p. 268.

54. Général de Monsabert, "Novembre 1951; Alerte à la France," *France-Illustration,* November 10, 1951, pp. 495-6. Statements by Joseph de Monsabert, *J.O.,* 1st session of November 19, 1953, pp. 5271-2; and 2nd session of November 19, 1953, pp. 5349-50.

55. Général Koenig, "Pour rendre efficace la défense de l'Occident, donnons à l'Europe son statut politique," *Carrefour,* October 22, 1952.

56. "Avec des faibles: guerre et catastrophes. Aves des forts: la vie et la paix. Discours prononcé par le général de Gaulle le 7 Janvier à Nîmes," *Le Rassemblement,* January 12-18, 1951, p. 3.

57. *La France sera la France,* pp. 284, 287-8; including excerpts from de Gaulle speeches of November 17, 1948 and March 29, 1949.

58. De Gaulle interview, *Le Rassemblement,* June 29—July 5, 1951, pp. 8-9.

59. Edmond Taylor, "The Communists' New Look in France," *The Reporter,* New York, (Vol. 10) March 30, 1954, pp. 19-22. André Philip, "The Interplay of Interests and Passions," in: D. Lerner and R. Aron, eds., *Op. cit.,* pp. 25, 27-32. Jacques

Vernant, "European Politics faces French Economics," *Loc. cit.*, pp. 40-4.

60. E. Taylor, *Op. cit.*, affirms that "in the last few months, French big business has poured over $3.5 million into the anti-E.D.C. campaign," but he offers no evidence or justification of this figure.

61. The question is touched upon in Manuel Bridier, "La C.E.D., les communistes et le 'Comité des Forges,' " *Le Rassemblement,* December 17-23, 1953.

62. There are some illuminating ramifications to this question. Thus according to *Le Crapouillot,* the crisis which at one time gripped the managing board of *Le Monde* over the neutralist policy of Beuve-Méry was resolved in favor of the latter by a certain stockholder, Johannes Dupraz, an MRP deputy and wealthy member of the financial *haut monde.* M. Dupraz, according to *Le Crapouillot,* was acting in the name of the company Descours and Gabaud which was engaged in a lucrative trade in metallurgical products with Communist China; see: "Comment on devient milliardaire—Les Gros: Tome II," *Le Crapouillot,* New Series, No. 23 (February, 1954), pp. 42-4.

63. *Ibid.,* pp. 31-2, 50-1. For an attack on the continuation of East-West trade which appeared in a Gaullist publication at a time when the RPF still stood for uncompromising hostility to any concessions towards the Communist powers, see: "Guerre et commerce: le ravitaillement de la Russie par le monde libre," *Le Rassemblement,* December 29, 1950—January 4, 1951, p. 7. This article is taken largely from an account of the trade between O.E.E.C. members and the Soviet Union in *U.S. News and World Report,* and from a study that appeared in the *Bulletin de l'Association d'Etudes et d'Information politiques internationalies,* (B.E.I.P.I.), Paris (no dates are given). According to the article, such trade at the time (pre-1951) amounted to something between one and a half and two billion dollars yearly. While exports to Communist countries from the franc zone ranked considerably behind those from Britain and the Commonwealth, they were nonetheless significant and allegedly included machine tools, industrial machinery, abrasives, wire, steel and iron tubing, boilers, pumps, motors, railroad equipment, electrical equipment and various metals, totalling fifty-one million dollars in all for 1948. This amount was said to have been doubled to one hundred and five million dollars for

1949, and, it was estimated, would reach an equivalent sum in 1950. For other Gaullist criticisms of East-West trade see: "Les falsifications du réarmement," *Le Rassemblement,* January 19-25, 1951; and: André Desmond, "Tandis que nos soldats tombent en Indochine, le Gouvernment livre de l'acier à Mao Tse Tung!," *Carrefour,* January 9, 1951.

64. Général de Monsabert, "Novembre 1951: Alerte à la France," *France-Illustration,* November 10, 1951, pp. 495-6. De Gaulle interview, *Le Rassemblement,* June 29—July 5, 1951, pp. 8-9.

65. Jacques Soustelle statement, *J.O.,* 2nd session of December 21, 1954, pp. 6696-702. Mme. Iréné de Lipkowski [ideologically a Gaullist, but at that time unaffiliated; de Gaulle, it will be remembered, had "released" RPF deputies in 1953.] *Loc. cit.,* 2nd session of December 29, 1954, p. 6936. Général de Gaulle, "Nous ne saurions accepter de noyer notre sécurité, notre indépendance dans des organismes qualifiés de collectif mais en fait dirigés par d'autres," *Le Rassemblement,* September 28—October 4, 1951, pp. 8-9. Louis Terrenoire, "Un crime à ne pas commettre," *Loc. cit.,* February 15-21, 1952. "L'Armée française dissoute. La Wehrmacht reconstituée," *Loc. cit.,* March 7-13, 1952, p. 5. "Ne laissons pas faire—Staline pour la reconstitution de la Wehrmacht—Schuman pour la dissolution de l'Armée française," *Loc. cit.,* March 21-27, 1952, back cover. "Michel Debré à M. Robert Schuman: 'Vous refaites la politique de Laval'—Armée allemande reconstituée armée française désorganisée, tel est le sens du traité d'armée européenne," *Loc. cit.,* June 20-26, 1952, p. 5. "L'Europe dénationalisée, c'est l'invasion du Germanisme," *Loc. cit.,* June 20-26, 1952, p. 5. Général de Gaulle, "Le projet d'armée européenne qui, en sacrifiant l'indépendance française prépare l'hégémonie allemande, doit être combattue par tous les moyens," *Loc. cit.,* November 19-25, 1953. "C.E.D.=Collaboration Et Défaitisme," *Loc. cit.,* November 12-18, 1953. Gaston Palewski, "Comment réarmer l'Allemagne," *L'Express,* September 11, 1954, p. 4.

66. De Gaulle maintained that the U.S. had adopted a peripheral strategy (see section: "L'attitude des Etats Unis," in " 'La France doit rechercher s'il est possible ou non d'obtenir un arrangement avec le monde soviétique' déclare le général de Gaulle," *Le Monde,* November 14, 1953, p. 5.) Commenting on *Le Monde's* publication of the apocryphal "Fechteler report," a report which appeared to indicate that a leading member of

the U.S. Supreme Command considered Europe indefensible against a Soviet attack (see: Chapter II), the Gaullist Claude Couband declared that, while the authenticity of the document was questionable and the motives of *Le Monde* criticizable, the "report" nonetheless did represent America's strategy (Claude Couband, "L'insécurité de L'Europe fait scandale," *Le Rassemblement,* May 16-22, 1952).

67. *Press Conference of General de Gaulle held in Paris, 7th of April 1954.* " 'Il appartient à la France de faire une réalité de la détente Est-Ouest' déclare le général de Gaulle," *Le Monde,* April 9, 1954, p. 4. See also: Jacques Soustelle "Nous n'accepterons pas la déchéance de la France," *Le Rassemblement,* January 29–February 4, 1953. Général de Gaulle, "L'armée européenne n'est que la camouflage d'une abdication," *Loc. cit.,* February 26–March 4, 1953. "Pour que ça change, il faut choisir entre la France libre ou asservie," *Loc. cit.,* November 5-11, 1953, p. 6.

68. Jacques Soustelle statement, *J.O.,* 1st session of October 8, 1954, pp. 4623-7.

69. Léon Noël statement, *J.O.,* 2nd session of November 17, 1953, pp. 5202-6. Henri Torrès, "L'armée européenne: organisation offensive," *Le Rassemblement,* June 20-26, 1952, p. 5. "Nous ne laisserons pas vendre la France. Michel Debré au Conseil de la République: 'Parceque nous voulons l'association de toutes les Nations d'Europe pour leur défense nous refusons la C.E.D. qui divise l'Armée et l'Union française en armant l'Allemagne pour la reconquête de l'Est,' " *Loc. cit.,* November 5-11, 1953.

70. "Le complot allemand avec le Kremlin" (discussion of Tete Harens Tetens' book by this title [U.S. edition: *Germany Plots With The Kremlin,* New York: H. Schuman, 1953]), *Le Rassemblement,* November 5-11, 1953.

71. J. B. Duroselle, "The Crisis in French Foreign Policy," *The Review of Politics,* October, 1954, pp. 412-37.

72. *Le Rassemblement,* December 17-23, 1953, p. 6.

73. Louis Terrenoire, "L'Europe des S.S. ne sera jamais la nôtre," *Le Rassemblement,* July 23-29, 1953. Jacques Soustelle, "Les anciens nazis partisans de la C.E.D. et leurs 'alliés' en France," *Loc. cit.,* April 28–May 5, 1954. "Les anciens nazis ont voté 'utile.' Adenauer plébiscité donne à l'hégémonie allemande le drapeau de l'Europe," *Loc. cit.,* September 10-16, 1953.

74. "Europe oui, Europa non," *Le Rassemblement,* November 26–December 2, 1953, p. 6.

75. Edmond Taylor, "The Communists' New Look in France," *The Reporter,* March 30, 1954, pp. 19-22. Jacques Soustelle, "Mon voyage en Pologne," *Le Rassemblement,* December 17-23, 1953.

76. Gaston Palewski statement, *J.O.,* 2nd session of December 27, 1954, pp 6936-7.

77. For an example of his attitude concerning East-West relations, see: Georges Loustaunau-Lacau statements, *J.O.,* 2nd session of December 27, 1954, pp. 6889-91; and 1st session of October 8, 1954, pp. 4631-4.

78. "Pour la France, pour la Republique: de Gaulle." *Le Rassemblement,* April 13-19, 1951.

79. Although by this time *Carrefour* was no longer specifically connected with Gaullism [its sympathies still may have tended in the same direction—see, for example, photograph of de Gaulle and caption, issue of December 8, 1954], it is interesting to refer to its article: "La future armée allemande veut être la plus démocratique du monde. Le restera-t-elle longtemps?," December 22, 1954. For an openly Gaullist opinion, see: "La France est en péril. C.E.D.=hégémonie allemande et rupture de l'Union française," *Le Rassemblement,* October 1-7, 1953.

80. Actually, the charge of "synarchy" was made primarily in connection with the European Coal and Steel Community, but that was long after the Schuman Plan had been ratified by the French National Assembly (December 13, 1951). The attack on the way the Coal and Steel Community was carrying on its functions, and the charge of a "technocratic" bureaucracy, were actually developed late in 1953 when the question of EDC had become a major concern, and they formed an integral part of the Gaullist campaign against the European army.

81. Louis Vallon statement, *J.O.,* 3rd session of March 24, 1953, pp. 2262-3. "La vérité sur le pool charbon-acier. Pour l'Allemagne ce sont des avantages, mais pour la France c'est un danger," *Le Rassemblement,* December 14-20, 1951, p. 12.

82. Félix Garas, "Le Plan Schuman devant l'opinion publique," *Carrefour,* April 24, 1951, p. 3.

83. Manuel Bridier, "L'armée dite européenne au service du capitalisme d'Etat," *Le Rassemblement,* December 31, 1953–January 6, 1954, p. 3. M. Bridier, "L'armée 'européenne,' enjeu

d'une guerre des synarchies," *Loc. cit.,* January 14-20, 1954, p. 3. Statement by Jean Nocher, *J.O.,* 3rd session of November 19, 1953, pp. 4392-7.

84. For Monnet's reply, see " 'L'Inspirateur' répond aux attaques du Président du R.P.F. 'Les conceptions du général de Gaulle reposent sur des notions périmées' nous déclare M. Jean Monnet," *Le Monde,* November 17, 1953.

85. *Press Conference of General de Gaulle held in Paris, 7th of April, 1954.* " 'Il appartient à la France de faire une réalité de la détente Est-Ouest' déclare le général de Gaulle," *Le Monde,* April 9, 1954, p. 4. For a ridiculously partisan expansion of this notion (and, incidently, for a violent attack on Jean Monnet in a non-Gaullist publication), see: "L'extension, de la synarchisation de la France et de l'Europe. Le Vatican, la Synarchie et l'Unité européenne. Histoire de M. Jean Monnet, dictateur occulte de la France et 'Imperator' de l'Europe," in R. Mennevée, *Les Documents politiques, diplomatiques et financiers,* Paris (roneotyped), March 1, 1953 (cited also in "Scandales de la IVe République," *Le Crapouillot,* new series special issue No. 27, pp. 67-75).

86. "La preuve est faite que les promoteurs européens du pool acier-charbon ont trompé les français," *Le Rassemblement,* October 29—November 4, 1953.

87. Marteau, "Le pool charbon-acier dans l'impasse?," *Le Rassemblement,* January 21-27, 1954.

88. "Les technocrates 'européens' sacrifient les ouvriers français," *Le Rassemblement,* December 3-9, 1953, p. 3.

89. Manuel Bridier, "Le Congrés F. O. et les fausses routes de la productivité," *Le Rassemblement,* November 20-27, 1952, p. 3.

90. Jacques Soustelle statement, *J.O.,* 1st session of October 8, 1954, pp. 4623-7. J. Soustelle statement, *Loc. cit.,* 2nd session of December 29, 1954, pp. 6959-60.

91. Mme. Iréné de Lipkowski statement, *J.O.,* 2nd session of December 29, 1954, p. 6936. " 'Nous vous demandons pardon de ce crime contre la paix' déclare Mme. de Lipkowski," *Le Monde,* December 31, 1954, p. 4. Louis Vallon statement, *J.O.,* session of October 12, 1954, pp. 4671-2.

92. "A French Farce . . . .," *Le Rassemblement,* January 16-24, 1952, p. 3.

93. George Slocomb, "If de Gaulle Returns to Power," *The New York Herald Tribune,* European Edition, January 14, 1952,

p. 4. Also published as: "De Gaulle on European Defense," *Ibid.*, New York Edition, January 26, 1952, p. 8.

94. "L'Attitude du général de Gaulle a encouragé les Soviétiques," in: Henri Pierre, "Washington craint que l'offre russe ne mette en danger l'unité occidentale." *Le Monde* November 29 & 30, 1953.

95. Albert Ollivier, "Après l'échec de la C.E.D. des décisions s'imposent," *Le Rassemblement,* December 3-9, 1953.

96. Highly prejudiced, the following account nonetheless is significant in view of the subsequent evolution of de Gaulle: Henri de Kerillis, *I Accuse de Gaulle,* New York: Harcourt, Brace & Co., 1946. See also: Lucien Galimand, *Origine et Déviations du Gaullisme; de Gaulle, Agent de Reynaud?*, Paris: Editions de la Couronne, 1950.

97. Winston S. Churchill, *The Second World War,* Boston: Houghton-Mifflin Co., Vol. IV: *The Hinge of Fate,* 1950, Ch. 11, 12 & 15. William L. Langer, *Our Vichy Gamble.* Charles de Gaulle, *Mémoires de Guerre,* Vol I: *L'Appel, 1940-1942,* Paris: Librairie Plon, 1954. *La France sera la France,* pp. 195-208.

98. "De Gaulle dit à ses compagnons," *Le Rassemblement,* July 18-24, 1952. Also: "L'alliance des Etats-Unis est devenue une espéce de protectorat," in: " 'La France doit rechercher s'il est possible d'obtenir ou non un arrangement avec le monde soviétique' déclare le général de Gaulle," *Le Monde,* November 14, 1953, p. 5.

99. Louis Terrenoire, "Le gaullisme est incompatible avec le séparatisme," *Le Rassemblement,* February 25—March 4, 1954.

100. *La France sera la France,* p. 241.

101. *Ibid.,* pp. 225-7; including excerpts from de Gaulle speeches of April 6 and 27, 1947. See also: "Le Pacte atlantique ne doit pas conserver l'ordre établi," *Le Rassemblement,* September 15-21, 1951, pp. 4-5; de Gaulle speech to Anglo-American Press Club in Paris; and: "Avec des faibles: guerre et catastrophes. Avec des forts: la vie et la paix. Discours prononcé par le général de Gaulle le 7 Janvier à Nîmes," *Loc. cit.,* January 12-18, 1951, p. 3.

102. "Pour les milieux d'affaires américains, l'Europe c'est l'Allemagne," *Le Rassemblement,* December 31, 1953—January 6, 1954.

103. Jacques Soustelle, "Le Quai d'Orsay à genoux devant la F.B.I.,?" *Le Rassemblement,* February 25—March 3, 1954.

104. Bernard Simiot, "La Vérité sur le Maroc," *Carrefour,* January 16, 1951.
105. J. Soustelle, "La 'libération' du Guatémala," *L'Express,* June 26, 1954, p. 6.
106. "Après les déclarations du général de Gaulle, M. Mendès-France doit affronter sans danger les interpellations sur l'Afrique du Nord et sur la ratification des accords de Paris," *Le Monde,* December 7, 1954.
107. R. de St. Jean, "Dans les coulisses de l'O.N.U., voici Irving Brown, ennemi juré de Staline . . . . et de la France en Tunisie," *Carrefour,* October 15, 1952, p. 6. André Maurois, "Pour mettre fin au malaise Franco-Américain," *Loc. cit.,* p. 6. Edouard Labessière, "Les Etats-Unis préparent-ils la conquête pacifique de l'Indochine? Dans cinq mille villages, une enseigne de la Crois Rouge ventera aux autochtones la générosité américaine," *Loc. cit.,* July 21, 1951, p. 5. Robert Bony, "S'il nous faut aujourd'hui recourir en Algérie à la manière forte c'est que depuis trop longtemps, s'éxercent contre la France des complicités etrangères!," *L'Aurore,* Paris, May 23, 1955. "A Saigon Diem négocie avec le général Collins envoyé d'Eisenhower et confère avec le haut-commissaire Malcolm MacDonald—Les U.S.A. mis en garde contre les décisions que pourrait provoquer la propagande anti-française," *Loc. cit.,* May 3, 1955.
108. For an idea of French sensitivity on this score, see: "Ce que les Français pensent de L'Amérique," *Réalités,* (French edition) August 1953, No. 91, pp. 18-22. For an interesting and open-minded account of the French colonial question as of 1954, see H. Leuthy, *Op. cit.,* Pt. III: "Overseas France."
109. *L'Express,* May 2, 1954, p. 7.
110. " 'Il appartient à la France de faire une réalité de la détente Est-Ouest' déclare le général de Gaulle," *Le Monde,* April 9, 1954.
111. For an earlier Gaullist view on peace negotiations with the Communists in the Far East, see: Claude Couband, "La paix des cimetières," *Le Rassemblement,* January 19-25, 1951, p. 5.
112. Général de Gaulle, "Nous ne laisserons pas briser l'Union Française par les passions étrangères ni par les actes diplomatiques," *Le Rassemblement,* March 12-18, 1953, p. 6. Général de Gaulle, "L'armée européenne n'est que le camouflage d'une abdication," *Loc. cit.,* February 26—March 4, 1953, pp. 1-6.
113. For an early expression of a similar attitude, see de Gaulle's

assertion that he would welcome U.S. aid to Indo-China so long as this aid was channelled through French authorities, *La France sera la France,* p. 191. See also: Louis Vallon statement, *J.O.,* session of May 4, 1954, p. 2094; Albert Ollivier, "Genève et Dien Bien Phu," *Le Rassemblement,* May 6-12, 1954; and above all: "Conférence de Presse du général de Gaulle, Paris, le 30 juin 1955," *Courrier d'Information. Le Rassemblement,* Paris, special issue (July 1955?), p. 6.
114. *Press Conference of General de Gaulle held in Paris, 7th of April 1954.*
115. *Ibid.*
116. *Ibid.* " 'Il appartient à la France de faire une réalité de la détente Est-Ouest' déclare le général de Gaulle," *Le Monde,* April 9, 1954, p. 4.
117. Claude Couband, "L'artillerie atomique à la rescousse," *Le Rassemblement,* May 18-24, 1951, p. 5.
118. "Les limites du repli américain en Corée," *Le Rassemblement,* January 19-25, 1951, p. 5. C. Couband, "Ce que la trêve en Corée représente pour la France," *Loc. cit.,* July 13-19, 1951. See also Robert de St. Jean, "Le match Truman-MacArthur," *Carrefour,* April 17, 1951, p. 5. Félix Garas, "Le procès d'un grand homme, *Loc. cit.,* May 15, 1951, p. 3.
119. R. de St. Jean, "Le match Truman-MacArthur," *Carrefour,* April 17, 1951, p. 5. F. Garas, "Le procès d'un grand homme," *Loc. cit.,* May 15, 1951, p. 3. R. de St. Jean, "Pour l'amour de M. Bevan, les soldats américains doivent-ils se laisser tuer gentiment par les Sino-Coréens?," *Loc. cit.,* July 2, 1952, p. 3.
120. R. de St. Jean, "Le match Truman-MacArthur," *Carrefour,* April 17, 1951, p. 5.
121. "Faire le C.E.D. serait trahir la France," *Le Rassemblement,* April 28—May 5, 1954, p. 6. "Ce qu'est l'armée dite européenne," *Loc. cit.,* November 12-18, 1953. See also: "A. comme Atome, B. comme Bombe. A 27 km. de Las Vegas, capitale des expériences nucléaires, une cinquantaine d'enfants sont entrés dans le monde atomique en faisant joujou avec la 'Bombe A,' " *Carrefour,* July 27, 1952. "Les Etats-Unis vont-ils commettre une nouvelle erreur en favorisant une grande Allemagne? Pour assurer la paix, un équilibre Orient-Occident doit être recherché," excerpts from an article by Phillippe Barrès reprinted from the financial paper *L'Information,* in *Le Rassemblement,* July 9-15, 1953.

122. Jean Moncey, "Le vrai 'ré-examen' que les Etats-Unis devraient faire," *Le Rassemblement,* May 20-26, 1954.
123. " 'La France doit rechercher s'il est possible d'obtenir ou non un arrangement avec le monde soviétique' déclare le général de Gaulle," *Le Monde,* November 14, 1953, p. 5. See also Gaston Palewski, "Comment réussir la négociation avec l'U.R.S.S.," *Le Rassemblement,* April 23-29, 1953. "Il faut organiser l'Europe," *Loc. cit.,* November 19-25, 1953, p. 4. Statement of policy, *Loc. cit.,* February 4-10, 1954, p. 6. Philippe Barrès, "L'enjeu de Berlin est grand pour la France," *Loc. cit.,* February 4-10, 1954. G. Palewski, "Pour rendre la paix possible (et d'abord en Indochine) il ne faut pas la compromettre avec la C.E.D.," *Loc. cit.,* February 25—March 3, 1954. Jacques Soustelle, "Pour la France, les questions d'Europe et d'Asie sont inséparables," *Loc. cit.,* March 11-17, 1954.
124. Manuel Bridier, "Réponse à un militant de l'armée européenne," *Le Rassemblement,* December 10-16, 1953, p. 4. "Le pire danger communiste," *Loc. cit.,* December 10-16, 1953, p. 4 (in reference to an article by M. J. Ellul, "Le péril est à l'intérieur," *Le Monde,* December 6-7, 1953, p. 3 ["Libres Opinions"]). "Le communisme peut conquérir l'Occident par les armes économiques," *Le Rassemblement,* March 11-17, 1954.
125. Gaston Palewski statement, *J.O.,* 2nd session of December 27, 1954, pp. 6936-7. "Après les déclarations du général de Gaulle, M. Mendès-France doit affronter sans danger les interpellations sur l'Afrique du Nord et sur la ratification des accords de Paris," *Le Monde,* December 7, 1954.
126. "De Gaulle souhaite la négociation avec l'Est avant l'application des accords de Paris," *Le Monde,* December 5-6, 1954. See also Louis Vallon statement, *J.O.,* session of October 12, 1954, pp. 4671-2; and: Gaston Palewski, "Une négociation s'impose entre les deux mondes," in "L'Assemblée Nationale a voté la confiance," *Le Monde,* October 14, 1954, p. 4.
127. Joseph de Monsabert, *J.O.,* session of January 6, 1954, pp. 12-3. " 'La France doit rechercher s'il est possible d'obtenir ou non un arrangement avec le monde soviétique' déclare le général de Gaulle," *Le Monde,* November 14, 1953, p. 5. Gaston Palewski, "Une négociation s'impose entre les deux mondes," in: "L'Assemblée Nationale a voté la confiance," *Loc. cit.,* October 14, 1954, p. 4. See also: Jean Mazé, "De Gaulle entre les deux Gaullismes, 1944-1952," in: "Le Pour et le Contre—

Pétain—de Gaulle," *Le Crapouillot,* new series No. 17 [no date], p. 51.
128. Gaston Palewski, "L'égalité des forces atomiques U.R.S.S. —U.S.A. rend nécessaire la négociation Est-Ouest," *Le Rassemblement,* September 10-16, 1953.
129. *Press Conference of General de Gaulle held in Paris, 7th of April, 1954.*
130. *Ibid.*
131. "De Gaulle souhaite la négociation avec l'Est avant l'application des accords de Paris," *Le Monde,* December 5-6, 1954. *J.O.,* 3rd session of December 23, 1954, pp. 6843-4. *Loc. cit.,* 2nd session of December 22, 1954, pp. 6756-9. "L'Assemblée se prononcera mercredi sur l'article Ier (repoussé vendredi) et sur l'ensemble des accords de Paris," *Le Monde,* December 29, 1954, p. 4. See also *L'Express,* September 11, 1954, p. 4. Gaston Palewski statement, *J.O.,* 1st session of November 17, 1953, pp. 5192-6. *Ibid.,* 2nd session of December 27, 1954, pp. 6887-9. In reply to a request of Premier Mendès-France, M. Palewski subsequently withdrew his amendment—*Loc. cit.,* p. 6893—but nonetheless joined the opposition on the final vote: *Loc. cit.,* 2nd session of December 29, 1954, pp. 6936-7; and: "Une immense défaite nationale," in: "L'Assemblée confirme son vote de lundi," *Le Monde,* December 31, 1954, p. 4.
132. "Après les déclarations du général de Gaulle, M. Mendès-France doit affronter sans danger les interpellations sur l'Afrique du Nord et sur la ratification des accords de Paris," *Le Monde,* December 7, 1954.
133. Manuel Bridier, "L'union de tous les Français peut seule sauver l'indépendance nationale menacée par le projet d'armée dite européenne," *Le Rassemblement,* November 5-11, 1953, p. 2.
134. M. Bridier, "La C.E.D., les communistes et le 'Comité des Forges,'" *Le Rassemblement,* December 17-23, 1953, p. 3.
135. "Des plat . . . itudes," *Le Rassemblement,* November 5-11, 1953.
136. M. Bridier, "L'armée dite européenne et le regroupement national," *Le Rassemblement,* January 28—February 4, 1954.
137. Louis Terrenoire, "Le gaullisme est incompatible avec le séparatisme," *Le Rassemblement,* February 25—March 3, 1954.
138. *L'Humanité,* May 9, 1953, p. 1. Marie-Louise Barron, "Emouvant hommage à Jeanne d'Arc et Danielle Casanova," *Loc. cit.,*

May 7, 1954, p. 4. Account of Joan of Arc celebration, *Loc. cit.,* May 12, 1954, p. 5.

139. Speech of Maurice Thorez to the National Congress of the French Communist Party at Ivry, *L'Humanité,* June 8, 1954. Jacques Duclos' speech opening the XIIIth National Congress of the French Communist Party, *Loc. cit.,* June 4, 1954.

140. "Au cours d'une conférence de presse, de Gaulle se prononce: Contre la C.E.D., Pour la détente internationale, Pour la fin de la guerre d'Indochine," *L'Humanité,* April 8, 1954, pp. 1, 5.

141. Jean Fabiani, "De Gaulle reste," *Combat,* October 21, 1954. See also: "M. Mendès-France abandonnera le quai d'Orsay à le mi-janvier pour se consacrer aux problèmes économiques. Le général de Gaulle souhaite une négociation avec l'Est avant l'application des accords de Paris," *Le Monde,* December 5-6, 1954.

142. "La France se souvient. Un jour de gloire ouvrait la marche triomphale de la délivrance," *Jours de France,* June 16-23, 1955, pp. 45-8.

143. *La France sera la France,* pp. 208-11. See also de Gaulle's evocation of the historic friendship between France and Russia and of the absence of any conflict between the two countries since the time of the Crimean War, in: *Press Conference of General de Gaulle held in Paris, 7th of April, 1954.* Note the reference to the U.S.S.R. as the ally of France in the "hypothetical case" of German aggression: "La France est toujours l'alliée de l'U.R.S.S.," in: " 'La France doit rechercher s'il est possible d'obtenir ou non un arrangement avec le monde soviétique' déclare le général de Gaulle," *Le Monde,* November 14, 1953, p. 5. See also the reference to the Franco-Soviet Mutual Assistance Treaty in: Jacques Soustelle statement, *J.O.,* 1st session of October 8, 1954, pp. 4623-7. According to a report in *Le Monde* de Gaulle's attitude in 1954 was marked "by the souvenirs of the fraternity of arms with Moscow:" "L'entretien Mendès-France—de Gaulle a porté sur les questions internationales," *Le Monde,* October 15, 1954.

144. *L'Express,* December 31, 1954, p. 4.

145. "L'entretien Mendès-France—de Gaulle a porté sur les questions internationales," *Le Monde,* October 15, 1954. "Aprés les déclarations du général de Gaulle, M. Mendès-France doit affronter sans danger les interpellations sur l'Afrique du Nord et sur la ratification des accords de Paris," *Loc. cit.,* December

7, 1954. *L'Express,* December 25, 1954, p. 10. *Ibid.,* December 31, 1954, p. 10. See also Daniel Lerner, "Reflexions on France in the World Arena," in D. Lerner and R. Aron, eds., *Op. Cit.,* p. 219.

146. André Malraux, "The 'New Left' Can Succeed!," *Yale French Studies,* No. 15: "Social and Political France," pp. 49-60. André Siegfried, "History of the Mendès-France Government," *Loc. cit.,* pp. 61-7.

147. Jacques Soustelle statement, *J.O.,* 1st session of October 8, 1954, pp. 4623-7. *Loc. cit.,* 2nd session of December 29, 1954, pp. 6959-60. For a discussion of this point, see Stanley Hoffmann, "The Postmortems," in: D. Lerner and R. Aron eds., *Op. cit.,* pp. 189-92 ff.

148. Gaston Palewski statement, *J.O.,* session of October 12, 1954, pp. 4670-1. *Ibid.,* 2nd session of December 29, 1954, pp. 6936-7; see also roll-call of vote on the motion of confidence, *Loc. cit.,* pp. 6959-60. "Une immense défaite nationale," in: "L'Assemblée confirme son vote de lundi," *Le Monde,* December 31, 1954, p. 4.

149. "Les gaullists déchirés" in: "L'Assemblée retarde de vingt-quatre heures le scrutin définitif sur les accords de Paris," *Le Monde,* December 31, 1954, pp. 2-3. "Les Républicains sociaux fixent des objectifs à la future majorité," *Loc. cit.,* January 11, 1956, p. 5.

150. Jacques Fauvet, "La géographie des partis après les élections," Pt. IV: "Des voix R.P.F. de 1951 se sont portées aussi bien sur le poujadisme que sur les listes mendèsistes," *Le Monde,* January 13, 1956, p. 5.

151. Raymond Barillon, "Réunis en Congrès à Asnières, les Républicains sociaux entendent rester fidèles au 'gaullisme,'" *Le Monde,* November 19, 1955, p. 6.

152. Jacques Fauvet, "Les cinq caractéristiques du scrutin," *Le Monde,* January 4, 1956.

CHAPTER FOUR

Some Conclusions

It has been seen that left-wing neutralism in France developed primarily as a response to American policy. Neutralists generally responded to the evolution of opinion in the United States, and to the development of American policy in Europe by moving closer to the open anti-Americanism of the *Progressistes* on the far left. At the same time, on three vital questions: EDC, American policy in the Far East, and the influence of the United States in France and in French possessions, the neutralists made contact with nationalist elements on their right. And the small circles of neutralists also reached, on these issues, a latent undercurrent of mass opinion. This mass segment remained an over-all minority,[1] but on one issue at least it brought to bear against the largely passive majority that acquiesced in EDC, a highly intense and active minority. The intensity of the opposing elements, whether neutralist of the left or nationalist, largely compensated for their lack of numbers against a relatively lukewarm coalition of supporters. Thus it is worth noting on the one hand that at the climax of the campaign against EDC a mass-opposition had undoubtedly developed, but a popular majority apparently favored the project or regarded it as a necessity, and on the other hand that the minority opposition contained far more active and convinced elements than were generally to be found among the supporters.

A result of these developments was that by 1954, neutralism had become politically "respectable" in France. It was now ingrained as one strand in the fabric of national reflexes and even influenced the reactions of some of its most declared opponents.[2] However, it did so not in the sharp anti-Americanism of the extreme left but rather in a reversion to the old concept of a neutralism that would remain essentially friendly to the non-Communist side, even while acting as a bridge to the other power bloc. The significance of this attitude depends upon the effect American policies appear to be having on the risks of war and on the chances of peace.

Meanwhile, on the other side of the political spectrum, a movement had mushroomed in the late forties which proclaimed a militant anti-communism as the chief element of its right-wing nationalism. As a result of developments inside France in the early fifties, the RPF lost much of its right-wing support to other political movements and was left with a relatively hard core of both nationalists and idealists who looked back to the left-of-center social philosophy of the Resistance. At about the same time the developing issue of EDC challenged the nationalism of the Gaullists from a new quarter. Emphasis on the Resistance meant automatically a greater stress on opposition to German rearmament. Germany now replaced the Soviet Union as the primary target of French nationalism, and the opposition to Germany spilled over in bitterness towards the U.S. which was regarded as Germany's principal supporter. This opposition eventually manifested itself in an ideological realignment in which the remaining Gaullists were cooperating with and agreeing with the foreign policy views of many of the neutralists they had previously anathemized.

The political evolution in France, which had deprived Gaullism of most of its right-wing support, in effect killed the movement as a political force. The latter survived, however, as a mystique, and in fact its very removal from the political scene enhanced its influence as the embodiment of an attitude, and as a nostalgic reminder of the period of national solidarity of the Liberation. As a consequence, Gaullist deputies were no longer isolated from all the other groups in French political life as they had been in the last years of the RPF. The ending of this isolation for a time more than compensated for their drastic decrease in numbers as regards their influence on parliamentary life. But the importance of these developments lies less in the field of political action than in the area of moods and of the political climate. In short, there had developed in France tendencies on the part of both the non-Communist left and the nationalist right to converge upon a joint policy of French "independence,"[3] of France as the mediator between East and West, and to generate a mood of hostility towards the "line" of Western policy and particularly towards the role of the United States. This general atmosphere may appropriately be termed pseudo-neutralist. Its elements include a distrust of America's political maturity and leadership, disagreement with regard to U.S. policies in the Far East, in North Africa and in Germany, and fear that American policies would increase the prospects of a nuclear war.

The particular policies which neutralists emphasize tend to vary with the political complexion of each individual faction. Yet a common denominator of demands and a joint hierarchy of values can be clearly perceived.

The first fundamental principle of neutralism is that peaceful co-existence of the Communist and non-Communist worlds is possible, and furthermore is a necessity for the survival of European civilization.[4] It is possible because the Soviet Union does not want war[5] since it considers war unnecessary to the world-wide victory of communism. In this situation, neutralists believe, it becomes the role of Europe and particularly of France to act as the international mediator between the two blocs. The more violent neutralists took this notion to the point of calling for an "independent bloc" in Western and Central Europe.[6] The majority were content with the demand that France exercise a neutralizing force in the Cold War by restraining the extremists in the Western camp from its place within the alliance.

All neutralists agreed that France[7] should resist the excesses of American anti-communism, especially those implied in the notion of a "roll-back" or in the illusion of a crusade.[8] Consequently, all neutralists could agree on a minimum program of greater "independence"[9] with which France would exercise a restraining influence upon the United States and carry out her mission to provide a bridge between the two worlds.

Such a role would require a new direction of French policy, both in domestic and foreign matters, both in Europe and in Asia.[10] In the political realm, it means that France would back the reunification of Germany under a freely elected government, bringing to an end the Communist regime in the Eastern zone. In return, France should accept the fact that a reunified Germany would have to remain disarmed and neutral.[11] Another aspect of such a role would be cultural. This means that France would act as an ideological bridge between the Soviet Union and the United States.[12] On the economic side, France would seek to reduce world tension by stimulating East-West trade.[13]

The second major principle of neutralism is that successful defense against the far-reaching appeal of communism is possible only if the Western powers adopt social and economic policies which offer material prospects for social progress as well as for an improvement in the standard of living in Europe and even more in under-developed areas.[14] In order to achieve this end, the Western powers would have to reduce their military expenditures, in any case unnecessarily high, and use this wealth instead in a vast "Point IV" type of program based on the recognition of "national" and "social" revolutions in Asia and Africa.[15] The outlines of this program, need it be said, combine the aspects of national pride and social idealism with which we have been concerned as the characteristic goals of neutralism.

Implicit in the political-ideological factors that figured prominently in the foregoing summary were social and economic considerations, and "cultural" questions, that may have had a less apparent but no less determining effect upon events. In particular, it was the prospect of an integrated Europe in which Germany, encouraged and supported by the United States, would become dominant that aroused fears about the social and economic implications of Western policies. On the right, these fears concerned the effect of a European market structure on certain French industries in which productivity is relatively low, especially compared with those of Germany. Would not a consolidation of European industry, and its concomitant removal of tariff barriers, set in motion a negative multiplier-accelerator effect within the particular investment and consumption ratios of French manufactures? The classical argument—that such a result, killing the large parasitical segment of marginal concerns, where the investment ratio in any case was very low, would be all to the good of the French economy—did not overcome the hostility of the particular groups whose interest would be affected.

For those on the left, the fear that American policy in Europe would result in a further handicap to French industry in contrast to the more efficient and hence favored factories of the Federal Republic was supplemented by the fear of a fascist-type synarchy in which a cartel structure would reappear in its worst form because now it would enjoy the backing of the economic resources and political pressure of capitalist America. The lot of the French worker, already burdened by "exaggerated" defense expenditures, would then be even worse. Thus the economic fear merged in with the ideological-political fear, which in turn found further expression in a cultural-ethical hostility to the United States, and in the intellectual "superiority complex" that grew out of the military-political inferiority complex of postwar France. This took form in the traditional, but now accentuated, contempt of American "culture" as well as in a self-righteous sense of moral superiority to the evolution of American democracy in the era of McCarthy, two issues which again offered a convenient meeting ground to the critics of both the right and left. A similar scorn of contemporary Germany, seen as a nation of hard workers generally devoid of intellectual and spiritual graces, raised the specter of an "axis" of the West running between its two technological leaders at the expense of the fundamental humanism which was considered the prerogative of France. Thus suspicion of Germany and suspicion of the United States ran along parallel lines. And fears of the danger to French civilization, inherent in a partnership of these two states inevitably had its repercussions in increasing resistance to the policy of European unity pushed by, and increasingly identified with, Washington.

The evolution of opinions and attitudes, and even more the change of values, with which this study has concerned itself, appeared to be for the neutralists of the left essentially the result of American policies and for the nationalism of the Gaullists primarily the effect of socio-political changes in France. The convergence of oppositions which occurred in mid-1954 was thus also a convergence of a line of internal developments in France and of the general evolution of Western policies. Rarely, for either Gaullists or neutralists except the extreme fringe, was Soviet policy a positive factor in the balance.

The historian is inevitably concerned with the interaction of unique elements in a particular situation with certain general patterns of relationships of a social-science character. The question thus arises, to what extent was this convergence essentially the product of a unique set of circumstances and to what extent did it represent fundamental characteristics which are inherent in the nature of the two components involved: the mystique of social revolution and the mystique of nationalism. In the former case, the implication is that the situation was probably unique,[16] in the latter, it suggests that the situation is likely to be repetitive under predetermined circumstances. The first hypothesis focuses attention on the particular function of individuals, such as de Gaulle with his traditional hostility towards France's English-speaking allies. The second consideration naturally focuses on the dynamics of the forces involved: the nature of French nationalism, the revolutionary ideal, and the logic of international relations in the present world conflict. In other words, the question is: what was the convergence of particular and general elements which led to the convergence of neutralism and nationalism.

Because the old Gaullism despite its internal contradiction was a movement which did have some structure and organization, and because it is possible to see it in the perspective of a political movement which has been "completed,"[17] it is simpler to consider this problem in regard to the history of the RPF.

The RPF began as a specific manifestation of the French right. It is difficult to exaggerate the significance that the particular nature of a movement has upon its history and its effectiveness. One need only compare the RPF, with Malraux, Soustelle, and with the idealism of Vallon or de Lipkowski to the mob of Poujade.[18] The difference between these two forces, both issued originally from the right, is a measure of the effect that the distinct dynamics and character of a movement and the personal attributes of its leaders have upon its policies and even more upon its "spirit."[19] Yet the psychological attitude of the right and the force of nationalism involved in both of these two movements are semipermanent realities[20] which reappear in the ever-changing manifestations that inevitably succeed any particular failure.

The point is especially meaningful in a situation marked since the Suez crisis by the accentuation of nationalist neutralism growing out of resentment of U.S. influence in French spheres of interest. For the past few years, the increasing tensions in North Africa and the Near East, combined with the anxiousness of the United States to avoid antagonizing the Moslem community, have strikingly increased the nationalist sensibilities of many Frenchmen and their suspicion of American policy. Thus the evolution of French opinion has tended in the direction of one of the forms of neutralism with which this study has been concerned. The relative permanence of the nationalist neutralism of the right is relevant to American policy in Europe because it bears upon a potential repetition of the convergence of oppositions in which the attitudes of one segment of neutralist opinion become the attitudes of all.

The question therefore arises: was the convergence of attitudes that has been discussed essentially an inherent characteristic of the nature of these two relatively permanent mystiques, brought out by a particular series of events, but at the same time "natural" to these two elements? This is the question to which the next chapter will suggest—it can do no more—a meaningful answer by comparing the dynamics of these movements in France with the dynamics of similar nationalist and neutralist forces in some other European countries.

At this point, the conclusion of the present study is the convergence in France of two mystiques which have been regarded in Western democracies in the twentieth century as primarily opposed to one another: nationalism, and the concept of Progress. In this perspective, a policy of neutralism in international afairs was also to be seen as the indispensable vehicle through which France would break loose from her disastrous social immobilism. We have seen both the neutralists of the left and the Gaullists proclaim that a change in the internal structure of French society could come about only by a break with the policies and obligations imposed upon the country by its subsidiary role to Washington. In other words, a nationalist neutralism was in a sense to produce a *tabula rasa* upon which could be forged a new *élan vital* that, by a reassertion of the mystique of Movement, would bring to an end the decline of France. Indeed, such a mystique had characterized the heroic periods of French republicanism and national consciousness, most recently that of the Liberation, but it had been crushed since 1948 by the weight of the economic, political and psychological effects of policies inherent in the role of France in the Cold War.

The interpretation of this mystique varied tremendously from one element in the nationalist-neutralist combination to another, but as long as these were the expression only of opposition movements, that fact did not matter very much. Furthermore, the real force of these emotions evoked by the mystique provided a psychological bond for groups whose political programs would have been incompatible. It also generated that fervor which, in contrast to the mood of most of the French supporters of Western policy, characterized many of its opponents.

It is a well-known point in history that the tradition of nationalism which grew out of the French Revolution was itself a revolutionary force, an expression of the left.[21] In the first half of the nineteenth century the identification of nationalism with liberalism,[22] although very different from the Jacobin ideal of 1795, still preserved the fundamental character of nationalism as a manifestation of Progress.[23]

Conservative nationalism,[24] which goes back even further as an historical tradition, was not a characteristic feature of the age of Metternich. The very connection between nationalism and the Jacobin and Liberal revolutions gave it a bad connotation to the conservative aristocracies of the Continent. As late as 1871, the Prussian junkers identified service to the state with the Prussian monarchy, not with a national Germany.[25]

It was after 1848 that the situation began to change, that traditional nationalism provided the emotional basis for an integral nationalism of the right, which became the characteristic of the nationalist mystique in Europe in the twentieth century.[26] Nationalism now was essentially associated with the mystique of Order and with the status quo of the social hierarchy.

Such was the mystique of the *Action Française,* and such has been the role of that totally different recent manifestation of the French right: Poujadism.[27]

Yet, in the thirties the ideological issue of National Socialism, which was itself a peculiar combination of social Movement and Nationalism, had attracted the sympathy of the French right.[28] It was the left which for ideological reasons became a somewhat battered symbol of French national resistance to the expansion of Nazi Germany.

The real significance of neutralism in France is that it again brought about a mystique of Nationalism that tied in with Progress, and a mystique of Progress that tied in with Nationalism.

Lying behind this combination of forces, frequently spoken but more often left unsaid, was the pervasive fear born of the instinct of self-preservation. Twice in two generations Europe had been devastated by war; it could not survive a third round. This feeling, although distinct from the ideological considerations which in large part motivated the nationalist right and the neutralist left, has reappeared as a continual under-current in these pages. It provided a sensitive film of basic emotions upon which the neutralist views were recorded. Seen in this light, it is a testimonial to the relative resilience of France that the coalition of neutralisms did not have a continuous effect upon the policies of the government.

Before drawing any conclusions about neutralism in general, we shall turn briefly to some other countries in order to see whether there are indications that the developments studied in France form part of a pattern. For the time being, it is possible to conclude that in France this combination was highly unstable, but that while it held together it generated great power and great intensity that imply a major challenge to Western policies.

Footnotes

1. "Résultats d'ensemble d'une enquête sur la Communauté Européenne de Défense," *Sondages,* 1953, No. 2, Supplement, especially pp. 1, 4, 9 ff.

2. "Un discours de M. Pineau devant la presse anglo-américaine," *Le Monde,* March 4-5, 1956, p. 3. Jacques Kayser, "Si les mots engagent . . . . Une diplomatie nouvelle?," *Loc. cit.,* March 8, 1956. See also Pierre Brisson's criticism of Pineau's statement: "La politique du trait-d'union est une chimère," in *Le Figaro,* cited in *Le Monde,* March 6, 1956, p. 2. Henri Pierre, "D'accord avec certaines des critiques de M. Pineau, les dirigeants américains regrettent surtout qu'il les ait exprimés publiquement," *Loc. cit.,* March 6, 1956. p. 2. Harold Callender, "Criticism from France; An Analysis of Aims Behind Comments on U.S. and Britain by Mollet and Pineau, *The New York Times,* April 4, 1956, p. 8. Elie Abel, "Capital Is Shaken by French Doubts on West's Policy; Pineau's Complaint of Flaws in Strategy Against East Displeases Officials," *Loc. cit.,* March 4, 1956. "Eden invites Mollet in Bid to Heal Rift over Policy; French Premier Accepts and Early Talk is Expected—Pineau's Attack on West's Aims is Held Basis of British Move," *Loc. cit.,* March 4, 1956. Yves Moreau, "Heureux changement," in *L' Humanité,* cited in *Le Monde,* March 6, 1956, p. 2.

3. Michel Debré, "Les Ultras Contre de Gaulle, *Le Monde,* June 15, 1957, p. 3. It should be noted that Daniel Lerner ("Reflexions on France in the World Arena," in D. Lerner and R. Aron, eds., *Op. cit.,* Ch. IX, pp. 216-8) holds that this factor did not play a primary role in the formation of French policy.

4. "Le paix possible," special issue of *Esprit,* March, 1951. See particularly the following articles: Jean Lacroix, "Faire la paix," pp. 326-32; Jean-Marie Domenach & Paul Fraisse, "De la peur à la coéxistence," pp. 333-43. Paul Ricoeur, "Pour la coéxistence pacifique des civilisations," pp. 408-19. Also, Albert "Pour la coéxistence pacifique des civilisations," *Esprit,* March,

Béguin, "Réflexions sur l'Amérique, L'Europe, la neutralité et quelques autres sujets de préoccupation," *Loc. cit.,* June, 1951, pp. 868-90. For some other sources, see: Gilles Martinet, "L'U.R.S.S. et les problèmes de la coéxistence," *La Nef,* (New series, No. 4), July, 1953: "La Guerre et la Paix," pp. 37-44. E. N. Dzelepy, "Réalité de la coéxistence," *Les Temps Modernes,* July, 1954, pp. 138-52. Jacques Armel, "L'Occident craint-il la coéxistence?," *L'Observateur,* March 12, 1953, pp. 12-3. Sirius, "Guerre ou paix," *Le Monde,* May 5, 1950. "Esquisses d'une politique," Pt. IV: "La paix sans communisme," *Loc. cit.,* June 12, 1951. André Fontaine, "La coéxistence pacifique en théorie et dans les faits," *Loc. cit.,* August 1-2, 1951. Maurice Duverger, "Dialectique de la paix," Pt. I: "L'apocalypse n'est pas fatale," *Loc. cit.,* September 6, 1951. M. Duverger, "Coéxistence ou croisade," *Loc. cit.,* April 12, 1952. Jacques Kayser "L'offensive pacifiste ne doit pas être jugée plus dangereuse que l'aggression militaire," *Loc. cit.,* April 1, 1953. Jean-Jacques Servan-Schreiber, "Nos buts de guerre en Asie," *Loc. cit.,* March 14, 1953. Sirius, "Si c'est un rève . . . .," *Loc. cit.,* April 25, 1953. Jules Isaac, "Guerre atomique ou coéxistence," *La Revue Socialiste,* July, 1954, pp. 113-28.

5. "Les nouveaux projets Soviétiques," *L'Express,* October 31, 1953, pp. 6-7. "Il est temps encore" (signed "Esprit"), *Esprit,* March, 1952, pp. 329-36. Claude Bourdet, "En U.R.S.S. et ici—Rehabilités et disqualifiés," *L'Observateur,* April 9, 1953, pp. 5-6. Gilles Martinet, "L'U.R.S.S. et les problèmes de la coéxistence," *La Nef,* July, 1953, pp. 37-44. Colonel "X," "Il ne faut pas contraindre l'U.R.S.S. à modifier sa stratégie 'atomique,' " *La Tribune des Nations,* October 22, 1954. Henri Bartoli, "Deux systèmes économiques," *Esprit,* March, 1951, pp. 357-74. [373-4].

6. Marcel Gimont, "Derrière la façade," *Combat,* January 12, 1951. "L'éhéance 1952" (signed "Combat"), *Loc. cit.,* August 28, 1951. Sirius, "Vers la troisième? . . .," *Le Monde,* June 11, 1952. Claude Bourdet, "L'Europe que nous voulons," *L'Observateur,* February 18, 1954, pp. 5-6. Gilles Martinet, "Leur Europe et la nôtre," *Loc. cit.,* Pt. II: November 18, 1954, pp. 9-10. G. Martinet, "Il faut rejeter l'ultimatum américain," *L'Observateur,* July 1, 1954, p. 6. H. de Galard, "Staline et l'indépendance de l'Europe," *Loc. cit.,* October 8, 1952, pp. 8-9. H. de Galard, "Eisenhower au pouvoir: Vive l'Europe indépendante!," *Loc. cit.,* November 6, 1952, pp. 8-9. Paul Ricoeur,

1951, pp. 408-19. J. W. Lapierre, "La neutralité française: utopie ou solution?," *Loc. cit.*, March, 1951, pp. 375-92 [386-92].

7. Roger Stéphane, "Les équivoques du neutralisme," in "Tableau politique de la France (1951)," special issue of *La Nef*, April—May, 1951, pp. 200-4.

8. Maurice Duverger, "Dialectique de la paix," Pt. II: "La toile de Pénélope," *Le Monde*, September 8, 1951. André Fontaine "La coéxistence pacifique en théorie et dans les faits," *Loc. cit.*, August 1-2, 1951. A. Fontaine, "La coéxistence des hérissons," *Loc. cit.*, August 8, 1952. M. Duverger, "Alliance ou protectorat," *Loc. cit.*, February 6, 1953, p. 2. Jean-Jacques Servan-Schreiber, "La guerre contre les Slavons," *Loc. cit.*, February 18, 1953. J. J. S. Schreiber, "Nos buts de guerre en Asie," *Loc. cit.*, March 14, 1953. André Fontaine, "Les deux coéxistences," *Loc. cit.*, Pt. I: "Est-Ouest," October 3, 1953. Claude Bourdet, "En U.R.S.S. et ici—Rehabilités et disqualifiés," *L'Observateur*, April 9, 1953, pp. 5-6. Sanford Gottlieb, "La politique des Etats-Unis en Extrème Orient," *Loc. cit.*, August 27, 1953, p. 16. Sanford Gottlieb, "Les réactions américaines à l'offensive de paix," *Loc. cit.*, April 16, 1953. Claude Bourdet, "Dulles contre la paix. Et Bidault?," *Loc. cit.*, June 25, 1953, pp. 5-6. Claude Bourdet, "L'esprit municho-'Européen,'" *Loc. cit.*, September 24, 1953, pp. 5-6. Jean Lacroix, "Faire la paix," *Esprit*, March, 1951, pp. 326-32. "Rapport du Sénat Américain sur le communisme mondial," *L'Express*, November 21, 1953, pp. 6-7. See also *L'Observateur*, issue of September 11, 1953; and: Marcel Gimont, "M. Dean Acheson dédaigne les pommes d'or que lui lancent les Russes," *Combat*, April 21, 1952, p. 4.

9. Louis Martin-Chauffier, "Les Etats-Unis et la politique française," *La Nef*, April—May 1952, pp. 184-9. Léo Hamon, "Réalité et vertus des forces intermédiaires," *Loc. cit.*, July, 1953, pp. 170-86. For an indication of the extent to which the neutralist demand for greater French "independence" reflected popular opinion, see J. B. Duroselle, *et al.*, *Op. cit.*, pp. 11-20.

10. Sirius, "Situations impossibles," *Le Monde*, February 20, 1952. Jean-Jacques Servan-Schreiber, "Un pacte de politique étrangère," *Loc. cit.*, May 30, 1953. Jean Fabiani, "Sur le chemin de la paix," *Combat*, October 19, 1954.

11. H. de Galard, "Les problèmes de la paix," Pt. II: "L'Allemagne," *L'Observateur*, April 23, 1953, pp. 7-8. B. Girod de l'Ain, "L'Allemagne occidentale pense à l'unité," *Loc. cit.*, July

16, 1953, pp. 10-1. Maurice Duverger, "Armée allemande ou unité allemande," *Le Monde,* September 28, 1951. Elie Gabey, "Unité allemande ou 'intégration,'" *L'Observateur,* April 20, 1950, p. 16. Jean Pouillon, "Après la mort de la C.E.D.," *Les Temps Modernes,* October, 1954, pp. 385-97.

12. Paul Rivet, "Neutralité européenne," *L'Observateur,* May 4, 1950, p. 3. Jean Lacroix, "Faire la paix," *Esprit,* March, 1951, pp. 326-32.

13. Elie Gabey, "L'appel de l'Est," *L'Observateur,* May 4, 1950, p. 5. "Ce que peut rapporter le commerce avec les Soviets," *L'Express,* January 30, 1954, pp. 6-7.

14. Jacques Armel, "L'Occident craint-il la coéxistence?," *L'Observateur,* March 12, 1953, pp. 12-3.

15. "Manuel pour Genève" (Based on Robert C. North's *Moscow and the Chinese Communists*), *L'Express,* May 8, 1954, pp. 8-9. Maurice Duverger, "Défendre Hanoï ou défendre Paris," *La Nef,* April–May, 1951, pp. 177-83.

16. Logically, it is quite possible for a particular attribute to be produced by certain factors in one case, and to be produced also by a totally different set of factors in another case, but the probability of this is in inverse ratio to the number of equivalent alternatives, which in this case is virtually unlimited.

17. Leonard Krieger, "The Horizons of History," *The American Historical Review,* (Vol. 63, No. 1), October, 1957, p. 72.

18. Herbert Luethy, "Poujade: Hitler or Pierrot?," *Commentary,* New York (Vol. 21, No. 4). April, 1956, pp. 301-10. M. S. Lipsedge, "The Poujade Movement," *Contemporary Review,* London, (No. 1082) February, 1956, pp. 83-8. Harry L. Turtledove, "Why the French Act That Way," *Harper's Magazine,* New York, (Vol. 162, No. 1272), May, 1956, pp. 71-6. See also: "Qui est M. Pierre Poujade," *Le Monde,* January 5, 1956, p. 4. Maurice Duverger, "Le ralliement," *Loc. cit.,* January 18, 1956. Jacques Fauvet, "La géographie des partis après les élections," Pt. III: "Le poujadisme a recruté à droite mais aussi parfois à gauche," *Loc. cit.,* January 12, 1956, p. 5. and Pt. IV: "Des voix R.P.F. de 1951 se sont portées aussi bien sur le poujadisme que sur les listes mendèsistes," *Loc. cit.,* January 13, 1956, p. 5.

For a breakdown of the election figures for all metropolitan France—the Poujadists polled 2,756,123 votes out of a total of 21,138,159 valid ballots—see: "Derniers chiffres et comparaisons," *Le Monde,* January 5, 1956, p. 2. See also: "Malgré un meeting agressif l'attitude des élus poujadistes reste encore mal définie," (with the accompanying comments of Raymond Barillon), *Loc. cit.,* January 18, 1956, p. 5. "Le Président du Bas-Rhin quitte l'U.D.C.A. et proteste contre le caractère anti-sémite du mouvement," *Loc. cit.,* January 26, 1956, p. 3. Pierre-Henri Simon, "L'appel du vide," *Loc. cit.,* January 25, 1956. See also: "M. Poujade se défend de tout anti-sémitisme; La déclaration du président de l'U.D.C.A.," and the interpolated commentary of Raymond Barillon, *Loc. cit.,* January 20, 1956. See especially: Robert C. Doty, "Mr. Poujade's Star Begins to Fade," *The New York Times* April 1, 1956, Section VI (*The New York Times Magazine*) pp. 17, 76, 78.

19. Harry L. Turtledove, *Op. cit.* H. Luethy, "Poujade: Hitler or Pierrot?," *Commentary,* April, 1956, pp. 301-10.

20. René Rémond, *La droite en France de 1815 à nos jours, continuité et diversité d'une tradition politique,* Paris: Aubier, 1954.

21. Boyd C. Shafer, *Nationalism: Myth and Reality,* New York: Harcourt-Brace, 1955, Ch. VI and pp. 143-7. Carlton J. H. Hayes, *The Historical Evolution of Modern Nationalism,* New York: Macmillan, 1950, (1st edit.: 1931), Ch. III. For the persistence of this mystique into the twentieth century, see: Harold Weinstein, *Jean Jaurès, A Study of Patriotism in the French Socialist Movement,* New York: Columbia University Press, 1936.

22. C. J. H. Hayes, *Op. cit.,* pp. 139-47. Hans Kohn, *The Idea of Nationalism; A Study of Its Origins and Background,* New York: Macmillan, 1944, pp. 595-6. For a summary of the various classifications of nationalism that have been worked out by various historians and social scientists, see: Louis L. Snyder, *The Meaning of Nationalism,* New Brunswick, N.J.: Rutgers University Press, 1954, Ch. V. C. J. H. Hayes maintains (*France, A Nation of Patriots,* New York: Columbia University Press, 1930) that nationalism is the dominant characteristic of French society, although he does not draw a clear distinction between nationalism, statism and patriotism (see Louis L. Snyder, *Op. cit.,* Ch. VIII). This book of Hayes should be used with reservations. Sections of it—for example Chapter II—fail to take into account counter-state tendencies and a streak of anti-nationalist anarchism which are inherent in French life as much as is the tendency to *étatisme.* Thus Hayes sees in France a pattern of conformity established by the various organs of the state, particularly the schools, which is often overlooked by those who

see only individualism in the French character. But Hayes, in explaining *étatisme,* does not take into account the *esprit frondeur,* the attitude that the government and the bureaucracy—"they"—are objects of suspicion and even resentment. In other words, Hayes does not give due consideration to the fact that love of *la patrie* does not necessarily imply respect or affection for either the government or the regime. Of course these tendencies may have been far less striking when the book was published a quarter of a century ago. The documentation in the appendices is particularly valuable.

For a more recent discussion on the nature of national sentiment in France, see David Thomson, *Democracy in France, The Third and Fourth Republics,* Ch. II, and especially pp. 147-63.

23. Roger H. Soltau, *French Political Thought in the Nineteenth Century,* London: E. Benn, 1931, Ch. V, especially pp. 93-7, and Ch. XIII, pp. 416-38, especially 424. David Thomson, *Op. cit.,* pp. 147-63.

24. René Rémond, *La droite en France de 1815 à nous jours,* pp. 151-7 ff. Roger H. Soltau, *Op. cit.,* Ch. II.

25. Alan J. P. Taylor, *The Course of German History; A Survey of the Development of Germany Since 1815,* New York: Coward-McCann, 1946, p. 113.

26. William C. Buthman, *The Rise of Integral Nationalism in France,* New York: Columbia University Press, 1939. Roger H. Soltau, *Op. Cit.,* Ch. XII. C. J. H. Hayes, *The Historical Evolution of Modern Nationalism,* pp. 173-212, 224-31. Denis W. Brogan, *France Under the Republic, The Development of Modern France (1870-1939),* New York: Harper, 1940, Books IV and VI.

27. See, for example, the position of the Poujadist deputies (the Poujadist group in the National Assembly adopted the name of *Union et Fraternité Française*) in the debates on French policy in Algeria: statements by: Jean-Marie Le Pen, *J.O.,* 1st session of March 8, 1956, pp. 753-7; Jean-Louis Tixier-Vignancour (independent, extreme-right deputy, close to the Poujadists and occasionally their unofficial spokesman), *Loc. cit.,* 2nd session of March 9, 1956, pp. 813-7; Jean Demarquet, *Loc. cit.,* 2nd session of March 9, 1956, pp. 821-6; Marcel Bouyer, *Loc. cit.,* session of March 12, 1956, pp. 855-6.

28. Charles A. Micaud, *The French Right and Nazi Germany, 1933-1939; A Study of Public Opinion.*

CHAPTER FIVE

International Comparisons: Bevanism — Nationalist Neutralism in Germany

> If the "cause" of the Free World is to spread colonialism and American rule everywhere with the help of napalm and atom bombs, then, argument runs, few Western people will find a cause worth dying for.[1]

As in France, there existed in postwar Britain circles of non-Communist intellectuals who regarded the policies of the United States with a critical view born of a suspicion of capitalism and of the Marxist axiom that the capitalist system inevitably breeds war.[2] At a time when the organized left in Britain, the Labor Party, had taken under the moderate, predominantly Christian-socialist leadership of Clement Attlee, Ernest Bevin and Sir Stafford Cripps a leading part in the formation of N.A.T.O., and had initiated a major British defense program, it was only the fringe of left-wing intellectuals[3] who sought their Socialist credentials in a criticism of American policies. This justification they found in the columns of the famous weekly *The New Statesman and Nation*. Here the *avant-garde* could express its equal contempt of the Soviet Union's concentration camps and of America's capitalist imperialism which, the notion was, appeared on the way to becoming the greatest danger to world peace, if it had not already done so.

> If war begins between China and the United States on the issue of Formosa, the aggressor will not be the Communists. Such a war, which could scarcely be confined to Asia would

> be the doing of General MacArthur who is making something like a private alliance with Chiang Kai-shek and the group of racketeers who surround him.[4]

As in France, non-Communist criticism of the United States had begun in the late forties in the form of an attack upon the methods and tactics of U.S. foreign policies only occasionally linked with an assertion of the moral and ideological alignment of social democracy with the free democratic states of the West. The argument was heard that the West's concentration of all efforts upon the military aspects of resistance to communism would disrupt the economies of the Western nations and end in disaster for them.[5]

> . . . by concentrating on rearmament as the instrument for combatting Communism, the Americans overlook the glaring fact that Communism wins its main victories by exploiting the economic and social weaknesses of its victims. Wholesale rearmament, and the concomitant diplomacy of strength is already creating positions of increasing weakness throughout the Western world.[6]

A radically new approach to the foreign policies of the Western nations was called for, concentrating more on social and economic measures that would raise living standards in the underdeveloped areas.[7] Even the creation of a neutralist Third Force was advocated, along with the refusal to participate in a deceptive front of "collective security," by at least some elements on the far left.[8]

The outbreak of war in Korea changed this attitude.[9] Thus it was now asserted that despite the wrongs of America's policy concerning Formosa and despite this country's support of Syngman Rhee, one could not get away from the fact that in Korea "an act of aggression has been committed and that one of the quickest ways to war—as the world knows in 1950—is unchecked acts of aggression leading to the humiliated state of mind of Munich, and, sooner or later, to that of 1939."[10]

Even this somewhat reluctant affirmation of an ideological

solidarity with the non-Communist bloc proved to be short-lived within the ranks of the militant left:

> Mr. Walker-Smith (Con.); ". . . After listening to some of the speeches made by the honorable members opposite, one might almost think it was us, or at any rate the United States who were the aggressors and the other parties who were on the defensive."
>
> Mr. Sydney Silverman (Lab. [left-wing]): "There came a moment when that was true."[11]

Again paralleling the evolution of neutralist opinion in France, the initial criticism of American methods was shifting, under the stress of American foreign policy in the Korean period and in response to the internal evolution of American opinion, to a general attack upon American aims.

> America is rapidly drifting to a point where "negotiation" does not imply genuine settlement but a virtual capitulation by the Russians to dictated terms.[12]

The charge was that in this context, any attempt at a peaceful settlement of international tensions was automatically branded by Americans as "appeasement."[13]

General MacArthur's activities in the Far East were seen as one edge of the sword of American "reaction" of which the other edge was the aggressive spirit of the Republican right.

> Several months ago—say at the time of the North Korean aggression—most people in the Labour Party would have been prepared to accept the view that the paramount cause of world tension was the policies pursued by the Soviet dictatorship. We believe that view was right. . . .
>
> It is equally necessary, however, to realize that a new situation has arisen. The danger of world war no longer arises solely from Soviet policy. It arises also from a temper which has been aroused in the United States and from the foolhardy policies into which the erstwhile more progressive

> Government in Washington has been launched at the bidding of an evermore raucous and hysterical reaction.[14]

Under pressure from this powerful interest-group, American policy had changed from a defense against aggression to an aggressive crusade.[15] American policy in the Far East appeared to be bent upon a deliberate provocation of China which would be the signal for a world war against communism, a war for which the United States would have to bear the guilt[16]—and a war which Britain could not survive.[17] Thus it was the moral justification of America's position which was under attack. "We are opposed to Russian expansion but also to an American victory" was the way R. H. S. Crossman put it.[18] While neutralist editorials in *Le Monde* were revealing the increasing bitterness of "Sirius," *The New Statesman and Nation* proclaimed:

> Lord Ismay said, no doubt truly, that 'There is no outrage against international law, against the laws of God or man from which the Soviet Union would shrink if they found it expedient so to do.' . . . so far, it is the Americans who have found it expedient to drop the atomic bombs, and who, at the present time, under the flag of the United Nations, are systematically destroying the towns and villages of North Korea with casualties among civilians so far estimated at somewhere between one and two million. . . . If the Russians do find it expedient to follow the example of the United Nations, they would undoubtedly do so.[19]

The Socialist left was becoming increasingly concerned with the "independence" of British policy—and of Britain—from the United States.[20] It advanced the concept of British leadership of the democracies of Western Europe.

> In effect, it is of prime importance to Britain as the potential leader of the democratic bloc in Western Europe, continually to affirm in action its independence of American influence.[21]

* * * * * * * *

> . . . the main justification for austerity and controls—that without them we cannot become independent of the U.S.A.—were entirely omitted from the [Labor Party] manifesto. . . .[22]

We find here a semi-conscious nationalism and national pride. This appears to be a natural development for the left under a government that was stressing fulfillment of the egalitarian evolution of the class structure accelerated by the war, and that was making of modern Britain a model of social legislation. The Labor government thus justified on the part of the left fringe of the Labor Party a new intellectual patriotism[23] in striking contrast with the latter's prewar attitude, a patriotism which ironically supported the left's criticism of the government's foreign policy.

While the significance of this trend within the British left could easily be exaggerated, it is nonetheless important to recognize its existence. The appeal to British "independence" which has loomed large in the campaign of the Socialist left, calls upon the same fundamental instinct of patriotism or national consciousness that we have seen involved in the nationalist neutralism across the Channel.

The parallelism between the development of neutralist views in Britain and in France is obvious to the point of suggesting an inherent connection. In fact, it would be an error to view neutralist sentiment in either country as directly affected by such sentiment in the other. To be sure, contacts between British and French neutralists multiplied. It has been seen, furthermore, that Bevanites found a sympathetic platform for their opinions in *L'Observateur* and *L'Express*. Such developments were themselves an indication of a general rise of hostility to American policy in Europe during the early fifties. But these international contacts between neutralists were essentially a result, not a cause, of the similarity of the development of opinion in the two countries; they offered opportunities less for formulating new prejudices than for confirming established ones. What had happened was essentially this: distinct groups of individuals schooled in similar political traditions reacted in a similar way to a common challenge: the effect on Europe of the general evolution of American attitudes.

The opinions we have considered so far were limited to small circles of intellectuals having little political power even within the Labor Party. As we have seen, the official policy of the Labor government in the early years of the Cold War was characterized by staunch defense of Western solidarity and close collaboration between the English-speaking democracies. The government controlled by a traditionally pacifist party launched an extensive arms program which was subsequently to be cut back by the new government of Winston Churchill.[24] A sign of the times was the fact that leading Communists and Communist sympathizers in the Labor Party such as D. N. Pritt, John Platts-Mills and Konni Zilliacus[25] were expelled—it was equally a sign of changing times when Zilliacus[26] was subsequently re-admitted. The anti-communism of British labor was clearly reflected in the diplomacy of Whitehall under foreign secretaries Ernest Bevin and Herbert Morrison.[27]

It was against this background that on April 22, 1951, the "stormy petrel" of the Labor Party, Aneurin Bevan, Minister of Health, resigned from the government. Ironically, this was the day after General MacArthur, symbolizing all that the left feared about America,[28] made his triumphal arrival in San Francisco. Within two days of Bevan's departure, two other left-wing members of the government resigned: Harold Wilson, President of the Board of Trade, and John Freeman, Parliamentary Secretary of the Ministry of Supply. The issue was free dentures and free eye-glasses.

In fact, underlying the schism which had come to a head over the principle of free medical service without qualification under the National Health Insurance Act was a deep and fairly long-standing disagreement over basic policies which had been sharpened under the stress of the Cold War. The leftists in the party who looked towards "Nye" Bevan as their leader had been chafing under the policies of the moderates in control of the party and of the government. Their disagreement ranged from the rate of nationalization to the central issue, the social and economic consequences of Western rearmament policies.[29]

The organ of this group, the left-socialist weekly *Tribune,* of which Bevan's wife, Jennie Lee, was one of the editors, had been developing serious doubts about the world policies of the Western democracies, and particularly of the United States.

One of the important points in the new development was that whereas *The New Statesman* appealed essentially to armchair Socialists in the professional classes, *Tribune* appealed directly to the militants in the rank-and-file of the Labor Party. Where the former spoke to political dilettantes, the latter addressed itself to professionals. Furthermore, *Tribune* had the "cover" of one of the party's most popular leaders, who had occupied an important seat in the cabinet. In other words, *Tribune* had access to one of the centers of power in British labor.

As long as Bevan had been in the government, his criticisms of its policy were necessarily muted, expressed in implications rather than in denunciations. The left of the party itself had maintained a certain circumspection in its discussion of government policy and a respect for the moderate leadership.[30] Thus while the left of the party had already grown restless ideologically, politically it was still a nonentity. The day that Bevan resigned, the veil was lifted. He proclaimed himself the champion of all those who felt that the policy of the cabinet was socially too "slow" and too near-sighted.[31] Above all, he proclaimed himself the champion of all those who disapproved of the foreign policy of Britain and the foreign policy of the United States.

Bevan's break with the Attlee government greatly altered the status of the neutralist left in the Labor Party.[32] Henceforth it had a leadership and an organization. Its efforts were to be concentrated on a struggle for power within the labor movement.

The fact that neutralist opinions in Britain were voiced by a group which operated within a major political party offers a distinct contrast with the early development of neutralism in France. This distinction has affected the history of neutralism as a political force in the two countries. French neutralists, not associated with a major political formation, were essentially involved in a propaganda campaign to win over French public opinion against EDC and against French support of American policy in the Far East. In Britain, however, the issue of public opinion concerned the Bevanites only incidentally—although they did not reject support when it happened to come their way—and the primary problem was to obtain control over the machinery of the Labor Party. This in turn involved largely a question of party maneuvers and bitter personal feuds within the labor movement. These feuds at one time threatened to tear the party apart.[33]

The core of the doctrinal issue separating the Bevanites from the party's center and right had been, at first, the question of the level of necessary arms expenditures. The Bevanites were concerned with the effects of the proposed military program on the social policies in which the left not only believed as a matter of principle but which, it felt, also constituted the primary deterrent to communism. "It has always been clear that the weapons of the totalitarian states are, first, social and economic, and only next military."[34]

According to the Bevanites, Western strategy was based "on a gross overestimate of Soviet strength and a cringing inferiority complex about Soviet political warfare. . . ."[35] This opinion became one of the crucial points in the Bevanites' stand on foreign policy. The Soviet Union's low level of industrial productivity, particularly in the crucial field of steel production, made a general military aggression on her part impossible, the Bevanites argued,[36] and Communist belief in the internal disintegration of capitalism made it unnecessary. Thus, the United States was desperately engaged in bolting the front door through which no one was trying to enter while it left open the back door to the "kitchen" through which intruders were coming in unmolested, to take over the food supply for the undernourished masses of Asia and Africa.[37] It followed that a curtailment of the arms expenditures of the Western powers would make it possible for the underdeveloped nations to carry out a necessary "social revolution."[38] Until such a drastic change in policy is carried out by the West, the argument ran on, the Cold War could not but be viewed by these underdeveloped nations as a world conflict between the exploiters and the exploited. By forcing these nations to use this particular yardstick, the Western powers were themselves confirming the claims of Communist propaganda about them:

> Poor men and women looking at the alignment of forces in the world today have far too much reason to believe that we have gone into Korea not in order to fight back aggression but rather as a part of a counter-revolutionary campaign to attack the legitimate nationalist and legitimate economic interests of poor people everywhere.[39]

The problem, Bevanites felt, was essentially that of a redistribution of the arms burden of Western nations according to the respective ability to pay of various countries,[40] and part of its solution lay in an international allocation of scarce raw-materials among Western states in order to avoid the disruptive economic consequences of hoarding by the wealthier nations[41]—that is to say, by the United States. Yet in the first period after their break with the policy of the leadership, Bevanite spokesmen affirmed that their group had no intention of destroying the Anglo-American alliance,[42] or of denying the necessity of some level of Western defense.[43] Nor could there be much question as to Bevan's own hostility to the form of "communism" practiced in the Soviet Union.[44] On the other hand, the Bevanites agreed in denouncing the basis of American foreign policy as well as this country's fitness to lead the Western powers. As has been noted, Bevan maintained that the United States had completely misunderstood the nature of the Communist threat.[45] The present line of Western strategy, the Bevanites asserted, would not only cause the Soviet Union to win the Cold War, it was also making of American policy itself the gravest threat to world peace.[46] ". . . the greatest danger of war arises from exaggerated American fears . . ." The conclusion was that it had become necessary to "restrain the Americans."[47] Bevan consequently demanded a complete reorientation of Western policy, a reorientation which the United States was unable to carry out under the circumstances of its own internal evolution and its "fear of communism" so that the moral and diplomatic leadership of the West had to be assumed by a Socialist Britain.[48]

We have come again to a position which, if not a reflection of nationalism, does certainly appeal to the nationalist instinct of those who would see their country, relegated to a secondary international power status, resume in some respects the leading role among nations.

It is natural to find the Bevanites in wholehearted agreement not only with the concept of "peaceful co-existence,"[49] but also with the policy of seeking an immediate detente in East-West relations through negotiation.[50] It was also to be expected that this group of Socialists living in a country which can survive only through its export, and feeling that economic pressures were jeopardizing the new social structure of the nation in which they prided themselves, should see in an international detente a hope for economic prosperity through a full-scale revival of East-West trade.[51]

The doctrinal cleavage in the Labor Party reached a climax with the questions of German rearmament and EDC. The causes of the Bevanite opposition were essentially the same as those we have already seen in France: fear of intensifying the Cold War, fear of a renascent German militarism,[52] and fear of provoking the U.S.S.R.[53] This attitude flew in the face of the position on Germany adopted by the Labor government and by the party majority.[54] The showdown came in '54 and '55. "Nye," who in the early years after his resounding departure from the Attlee government had won the popularity contest in the so-called "constituency" sections of the Labor Party by significant margins, now found himself under counter-attack from the slow-moving but steam-roller weight of the center and right-wing elements in the labor movement, particularly the leadership of the massive "general" unions in the TUC.[55] It was largely the unions which controlled the party; they had both the funds and the votes. While it would be a gross error to supose that Bevan had no following among union men—some of the left-wing unions, particularly among the railway workers, the engineering trades, electrical trades, and the Scottish miners gave him strong support—the center of gravity in the TUC lay in such anti-Bevanites as Arthur Deakin of the General Transport Workers Union.

In the critical test of power in 1955, Bevan was decisively defeated. He missed expulsion from the party, through action of the executive committee, by a very narrow margin; only the last-minute shift of Attlee himself to the center faction which was seeking a compromise averted an outright schism.

It has been mentioned earlier that in this internal party feud, the actual issues gradually came to hold second place in a quarrel which was degenerating into a bitter conflict of personalities.[56] The issue on which the anti-Bevanite counter-attack had finally gotten rolling, and had enlisted the support of much of the center, was not a matter of ideological questions but the point of Bevan's lack of loyalty to the party. At the very time that Bevan faced the most critical challenge in the party, many of his opponents had moved perceptibly closer to some of his chief demands regarding foreign policy. Partly this reflected the desire of stealing the Bevanites' thunder, and in this sense it is an indirect tribute to the popularity within labor ranks of some of his views. And partly, no doubt, it reflected the changing convictions in the Labor Party's center. In fact, ever since Prime Minister Attlee's eleventh-hour visit to Washington in December, 1950, at a critical point in the Korean crisis, British Labor has shared the feeling of the left-wing that it was their leader who, by restraining the United States, had prevented the immediate outbreak of World War III.[57] In the ensuing years, under the stress of events that have been described in these pages, suspicions of the motives of American policy grew in Labor, and even in non-Labor, circles which were far removed from the Bevanites.[58] This does not mean that the Labor Party became neutralist; it means that the party's center came to express more forcefully the basic criticism of Western policy formulated by the left. For example, at the time of the visit, in the summer of 1954, of the party's leadership, including both Attlee and Bevan, to Moscow and Peking,[59] Labor was emphasizing an approach to East-West relations of which the tone had shifted considerably towards the Bevanite position. In February, 1955, it was none other than "Clem" who directed a particularly sharp attack on American foreign policy.[60] This development was part of the generally growing criticism in Western Europe of the role of the United States, a criticism of which neutralism was both a reflection and a cause. The evolution of American policies in the early fifties lent itself to basic criticism from such non-neutralist sources as *The Manchester Guardian*.[61]

Thus, at the time in 1955 when Bevan's challenge to the moderate leadership of the Labor Party was decisively defeated and he narrowly missed expulsion, some of the ideas he advocated had become public property. This situation undoubtedly contributed to the reconciliation between the two factions in the Labor movement that followed the selection of Bevan's arch-rival, the right-wing Hugh Gaitskell, as the party's new leader, and that enabled the former Minister of Health to step into the second place in Labor's "shadow cabinet."

A conclusion for Britain similar to one reached on France seems inevitable: a certain form of moderate neutralism had become politically "respectable." Thus in the different political soil of Britain, ideas similar to those developed in France had taken root. This suggests that in both countries the "seed" was the same: an American policy which appeared to justify the increasing suspicions of the ideological left at the same time that it made possible an appeal to opposition based on national consciousness, both invoking the fundamental desire for the relaxation of international tension and for world peace. The surprising fact is not that such an attitude developed. It is rather that in the face of weapons which threaten Western Europe in the event of war with annihilation,[62] this attitude did not sweep every other opinion before it.

In France, we had seen neutralism, with its call for "independence" from the United States, appeal to one strand of nationalists of the right. A question naturally arises concerning the comparable element in Britain, the extreme right of the Conservative Party, the neo-Tories[63] who live in a world of the continued British grandeur of the Victorian, or at least the Edwardian, age. To this element, glorying in the traditions of Empire and the Navy, American power and policies are suspect *per se*,[64] and even more so when they seem to challenge British interests overseas. Categorically anti-bolshevik, this group nonetheless responds to the idea that Britain must free itself from

American influence[65]—whether, as one suspects, in the corruption of language, the corruption of taste, not to be confused with the art of British Academy painting, or in the general degeneration of standards. To this group, it seemed proper that Britain should resume the diplomatic leadership of the civilized world.[66]

The type of opinion described above has not played a major role in postwar British politics. Yet at certain times of crisis involving affairs of Empire and prestige,[67] the undercurrent of national sentiment upon which this opinion can play could not be discounted. It is not without significance that during a Commons' debate in which Bevan said:

> We are prepared to abrogate British sovereignty for an over-riding national purpose, but we are not prepared to do it merely to add to the sovereign power of another nation,

the spokesman of the extreme-right Independent Conservatives, Viscount Hichingbrooke, stated that "American liberalism" was:

> remorselessly depriving us of our independence, maneuvering against our empire and against our points of military strength overseas and at this moment in N.A.T.O. is hauling us on board a Juggernaut which they have created against an enemy of their choice. We believe it is time that this country woke up to the full significance of the facts that range around us, and decided that we are no longer content to be conscripted for an ideological cause not our own.[68]

In short, nationalism, whether in the implicit form of Bevanite anti-Americanism or of neo-Tory "independence,"[69] has not, on the whole, played as big a part in British criticism of "Western" policy as it has in French opinion, no doubt because Britain has felt itself closer to being an equal partner with the United States. But the germ of the emotion is there, and an environment has been cultivated for it, awaiting a potential opportunity in the sudden development of a new power relationship or in a gradual policy which appears to increase the danger of war.

* * * * * * * *

It was stressed in a previous chapter that it is meaningless to talk about "neutralism" in a country without reference to the context which gives this word a different meaning in each individual case. It is not possible, before discussing neutralism and nationalism in the Federal Republic, to cover the history of postwar Germany, but it is necessary to mention some of the main features which provide the framework for the particular movements with which we are concerned.

When Germany emerged from the war, the dominant fact in her life was that she had been defeated in war, but more than that, had been devastated, invaded and occupied. Within half a generation, the Thousand-Year Reich had installed a Soviet military government in East Berlin. The Potsdam agreement ratified what, militarily speaking, was the actual situation: the division of Germany, shrunk on its Eastern border, into two parts. While some 48 million people, and most of Germany's ports and industrial potential were located in the three zones that were soon to be incorporated into the territory of the Bonn government, some 16 million inhabitants, including farmers in East Prussia and industrial workers in Silesia, lived in what was to become the "German Democratic Republic." The Cold War transformed an administrative division into a barrier between two worlds, a barrier that ran through German towns and villages. It also transformed Western Germany from a defeated enemy into a courted ally of the West. German factories were to provide the industrial backbone of Western Europe.

From an occupied territory, Germany was now to become, by virtue of the *Generalvertrag,* a provider of military force for the West and, by virtue of EDC, a partner in its defense.

Largely an outgrowth of this situation are the two dominant facts of contemporary Western Germany: the political "miracle" of Adenauer and the economic "miracle" of prosperity.[70] These, in turn, are inter-related facts, and indeed some students of contemporary German attitudes consider a continuation of the democratic regime that the "Old Man" represents—with a parliamentary authoritarianism perhaps vindicated by its Bismarckian success[71]—a direct function of economic prosperity.

Any significant Communist sympathies which might have

survived the long decade of National Socialism, or more likely would have been born of its defeat, were effectively dealt with by the Soviet occupation. Besides, the streak of German contempt for the Slav goes back to long before Karl Marx.[72] Thus, anti-Soviet sentiment is undoubtedly overwhelming in the territory ruled by Bonn, perhaps second only to that in the territory ruled by Pankow.[73]

Against this situation must be reckoned the fact that first in the line of fire of Soviet weapons, should a third World War come about, are the prosperous and the not-so-prosperous citizens of the Federal Republic.[74] Against this situation must also be set the fact that reunification with the provinces of the East, a goal perhaps more talked about[75] than actually desired by those who have achieved material comfort under the existing status quo but nonetheless an important psychological factor in German attitudes, can be realized in peace-time only with the consent of Moscow. Thus, the international situation is the key to the "German problem," and vice versa.[76]

Such, in brief, are some of the considerations without reference to which a discussion of "neutralism" and "nationalism" in contemporary Germany can have no real meaning.

In Germany as in the other countries we have considered, neutralist protest against alignment with the Western camp began with the intelligentsia. The names of Professor Ulrich Noak and the *Nauheimer Kreis,*[77] of Joseph Wirth, Alfred Weber and the *Heidelberger Kreis,* or especially of Gustav Heinemann—who called attention to German neutralism in a spectacular manner when he resigned as Minister of the Interior of the Bonn government in 1950 over his opposition to the new policy of militarization—of Theodor Kögler and Helene Weber, or of Frau Wessel of the *Federalistiche Union* and the *Gesamtdeutsche Partei,* these need not detain us further.[78] Undoubtedly a more significant factor in the limited circles of German opposition to Western policy was a name which had become a legend: Pastor Martin Niemöller.

The bases of Niemöller's postwar attitude on foreign affairs, which at times appeared to be a scarcely veiled pro-communism, are not too clear.[79] Perhaps they include a certain element of pacifism and negation of Erastianism intended as an atonement for the former policy of the Lutheran Church in Germany which brought Niemöller to the concentration camp.[80] Perhaps they also include a continuation of that nationalism which had led Niemöller to await, under the Republic, the rejuvenating impact on Germany of Hitler. It is in this sense that one may compare Niemöller's neutralism to that of an active former Nazi who had turned against National Socialism: Hermann Rauschning. The erstwhile Nazi leader in Danzig became an ardent advocate in the fifties of opposition to the rearming of Germany and of the belief that Germany must act as the guardian of world peace by bringing about an international detente and by refusing to participate in an anti-Soviet coalition[81]—a theme which obviously carries us around to French neutralist views.

Niemöller's militant espousal of a neutralist position in the early fifties brings in the larger question of the attitudes in the Lutheran Church on the issue of East-West relations. Niemöller himself had an influential rank among German Protestants, especially as he received support for his neutralist position from the Swiss theologian Karl Barth.[82] This form of opposition, and that of some of the Evangelical elements such as the movement around *Unterwegs*,[83] represent an expression of German neutralism that is significant not by the numbers of their followers but because of their influence among the most idealist groups of German youths and students.

Of course, German Protestantism as such, with its strong Erastian streak, cannot be associated with the anti-government attitude of neutralism. Adenauer's party, while predominantly Catholic—perhaps the existence of the large potentially counterbalancing Protestant elements in Eastern Germany partly accounts for some of the Protestants' emphasis on rapid reunification through neutralization—includes a Protestant element. In fact, the CDU leader, Dr. Hermann Ehlers, was a leading Protestant figure. In 1950, a major issue developed at the United Synod of the Evangelical Churches over Niemöller's position. It should be noted that if Niemöller's name gives him particular influence among German Protestants, the official voice of the

Lutheran Church is that of the staunchly anti-Communist and anti-neutralist Bishop Otto Dibelius. Meanwhile a small minority of left-Catholics, generally associated with the *Pax Christi* movement, were brought from their opposition to German remilitarization to a more or less neutralist position in foreign policy comparable to the left in the Church in France.

At the other end of the political spectrum, the extreme nationalists also developed a form of neutralism of their own.[84] The postwar revival of a movement patterned on National Socialism came to a climax early in 1953. It was the short-lived *Sozialistische Reichs Partei* under the old Nazi Remer which, hating the Western democracies as much as bolshevism,[85] developed the idea of *Ohne uns.* The first postwar crisis of neo-Nazism, represented by the *Deutsche Partei* of Naumann, and by Middelhauve of the *Frei Deutsche Partei,* was weathered by the Federal Republic. The extreme right manifestations which have continued in existence do not follow a line of nationalist neutralism. Thus the weekly paper *Der Stahlhelm* (Cologne)—its name is a manifesto!—has strongly supported EDC and the *Generalvertrag,* while insisting upon German rights in the European community. The question may well be raised whether this belated support by neo-Nazis did not contribute to the mistrust of that policy by those on the left.

The names that have appeared thus far were found for the most part on the fringes of German national life. The dominant fact in the history of German neutralism has been the absorption of neutralist elements into the ranks of a mass political movement, the second party of the Federal Republic: the *Sozialdemokratische Partei Deutschlands.*

Re-created after the end of the Hitler regime, the SPD has been a significant political force in postwar Western Germany. While it has not been able to exceed a stable plateau of about 25% of the electorate, there is little doubt that it has a mass-following among the workers in the Federal Republic and in Berlin. As Adenauer has dominated the CDU, so Kurt Schumacher, until his death in August, 1952,[86] dominated the SPD.

Schumacher was a bitter foe of the Communists,[87] particularly of the Communist regime in Eastern Germany and of its official party, the *Sozialistische Einheitspartei Deutschlands.* In the Bundestag, Schumacher was a biting opponent of the Communists. But perhaps the dominant trait which characterized the former victim of Nazi concentration camps was a militant defense of German nationalism.[88] This manifested itself not only in demogogic demands for German "rights" vis-a-vis the Allies, but expressed itself primarily in a violent hostility to all forms of West-European union, the *Montanunion,* the *Europarat* (Council of Strasbourg),[89] the Schuman Plan,[90] and, of course, the *Europäische Verteidigungs Gemeinschaft*—EDC.

As did the neutralists in France, so the Socialists in Germany claimed that they were opposing not the spirit of international solidarity and of a united Europe but only its caricature of a "little Europe" which would prevent the realization of the ideal.[91] However, the position of Schumacher and the SPD on such questions as the Saar,[92] or its reaction to French fears of future aggression by a nationalist Germany,[93] make it impossible to characterize the position of German Socialists, who in the twenties had prided themselves on their internationalist ethics, as anything but an assertion of German chauvinism.

The position of the SPD was anti-"European," anti-EDC and even anti-N.A.T.O.,[94] but at first it did not merit the qualification of neutralist. Schumacher, bitterly opposing EDC and the *Generalvertrag* which would grant sovereignty to the Bonn government but also provided for a German defense contribution, stated clearly that he opposed the creation of German forces not as a matter of principle but only as a tactical device[95] in order to gain complete equality of treatment for his country. He rejected the idea of pacifism. Speaking for the SPD in the Bundestag, the new Socialist leader, Erich Ollenhauer, stated that the issue between his party and the government was not Western defense but the modality thereof.[96] Thus German Socialists proclaimed, like the Bevanites and "Gilsonites," that essentially they belonged in the anti-Communist camp[97] but that concentration on the military aspects of defense was not the way to fight the Communist threat.[98] The primary weapons, the SPD asserted, were economic, social and ideological ones.[99]

It is appropriate to characterize this as an opposition to the policies of the democracies, not to their principles.

From 1952 to 1954, the SPD came to concentrate its opposition increasingly upon the *Generalvertrag* and EDC as the cornerstones of German rearmament. For the Socialists, this issue came to dominate all other political considerations.[100] The trend was particularly accentuated under Schumacher's successor Ollenhauer.[101] While a faction, the "mayor's faction," best represented by Ernst Reuter of Berlin, and occasionally supported by Carlo Schmid, stood for a more "Western" policy and for the cooperation with European integration,[102] the dominant party machine under Ollenhauer came to pour ever greater energies into the anti-rearmament campaign,[103] and to take on an ever more anti-N.A.T.O. attitude. The predominant motive of this point of view was nationalism,[104] and particularly the demand for the national reunification of Germany.

Time after time, Schumacher, Ollenhauer and other SPD speakers stressed that for them the first, the cardinal element of foreign policy was the reconstitution of a united German nation.[105] The political balance, which concentrated the strength of the CDU in Southwestern Germany, undoubtedly was a primary factor that caused the political rivals of the CDU, unable to win a majority in the Federal Republic, to hope for political recruits from the East in a reunited country. Since the Soviet Union obviously would never allow the Pankow regime to be absorbed in a united Germany that would be part of the Western camp, *the inevitable consequence of placing German unification above every other goal was to demand a policy of peaceful reconciliation with the U.S.S.R.*[106]

From Schumacher's opposition to the conditions of a West German defense contribution[107] we have moved to Ollenhauer's opposition to the principles of Western defense policies.[108] From the earlier attitude that Germany's participation in Western defense must be bought, we have moved to the view that Germany must not participate in *any* coalition which could be regarded as hostile by either side.[109] In practice, this meant that Western Germany seeking peaceful unification with the Eastern zone which only Moscow could grant, must avoid any act that might deepen the cleavage between the two blocs.[110] Indeed, Germany must put to use its central location on the Continent in order to bring about an international detente and to act as a bridge between East and West.[111]

Paralleling the evolution we had seen in France and Britain, the SPD had moved from an opposition to particular Western policies to a fundamentally neutralist position strongly reminiscent of the "friendship" for the United States, morally and culturally,[112] yet "independence" of it militarily and diplomatically[113] that had also characterized Gilsonism.

This *de facto* neutralism growing out of an expression of nationalism also fitted in with another psychological motive characterized by the neutralist slogan, *Ohne uns*. Not a Socialist invention, the *Ohne uns* mentality nonetheless contributed to the Socialists' appeal against German participation in EDC.[114] It was Schumacher who once remarked, with the logic of a period in which intercontinental ballistic missiles appeared only in science-fiction, that the first battle in a new world war would not devastate the reserves of either of the super-powers but would spell the end of Central Europe.[115] Consequently the needs of the United States and those of Germany were quite different; each country should follow the distinct policy suited to its own situation.[116] A European "Third Force," representing in its diplomacy the essential requirement for the survival of Europe—peace[117]—must be created to act as a buffer[118] between the other forces.[119] As a neutralist put it, Germany must avoid the "show-down" policy of the United States and take the initiative in restoring an international balance of power.[120] The argument, it is clear, could have been found in many an editorial of "Sirius."

Small wonder that the SPD in its evolution came to absorb the various neutralist splinter factions whose principal demands[121] it now embodied in a political medium which was much more effective than they could be themselves. "How effective?" one may well ask in view of the successive electoral victories of Adenauer. Among the observers of contemporary Germany who agree that the nation's mood and policies are likely to present little danger to the West as long as the country's relatively high level of production continues, there are a few, at least, who ask what will happen if, or when, the "miracle" of German productivity gives way to a period in which material comforts are relatively less great? Will the pattern of the past reassert itself?[122] In an age of potentially total devastation, will the emotional appeal of nationalism, combined with the particular idea of security of the *Ohne uns* attitude, then find a more receptive audience?

All these are questions of the future. For the moment, one may say that with the position of the SPD we have come to that merger of neutralist and nationalist psychological motives which we had found in France. On the one hand we are reminded of Gaullism, moving from a nationalist stand against the Schuman Plan to the opposition in principle to the foreign policy of the United States. On the other hand, we are reminded equally of the neutralist left in France, or of Bevanism, moving from the idea that the primary defense against communism lies in the social and economic realm[123] rather than in the military field to an attack on German rearmament,[124] and eventually to a fundamental criticism of the emphasis on Western defense policy.[125]

It would be very superficial to conclude that neutralism in France and in Germany are essentially similar manifestations, not affected by the particular circumstances of each country. We have seen that among the various tendencies towards neutralism in Germany there existed certain idealist elements,[126] Christians and pacifists who saw German neutralism as the saving factor[127] in a world torn between two irresponsible superpowers.[128] "To destroy men, in order supposedly to rescue humanity, that is cannibalism."[129] These are Niemöller's words.

But we have also seen that nationalist neutralism in Germany developed largely out of the emphasis upon reunification.[130] In this sense, German neutralism takes on the aspect of a parochial policy appealing to certain local circumstances,[131] rather than a supra-national combination of ideological factors. One of the aspects of this particular situation has been the relative absence of a "cultural" anti-Americanism[132] not only in the SPD but among many other neutralist groups themselves.

In fact, their quarrel was less with the general line of American policy as such[133] than with Germany's participation in that policy.[134] For most of these neutralists, even the alternative policies of "independence" or the creation of a neutral "Third Force" were to rely in last analysis, as did Gilsonism in France, upon a Western guarantee.[135] Perhaps all this is saying no more than that the psychological basis of German neutralism was nationalist.[136]

Yet it is not accidental that neither neutralists nor Gaullists in France talked in terms of *sans nous*. In one case, we have essentially a program of intended world pacification and an ideological reassertion of social progress against the international conservatism of American policy. In the other, we have largely a question of national interests[137] and the hope of prosaic political-party advantages. In line with this difference was the fact that whereas in France the convergence of nationalism and neutralism was essentially oriented towards the left—witness the temporary evolution of Gaullism—in Germany this convergence was the outcome of an evolution which had taken the dominant left-of-center party far towards the right. Thus the question arises again: can any general conclusions be found about the evolution of neutralism in Europe.

* * * * * * * *

Whether the respective neutralist and nationalist manifestations we have considered in various countries are inherently similar, though revealing certain striking differences, or whether they are inherently different, though revealing certain striking similarities, this is a problem in semantics. The historian is interested in the specific nature of the similarities and of the differences. The differences that have appeared between the tendency towards neutralism of Gaullist nationalism, the essentially Socialist neutralism in England, and the tendency towards nationalism of the Socialists in Germany suggest that there is no single, general "answer" to neutralism, and that the term itself has as many meanings as there are different socio-political situations.

On the other hand it is remarkable that in different countries of Europe, and even among mutually hostile political groups in the same country, strikingly similar reactions to American policies developed and strikingly similar demands for a "different" policy and attitude by the Western powers were evolved. The similarities between the ideas and programs of Ollenhauer and of Jacques Soustelle, for example, are all the more noteworthy for the fact that they grew up independently of each other and spontaneously. There is no evidence of neutralism in one country having a direct effect upon the evolution of neutralism in another. As we have seen, when the views of Bevan or of Karl Barth were cited in a French neutralist organ, they appeared essentially as *a posteriori* support of established doctrines, not *a priori* arguments for new ones. What factors explain the similarities and the spontaneous development of comparable attitudes while at the same time accounting for their differences? One must conclude that certain general forces were operating within each of these countries in particular, different contexts.

What are these general forces? They have appeared implicitly in these pages:

1) an ideology inclined to the left, to some form of Socialist criticism of America's "capitalist" policies and their conservative effect upon European society, particularly at a time when opinion and the government in this country had shifted to the right;

2) a nationalist opposition to American "interference," or a resentment of American power, and an assertion that the strategic interests of Europe were basically different from those of the United States;

3) a general, underlying fear of war, and particularly of American policies as a potential provocation to war.

It is when circumstances bring about a merger of these divergent attitudes and emotional motives, when the instinctive reactions of a mass-segment of the population and the campaign of a neutralist élite or of a nationalist party find a common cause, that significant repercussions in foreign affairs are likely to occur. This consideration assumes added significance in the context of a period that has seen two major developments relevant to these attitudes:

1) the accentuation, since the Suez crisis, of nationalist hostility in France and Britain to America's policy towards independence movements in colonial territories, and:

2) the increased opposition in Western Europe, since the dramatic scientific achievements of the Soviet Union, to the United States' attitude on East-West relations.

One may well raise the question, while taking full account of the basic differences between the conditions studied in France and those existing in former colonial areas in Asia or in the Near East, whether the particular combination of ideological leftism with a sense of national pride and with an underlying fear of provocation to war are not also the essential ingredients in the neutralist attitude of, for example, Prime Minister Nehru or President Nasser.[138] We have seen in France that, harking back to the nationalist-Jacobin and nationalist-liberal combinations of the late 18th and early 19th centuries, neutralism was a factor in the partial reconciliation of the mystique of movement and the mystique of nationalism. That nationalism and social reform, or revolution, should again be joined as twin forces resolving themselves in a neutralist attitude in some of the old countries but new nations of the "Asian-African" bloc does not appear surprising.

To leave the realm of imagination and return to that of history—although without imagination, "history" would be a senseless drill—we have noted in France a convergence of an ideological neutralism of the left and a nationalist mystique of the right. In Britain, we had seen that this pattern applied in its general outline, although the role of nationalism here was much attenuated. In Germany, where the nationalist character of the corresponding movements was clearly in evidence, the internationalist-ideological aspect was relatively less significant. Thus we noted that while the striking similarities between the program of the Bevanites, the SPD and *Le Monde,* or of *The New Statesman* and *L'Observateur*—ideas which we saw grew up spontaneously in the three countries out of similar reactions to a general situation—suggested a "pattern" of neutralism, the differences between the movements indicated the danger of thinking in terms of some neutralist-nationalist "formula." In brief, it appears that the development of a neutralist-nationalist attitude can be understood only by studying the responses of groups in different historical contexts to a similar general challenge. At the same time, we have seen that such a challenge was inherent in the world situation, both in the general threat to peace and in the particular direction of past American policies.

It has been observed that the combination of psychologically opposite elements tended to be unstable. But it was also observed that this combination had potentialities of great significance depending upon the nature of the external challenge, precisely because it appealed to a combination of emotional forces associated with a variety of political opinions. Above all, it has been observed that an attitude based on the ideologies of social progress and national "independence" in the name of co-existence, that is to say of the preservation of peace, makes appeal to the most powerful socio-political sentiments and ideological forces in the contemporary world.

Footnotes

1. Alexander Werth, "The Soviet Line," *The New Statesman and Nation,* (London), April 21, 1951, pp. 442-3. (Henceforth, this source will be referred to as *The New Statesman.*)

2. The question of opposition in Britain to American policy has been thoroughly examined by Leon Epstein, *Britain—Uneasy Ally,* Chicago: University of Chicago Press, 1954. For the particular issue raised, see *Ibid.,* pp. 99-107.

3. Elaine Windrich, *British Labour's Foreign Policy,* Stanford, Cal.: Stanford University Press, 1952, pp. 181-93.

4. "The Menace of General Mac Arthur," *The New Statesman,* August 12, 1950, (Vol. 40, No. 1014), p. 161.

5. Aneurin Bevan, *In Place of Fear,* London: William Heinemann Ltd., 1952-New York: Simon and Schuster, 1952, Ch. VIII: "World Leadership." "How Strong Are the Russians," *Going*

Our Way?, London: Tribune (1951). John Freeman, "Arms and the Right Priorities," *Loc. cit.* "Positions of Strength," *The New Statesman,* December 9, 1950 (Vol. 40, No. 1031), p. 576. Ian Mikardo, "Arms and the Consequences," *Tribune* (London), February 23, 1950. "Economic Sense or Military Nonsense?," *Loc. cit.,* March 7, 1952. Dudley Sears, "How Near is the World Slump?" *Loc. cit.,* June 13, 1952. A. Bevan statement, in: Great Britain, *Parliamentary Debates* (*Hansard*); *House of Commons; Official Report* (will be referred to henceforth as *Hansard*), (London), Vol. 487, April 23, 1951, cols. 34-46. Richard Crossman statement, *Loc. cit.,* Vol. 497, March 5, 1952: "Defence," cols. 480-93. R. H. S. Crossman statement, *Loc. cit.,* Vol. 494, November 20, 1951: "Foreign Affairs," cols. 283-92. Ian Mikardo statement, *Loc. cit.,* Vol. 487, May 1, 1951: "Defence Program (Raw Materials and Production)," cols. 1117-8.

6. "Positions of Strength," *The New Statesman,* December 9, 1950, p. 576.

7. A. Bevan, *In Place of Fear,* Ch. VIII, especially pp. 130-2 (New York edition). A. Bevan statement, *Hansard,* Vol. 484, February 15, 1951: "Government Policy," cols. 735-7. A. Bevan statement, *Loc. cit.,* Vol. 496, February 26, 1952: "Foreign Affairs," cols. 994-1000. R. H. S. Crossman statement, *Loc. cit.,* Vol. 494, November 20, 1951: "Foreign Affairs," col. 290.

8. *Keep Left, By A Group of Members of Parliament,* London: New Statesman and Nation, May, 1947, pp. 31-2, 33-5, 40-1. See also the changed attitude of R. H. S. Crossman described in Leon Epstein, *Op. cit.,* pp. 124-6.

9. It is interesting, in this regard, to follow the evolutions of one of the leading left-wing intellectuals in Britain, R. H. S. Crossman, assistant editor of *The New Statesman* and member of parliament. In 1947 and 1948, Crossman was one of the leading figures in the "Keep Left" movement, demanding a neutralist policy and the refusal of collective security against communism. By 1951, Crossman had completely reversed his attitude. He now rejected a policy of British "independence" or neutralism, and said that Britain could play its necessary role of influencing American policy only as a sincere partner in joint defense: R. H. S. Crossman and Kenneth Younger, *Socialist Foreign Policy,* Fabian Tract No. 287, London: Fabian International Bureau, Spring, 1951, pp. 1-4, 6-7. Subsequently,

in line with the evolution of the British left, Crossman again reverted to a militantly neutralist position. See also L. Epstein, *Op. cit.,* pp. 109-12.

10. "Korea and the Powers," *The New Statesman,* July 1, 1950 (Vol. 40, No. 1008), pp. 1-2.

11. *Hansard,* Vol. 495, February 5, 1952: "Foreign Affairs," cols. 883-4. Also: Aneurin Bevan statement, *Loc. cit.,* Vol. 496, February 26, 1952: "Foreign Affairs," cols. 994-1000; and: Tom Driberg statement, *Loc. cit.,* Vol. 496, February 26, 1952, cols. 1041-6. See also: "Strength For What End?" *The New Statesman,* August 18, 1951 (Vol. 42, No. 1067), pp. 169-70.

12. *Ibid.*

13. T. Balogh, "Report From America," *The New Statesman,* Pt. II: "The Politics of Panic," August 4, 1951 (Vol. 42, No. 1065), pp. 116-7. See also L. Epstein, *Op. cit.,* pp. 143-8.

14. "The Fight to Save the Peace," *Tribune,* February 9, 1951. See also: Sydney Silverman statement, *Hansard,* Vol. 502, June 25, 1952: "Supply Committee: Korea," cols. 2303-14.

15. Aneurin Bevan statement, *Hansard,* Vol. 496, February 26, 1952: "Foreign Affairs," cols. 994-1000. Sydney Silverman statement, *Loc. cit.,* Vol. 502, June 25, 1952: "Supply Committee: Korea Campaign," cols. 2303-14. A. Bevan statement, *Loc. cit.,* Vol. 502, June 25, 1952, cols. 2039-49. Michael Foot statement, *Loc. cit.,* Vol. 503, July 1, 1952: "U. N. Policy—Far East (consultation)," cols. 288-301. Mrs. Barbara Castle statement, *Loc. cit.,* Vol. 503, July 1, 1952, cols. 325-35. See also: T. Balogh, "Why Don't We Stand Up To The Americans?," *Tribune,* September 21, 1951; and: "Where Labour Must Say 'No,'" *The New Statesman,* January 26, 1952 (Vol. 40, No. 1090), p. 85. See also L. Epstein, *Op. cit.,* Ch. X, especially pp. 215-6, 218-21, 228-31.

16. "The Menace of General Mac Arthur," *The New Statesman,* August 12, 1950, p. 161.

17. Captain B. H. Liddell-Hart, "Military Knowledge is Out of Date," *In the Shadow of the H-Bomb; A Reprint of the News Chronicle Articles of March 1st-11th with Additional Material,* London: News Chronicle Book Department, 1955, pp. 10-3.

18. R. H. S. Crossman, "Towards a Philosophy of Socialism," in: R. H. S. Crossman, ed., *New Fabian Essays,* London: Turnstile Press, 1952, p. 31.

19. "An Expert Warning," *The New Statesman,* March 3, 1951. (Vol. 41, No. 1043), pp. 236-7.

20. L. Epstein, *Op. cit.,* pp. 53-6.

21. "Socialist Foreign Policy," *The New Statesman,* January 14, 1950 (Vol. 39, No. 984), pp. 27-8. See also: T. Balogh, "Why Don't We Stand Up To The Americans?," *Tribune,* September 21, 1951.

22. R. H. S. Crossman, "Britain and the Outside World," *The Political Quarterly,* London, (Vol. 24, No. 1), 1953, pp. 28-38. "Lesson of the Election," *The New Statesman,* Pt. II: "The Election Manifesto," April 22, 1950 (Vol. 39, No. 998), pp. 448-9.

23. Michael Foot and Donald Bruce, *Who are the Patriots?,* London: Gollancz, 1949. John Strachey, "British Defence Policy," in: T. E. M. McKitterick and Kenneth Younger, eds., *Fabian International Essays,* London: Hogarth Press, 1957 pp. 85-6.

24. *Hansard,* Vol. 494, December 6, 1951: "Defence," cols. 2611-3.

25. L. Epstein, *Op. cit.,* pp. 81-3.

26. For an example of Zilliacus' position, see: Konni Zilliacus, "A Policy For Peace," *Tribune,* August 24, 1951.

27. M. A. Fitzsimons, *The Foreign Policy of the British Labour Government, 1945-1951,* Notre Dame, Ind.: University of Notre Dame Press, 1953.

28. "The Menace of General Mac Arthur," *The New Statesman,* August 12, 1950 (Vol. 40, No. 1014), p. 161. "Ourselves and America," *Loc. cit.,* December 16, 1950 (Vol. 40, No. 1032), p. 616. Norman MacKenzie, "The Mac Arthur Drift," *Loc. cit.,* February 9, 1952 (Vol. 43, No. 1092), p. 148. R. H. S. Crossman, "The War Against China," *Loc. cit.,* January 26, 1952 (Vol. 43, No. 1090), p. 88. "Where Labour Must Say 'No,'" *Loc. cit.,* January 26, 1952. "The Road to War In the Far East," *Loc. cit.,* January 29, 1955 (Vol. 49, No. 1247), pp. 121-2. "The Fight to Save the Peace," *Tribune,* February 9, 1950. See also: Jennie Lee statement, *Hansard,* Vol. 495, February 5, 1952: "Foreign Affairs," cols. 887-9. See also Elaine Windrich, *Op. cit.,* pp. 212-33.

29. A. Bevan statement, *Hansard,* Vol. 487, April 23, 1951, cols. 34-46. The text of Bevan's address is given also in: *Tribune,* May 4, 1951.

30. "Ourselves and America," *The New Statesman,* December 16, 1950 (Vol. 40, No. 1032), p. 616.

31. Norman Ira Gelman, "Bevanism: A Philosophy For British Labour?," *Journal of Politics,* Gainesville, Fla., November, 1954 (Vol. 16, No. 4), pp. 645-63. John P. Roche, "The Crisis in British Socialism," *The Antioch Review,* Yellow Springs, O., 1952, (Vol. 12), pp. 387-97.

32. The ineffectual minority of out-and-out pacifists, who accepted an eventual subjection to a Communist dictatorship as preferable to atomic war—for example, Emrys Hughes, *Bomb over Britain,* Glasgow: Civic Press, 1953—rejected the endorsement of a limited British defense program implicit in the Bevanite stand: see Emrys Hughes, *Arms and Mr. Bevan.* Glasgow: Unity Press, 1952. For the Christian pacifist position on defense, see: Reverend Donald O. Soper, "Arms? Britain Should Scrap the Lot," *In the Shadow of the H-Bomb,* pp. 19-20.

33. "Our Great Debate," *The New Statesman,* May 19, 1951 (Vol. 41, No. 1054), pp. 551-2. "A Crisis of Confidence," *Loc. cit.,* March 8, 1952 (Vol. 43, No. 1096), p. 264. "Who Are the Conspirators?," *Loc. cit.,* August 16, 1952 (Vol. 44, No. 1119), pp. 175-6. "So They Say . . .," *Loc. cit.,* October 9, 1954 (Vol. 48, No. 1231), p. 430. John Freeman, "After the Scarborough Conference," *Loc. cit.,* October 9, 1954, p. 424.

34. A. Bevan statement, *Hansard,* Vol. 487, April 23, 1951, cols. 34-46. See Harold Wilson's appeal for the relatively advanced countries of the West to help alleviate poverty and starvation in Asia: *The War on Poverty; An Appeal to the Conscience of Mankind,* London: Gollancz, 1953; and two pamphlets of his: *Today They Die; The Case for World Cooperation,* "Peace Aims Pamphlet, No. 54," London: National Peace Council, 1953, and: *Two out of Three; The Problem of World Poverty,* "Peace Aims Pamphlet, No. 57," London, 1953.

35. "Deter the Russians," *Going Our Way?* "How Strong Are the Russians?," *Loc. cit.* See also: A Bevan, *In Place of Fear,* Ch. VIII, pp. 131-5.

36. *Ibid.,* Ch. VIII, pp. 138-40. "How Strong Are the Russians?," *Going Our Way?* Some of the Bevanites came to realize, after the development of the hydrogen bomb and of missiles, that the new offensive weapons made the argument of economic "staying power" as the decisive factor of victory entirely obsolete. But they argued that this only increased the necessity of

opposing communism primarily with social and economic weapons; see: Thomas Balogh, "Political Economy in the Cold War," in: T. E. M. McKitterick and Kenneth Younger, eds., *Op. cit.*, pp. 41-77.

37. "The Death of Point IV," *Tribune,* September 21, 1951.

38. "War on Poverty," *Going Our Way?* John Freeman, "Arms and the Right Priorities," *Loc. cit.*, "Our Great Debate," *The New Statesman,* May 19, 1951 (Vol. 41, No. 1054), pp. 551-2. "Strength For What End," *Loc. cit.*, August 18, 1951 (Vol. 42, No. 1067), pp. 169-70. See also note 11 of this chapter.

39. Jennie Lee, excerpt from address to Parliament, *Hansard,* Vol. 495, February 5, 1952: "Foreign Affairs," col. 892; also cited in: *Quo Vadis?* London: *Tribune* (1952). For another expression of the same opinion, see: "Socialist Foreign Policy," *The New Statesman,* January 14, 1950 (Vol. 39, No. 984), pp. 27-8. L. Epstein, *Op. cit.*, p. 17, suggests that this stand by the Bevanites may have been little more than a formula tailored to British attitudes and in the vein of "some-of-my-best-friends-are-Americans" attitude.

40. Harold Wilson, "Neither Guns Nor Butter," *Going Our Way?* A. Bevan, *In Place of Fear,* Ch. VIII.

41. *Ibid.*, Ch. IX: "Raw Materials, Scarcities and Priorities."

42. "Our Great Debate," *The New Statesman,* May 19, 1951 (Vol. 41, No. 1054), pp. 551-2. "Restrain the Americans," *Going Our Way?*

43. "The Crime of 'One Way Only,'" *One Way Only,* London: Tribune, 1951.

44. George Lichtheim, "Behind the 'Anti-Americanism' of Mr. Bevan; How Far Will It Take Him—and British Labour?," *Commentary* (New York), July 1952 (Vol. 14, No. 7), pp. 15-20. A. Bevan, *In Place of Fear,* Ch. VIII.

45. *Ibid.*

46. T. Balogh, "Why Don't We Stand Up To the Americans?," *Tribune,* September 21, 1951.

47. *Ibid.* "The Dark Clouds of Rhetoric," *The New Statesman,* March 5, 1955 (Vol. 47, No. 1252).

48. A. Bevan, *In Place of Fear,* Ch. VIII.

49. A. Bevan statement, *Hansard,* Vol. 500, May 14, 1952: "The European Situation," cols. 1523-5. Mrs. Barbara Castle statement, *Loc. cit.*, Vol. 503, July 1, 1952: "U. N. Policy—

Far East (consultation)," cols. 325-35. Michael Foot statement, *Loc. cit.,* Vol. 503, July 1, 1952, cols. 288-301.

50. Aneurin Bevan, "Talk With Russia Now," *In the Shadow of the H-Bomb,* pp. 17-8. "Socialist Foreign Policy," *The New Statesman,* January 14, 1950 (Vol 39, No. 984), pp. 27-8. "Strength For What End?," *Loc. cit.,* August 18, 1951 (Vol. 42, No. 1067), pp. 169-70.

51. "The Flat-earthers," *The New Statesman,* October 6, 1951 (Vol. 42, No. 1074), pp. 356-7. "Even Bearing Gifts," *Loc. cit.,* April 19, 1952 (Vol. 43, No. 1102), pp. 451-2. G. D. H. Cole, "Trade With China," *Loc. cit.,* July 17, 1954 (Vol. 48, No. 1219), pp. 65-6. "Socialist Foreign Policy," *Loc. cit.,* January 14, 1950 (Vol. 39, No. 984), pp. 27-8.

52. Stuart Morris, *Neutrality, Germany's Way to Peace,* London: Peace News Pamphlet, 1953. "Rearming Germany," *Tribune,* September 21, 1951. See also L. Epstein, *Op. cit.,* pp. 258-63.

53. R. H. S. Crossman statement, *Hansard,* Vol. 494, November 30, 1951: "Foreign Affairs," cols. 283-8. R. H. S. Crossman statement, *Loc. cit.,* Vol. 504, July 31, 1952: "Germany," cols. 1773-80. A. Bevan statement, *Loc. cit.,* Vol. 500, May 14, 1952: "European Situation," cols. 1523-5. G. D. H. Cole, "The Case Against German Rearmament," *The New Statesman,* December 15, 1951 (Vol. 42, No. 1084), pp. 696-7. "Ourselves and America," *Loc. cit.,* December 16, 1950 (Vol. 40, No. 1032), p. 616. "Mobilising the IV Reich," *Loc. cit.,* August 4, 1951 (Vol. 42, No. 1065), p. 116. John Freeman, "After the Scarborough Conference," *Loc. cit.,* October 9, 1954 (Vol. 48, No. 1231), p. 424. "Agreement on Germany," *Tribune,* March 21, 1952. See also: Jennie Lee: "The Nazis Are Back," *Loc. cit.,* January 25, 1952.

54. Labour Party, *In Defence of Europe,* London: Labour Publications Department, June, 1954. Socialist Union, *Socialism and Foreign Policy,* London: Book House, May, 1953, pp. 63-4. Denis Healey, "Power Politics and the Labour Party," in R. H. S. Crossman, ed., *New Fabian Essays,* pp. 161-79. For a secondary account of Labour's foreign policy, see M. A. Fitzsimons, *The Foreign Policy of the British Labour Government, 1945-1951.*

55. "Waiting," *The Times,* London, October 14, 1955, p. 9. See also L. Epstein, *Op. cit.,* pp. 263-4, 268-9.

56. "So They Say . . .," *The New Statesman,* October 9, 1954 (Vol. 48, No. 1231), p. 430. "Who Are the Conspirators?," *Loc. cit.,* August 16, 1952 (Vol. 44, No. 1119), pp. 175-6.

57. "Ourselves and America," *The New Statesman,* December 16, 1950 (Vol. 40, No. 1032), p. 616. John Freeman and Denis Healey, *Rearmament—How Far?,* Fabian Tract, No. 288, London: Fabian International Bureau, Summer, 1951, p. 9. T. E. M. McKitterick, *Conditions of British Foreign Policy,* Fabian Tract, No. 289, London, 1951, p. 20.

58. Kenneth Younger statement, *Hansard,* Vol. 496, February 26, 1952: "Foreign Affairs," cols. 1056-9. K. Younger statement, *Loc. cit.,* Vol. 494, November 20, 1951: "Foreign Affairs," cols. 335-9. K. Younger statement *Loc. cit.,* Vol. 503, July 1, 1952: "U. N. Policy—Far East (consultation)," cols. 359-70. Clement Attlee statement, *Loc. cit.,* Vol. 502, June 25, 1952: "Supply Committee—Korean Campaign," cols. 2257-63. See also: "Parliament—Peaceful Settlement on Formosa," *The Times* (London), January 27, 1955, p. 6.

59. "Mission to the Forbidden City," *The New Statesman,* August 21, 1954 (Vol. 48, No. 1224), pp. 197-8. "The Road To War In the Far East," *Loc. cit.,* January 29, 1955 (Vol. 49, No. 1247), pp. 121-2.

60. "Mr. Attlee and Formosa," *The New Statesman,* February 5, 1955 (Vol. 49, No. 1248), p. 161.

61. "Quemoy and Matsu," *The Manchester Guardian Weekly,* Manchester, January 27, 1955. "Tachen and After," *Loc. cit.,* February 10, 1955. "Other Islands," *Loc. cit.,* February 17, 1955.

62. Capt. B. H. Liddell-Hart, "Military Knowledge is out of Date," *In the Shadow of the H-Bomb,* pp. 10-3.

63. George Orwell, "Notes on Nationalism," in: G. Orwell, *England Your England, And Other Essays,* London: Secker & Warburg, 1953, pp. 56, 64 (this particular essay is dated 1945).

64. Enoch Powell, "The Empire of England," *Tradition and Change; Nine Oxford Lectures,* London: Conservative Political Centre, December, 1954, p. 52.

65. Professor Hugh Sellon, "Peace With Honour," *Tradition and Change,* pp. 32-3, 34-5, 39.

66. Julian Amery statement, *Hansard,* Vol. 549, February 28, 1954, "Defence," col. 1092.

67. Julian Amery statement, *Hansard,* Vol. 510, February 5, 1953, "Far Eastern Situation," cols. 2142-4. Mr. Amery expressed pro-American sentiment, but demanded "equality" in the partnership between Britain and the U.S. A year later, his tone was more critical: Julian Amery statement, *Loc. cit.,* Vol. 529, Febru-

ary 22, 1954, "Supply: Civil Estimates—Foreign Affairs," cols. 419-501, especially 499-500.

68. Statements by A. Bevan and Viscount Hinchingbrooke, *Hansard,* Vol. 580, No. 34, December 20, 1957, "Foreign Affairs," cols. 755, 804-5. Also cited in Drew Middleton, "Commons Backs U. S. Missile Bases in Britain, 289-251; Rightist Conservatives Join Labor Drive at Macmillan Policies in Long Debate," *The New York Times,* December 21, 1957.

69. Most of the right wing of the Conservative Party did not express any hostility to the U.S. In certain instances, for example the Far Eastern situation and Western defense, they were usually the staunchest defenders of American policy. But the nationalist basis of their attitude meant that in any crisis which opposed British imperial interest, as they saw it, to the attitude of the U.S., a bitter disillusionment about having been "let down" by the Americans would assert itself. Apart from Hinchingbrooke's open criticism (see footnote 68), one finds, for example, in Julian Amery's statements in parliament defending the U.S. both the hope that America will support British interest in the Near East, and, more significantly, an expression of growing uneasiness when the State Department failed to do so.

The supposedly great gulf in attitudes between the Americans and the British is underlined in a lecture by the well-known writer and scholar, Max Beloff, "The American Role," *World Perspectives; Seven Oxford Lectures,* London: Conservative Political Centre, November, 1955, especially pp. 52, 54-7. Mr. Beloff is not a Conservative; nonetheless, his views were printed in a Conservative propaganda organ without qualifications and thus cannot be entirely disassociated from the party, even though they do not, of course, represent its official position. Mr. Beloff begins by citing a Soviet comment to the effect that certain "moderate" elements in the Conservative Party resented Britain's subservient role to the U.S. He rejects this caricature of the situation, but suggests that it contains some element of truth (*Ibid.,* p. 52). After discussing the different economic backgrounds and the different political traditions of the British and Americans, Mr. Beloff goes on to point out the divergence in their international policies (*Ibid.,* pp. 58-9) and the continuous problem of reconciling the two nations (*Ibid.,* pp. 60-1), except in the emergency of war—which is precisely the "solution" to be avoided. He concludes by suggesting that some other policy may be an easier way for Britain to secure its international objectives (*Ibid.*, p. 61).

It would be a clear distortion of the evidence to try to make of the statement of an individual who was member of the ardently "Anglo-American" English-Speaking Union, and who was not even a Conservative, a case of Tory anti-Americanism. It is only intended here to suggest that the psychological and national bases exist within certain elements of the British right for a fundamental opposition to American policies, as reflected in Hinchingbrooke. In this connection, it is also instructive to see the virtual glee with which Julian Amery referred to the existence of the hydrogen bomb that, by making America as vulnerable to attack as Britain had been in the A-bomb period, had eliminated the power differential between them, and thus had brought the United Kingdom back to the front rank of nations—a rather curious line of reasoning (Julian Amery statement, *Hansard,* Vol. 540, February 28, 1956, "Defence," col. 1092).

70. Alfred Grosser, *West Germany from Defeat to Rearmament,* London: Allen and Unwin, 1955, Chs. III and VI.

71. Charles W. Thayer, *The Unquiet Germans,* New York: Harper & Bros., 1957, pp. 122-5. In a critical comment on Adenauer, Reimer Siemsen writes ("Des Kanzlers geistiger Standpunkt," *Die Kultur,* Stuttgart [5th year, No. 91], September 1, 1957) that Adenauer in the West inevitably "begets" Ulbricht in the East, that the Communist and CDU leaders each "justify" the other.

72. At the time of the Crimean War, Marx hated Russia with an intensity that seems almost obsessive (Karl Marx, *The Eastern Question; A Reprint of Letters Written in 1853-1856 Dealing with the Events of the Crimean War,* ed. by Eleanor Marx Aveling and Edward Aveling, London: S. Sonnenschein, 1897, throughout). In a sense, this bitterness was directed against the Czarist regime. But it appears that in this period Marx' antipathy extended to the Russians (*Ibid.,* pp. 593-6) and beyond them to the "Slavonic races"—excepting the Poles. In fact, Marx stated that he considered pan-Slavism, under Russian aegis, a racial threat to the Germanic-Celtic civilization of Europe (*Ibid.,* pp. 543-4). This attitude appears very strikingly

in a more recent compilation: Karl Marx and Friedrich Engels, *The Russian Menace to Europe; A Selection of Articles, Speeches, Letters and News Dispatches,* Selected and edited by Paul W. Blackstock and Bert Hoselitz, Glencoe, Ill.: The Free Press, 1952. These documents make it apparent that if Marx and especially Engels developed in later years a keen interest in the social and economic changes occuring in Imperial Russia, their earlier contempt of Slavs generally, always with the striking exception of the Poles, had involved a kind of "Kultur"—nationalism (*Ibid.,* pp. 67-90) in accordance with their German background rather than their Socialist ideals. See also E. H. Carr, *The Romantic Exiles; A Nineteenth Century Portrait Gallery,* Harmonsworth-Middlesex: Penguin Books, 1949, note, p. 161.

73. Taking the events of June 17, 1953 as a tragic indication.

74. Wilhelm Wolfgang Schütz, *Deutschland am Rande zweier Welten; Voraussetzungen und Aufgabe unserer Aussenpolitik,* Stuttgart: Deutsche Verlags-Anstalt, 1952, pp. 33-4, 46-7.

75. For a criticism of the "taboo" on unity in contemporary Germany, see: * * * "Auf dem Prüfstand; Zur Pathologie des politischen Denkens der Deutschen," *Wort und Wahrheit, Monatsschrift für Religion und Kultur,* Freiburg im Breisgau, (2nd year, No. 2) February, 1957, pp. 99-100. Bernhard Roegele, "Herbst der Illusionen," *Neues Abendland* (Vol. 12, No. 2), 2nd quarter, 1957, pp. 101-3.

76. Alfred Grosser, *La situation en Allemagne en 1955; Rapport du Congrès international de Bruges, 1955,* Brussels: Institut des Relations internationales, 1955. See also note 131.

77. Nauheimer Kreis, *Die Nauheimer Protokolle; Diskussionen über die Neutralisierung Deutschlands,* Würzburg: Nauheimer Kreis—Dr. Ulrich Noak, 1950, especially pp. 55-7.

78. Report of Mr. Perlacky-Kasa to the Mutual Security Agency, Office of the Special Representative (Paris), Information Division, Research and Analysis Branch, Paris: MSS, 1953.

79. Martin Niemöller, *Deutschland Wohin? Krieg oder Frieden?,* Darmstadt: Jupiter, 1952. Reprint of a major speech Pastor Niemöller delivered in Darmstadt on January 17, 1952.

80. Alfred Grosser, *West Germany from Defeat to Rearmament,* pp. 158-61. Martin Niemöller, *Deutschland Wohin? Krieg oder Frieden?,* especially p. 9.

81. Hermann Rauschning, *Deutschland zwischen West und*

Ost, Berlin: Christian Verlag, 1950. H. Rauschning, *Die Deutsche Einheit und der Weltfriede,* Hamburg: Holstein, 1955.

82. Karl Barth, " 'Ne craignez point,' Lettre ouverte de Karl Barth sur la remilitarisation de l'Allemagne," Bâle, October 12, 1950., in: "Les Protestants allemands et le réarmement," *Esprit,* January, 1951, pp. 105-13.

83. "Les Protestants allemands et le réarmement," *Esprit,* January, 1951, p. 103.

84. Walter Büttner, *Verschwörung gegen Deutschland,* Kahl: Hohe Warte, 1953.

85. Statement by Dr. Dorls, in: Germany, Federal Republic, *Verhandlungen des Deutschen Bundestages, I. Wahlperiode 1949., Stenographische Berichte,* Bonn: Bonner Universitäts-Buchdruckerei, 1950 . . ., 98th sitting November 8, 1950 (Vol. 5), p. 3593. Henceforth this source will be referred to as *V.D.B.* Unless otherwise specified, the volume numbers will refer to the *I. Wahlperiode 1949.* For a similar expression of Nazi hostility to the U.S., see the statement of von Thadden (Deutsche Reichspartei), *Loc. cit.,* pp. 3587-90.

86. See the edition of the *Neuer Vorwärts; Zentral Organ der Sozialdemokratischen Partei Deutschlands,* Hanover, August 22, 1952. Henceforth, this source will be referred to as *Neuer Vorwärts.*

87. Schumacher statement, *V.D.B.,* 98th sitting, November 8, 1950. (Vol. 5), p. 3576. See especially Schumacher statement, *Loc. cit.,* 125th sitting, March 9, 1951. (Vol. 6), pp. 4761-6. "Die Wahrheit muss ans Tageslicht," *Neuer Vorwärts,* March 23, 1951.

88. Schumacher statement, *V.D.B.,* 68th sitting, June 13, 1950. (Vol. 4), pp. 2477-8. Ollenhauer statement, *Loc. cit.,* 255th sitting, March 10, 1953 (Vol. 15), pp. 12318-23. See also Kurt Schumacher, "Keine Verewigung des Unrechts," *Neuer Vorwärts,* April 27, 1951. "Schumanplan verewigt Besatzungsrecht," *Loc. cit.,* May 25, 1951.

89. Schumacher statement, *V.D.B.,* 68th sitting, June 13, 1950 (Vol. 4), pp. 2472-5.

90. *Ibid.* Kurt Schumacher, "Keine Verewigung des Unrechts," *Neuer Vorwärts,* April 27, 1951, voices the familiar argument that the European Coal and Steel community would be a reactionary cartel. See also: "Schumanplan verewigt Besatzungsrecht," *Loc. cit.,* May 25, 1951. "In den Wind gesprochen?,"

Loc. cit., January 4, 1952. "Die Wahrheit muss ans Tageslicht," *Loc. cit.,* March 23, 1951. Willi Eichler, "Mutter Europa und ihre Rabenkinder," *Loc. cit.,* May 18, 1951.

91. Erich Ollenhauer speech to the Bundestag, "Falscher Start nach Europa," *Neuer Vorwärts,* January 18, 1952. "Europäische Wirklichkeit," *Loc. cit.,* August 6, 1954. Schumacher statement, *V.D.B.,* 68th sitting, June 13, 1950 (Vol. 4), pp. 2476, 8. Erler statement, *Loc. cit.,* 242nd sitting, December 5, 1952 (Vol. 14), p. 11482. See also the comments by Rudolf Mettmann about the SPD, in "Carlo Schmid, Revolutionär oder müder Troubadour?," *Das Neue Journal,* Wiesbaden, 6th year, October 9, 1957, p. 2.

92. Dr. Karl Mommer, " 'Europäisierung'—Separierung," *Neuer Vorwärts,* August 1, 1952. Schumacher statement, *V.D.B.,* 68th sitting, June 13, 1950 (Vol. 4), pp. 2470-2. Ollenhauer statement, *Loc. cit.,* 190th sitting, February 7, 1952 (Vol. 10), p. 8115. *Ibid.,* 255th sitting, March 10, 1953 (Vol. 15), p. 12320.

93. Kurt Schumacher, "Keine Verewigung des Unrechts," *Neuer Vorwärts,* April 27, 1951. Willi Eichler, "Mutter Europa und ihre Rabenkinder," *Loc. cit.,* May 18, 1951. Erler statement, *V.D.B.,* 242nd sitting, December 5, 1952 (Vol. 14), p. 11477. Ollenhauer statement, *Loc. cit.,* 255th sitting, March 10, 1953 (Vol. 15), p. 12322.

94. Rudolf Mettmann, "Carlo Schmid, Revolutionär oder müder Troubadour?," *Dae Neue Journal,* October 9, 1957, p. 21.

95. Schumacher statement, *V.D.B.,* 68th sitting, June 13, 1950 (Vol. 4), p. 2477. See especially Schumacher statement, *Loc. cit.,* 98th sitting, November 8, 1950 (Vol. 5), p. 3571.

96. Ollenhauer statement, *V.D.B.,* 191st sitting, February 8, 1952 (Vol. 10), pp. 8237-8.

97. Schumacher statement, *V.D.B.,* 98th sitting, November 8, 1950 (Vol. 5), pp. 3574-6.

98. S[ozialdemokratische] P[artei] D[eutschlands], *Annahme bedeutet nicht Ratifizierung! Der Kampf um die Verträge geht weiter!,* Bonn: Vorstand der SPD, 1953, pp. 9-11; reprint of a speech by Erich Ollenhauer delivered on March 19, 1953. Henceforth, this source will be referred to by its title: *Annahme bedeutet nicht Ratifizierung!* See also statement of Dr. Arndt for the S.P.D., *V.D.B.,* 191st sitting, February 8, 1952 (Vol. 10), p. 8154, and Ollenhauer statement, *Loc. cit.,* p. 8238.

99. Erich Ollenhauer, "Die Mai-Botschaft verwirklichen!," *Neuer Vorwärts,* May 1, 1954. Statement of Ollenhauer, *V.D.B.,*

24th sitting, December 16, 1949 (Vol. 1), pp. 735-6. Schumacher statement, *Loc. cit.,* 98th sitting, November 8, 1950, (Vol. 5), pp. 3572-3. Erler statement, *Loc. cit.,* 242nd sitting, December 5, 1952, (Vol. 14), pp. 11482-3. Ollenhauer statement, *Loc. cit.,* 255th sitting, March 10, 1953 (Vol. 15), p. 12327.

100. Ollenhauer speech, "Kampf der Verzichtpolitik," *Neuer Vorwärts,* April 11, 1952. "Nicht Ratifizieren!," *Loc. cit.,* May 30, 1952. "Kampf der Zerreissung—Hilfe den Opfern," *Loc. cit.,* June 20, 1952. Ollenhauer speech in Berlin, "Kalter Krieg fordert feste Demokratie," *Loc. cit.,* October 17, 1952. "Einheit, Freiheit und soziale Gerechtigkeit," *Loc. cit.,* December 24, 1953. "Verstärktes Nein zu den Verträgen," *Loc. cit.,* March 20, 1953. Ollenhauer statement, *V.D.B.,* 190th sitting, February 7, 1952 (Vol. 10), pp. 8111-4. *Ibid.,* 191st sitting, February 8, 1952, pp. 8236-7.

101. *Annahme bedeutet nicht Ratifizierung!,* especially p. 5. Ollenhauer had taken a more militant position against German participation in Western defense than had his chief. See, for example, Erich Ollenhauer statement, *V.D.B.,* 24th sitting, December 16, 1949 (Vol. 1), pp. 735-6.

102. Rudolf Mettmann, "Carlo Schmid, Revolutionär oder müder Troubadour?," *Das Neue Journal,* October 9, 1957.

103. Ollenhauer speech, "Kampf der Verzichtpolitik," *Neuer Vorwärts,* April 11, 1952.

104. It is interesting to compare this attitude with that of a well known non-socialist, conservative-nationalist, and very popular postwar publication, *Der Spiegel* (Hamburg). A weekly "news magazine" consciously and successfully modelled on the American *Time, Der Spiegel* is essentially noted for its sensationalist exposés, and its brittle, cynical style. Its position on political issues has tended to be eclectic, repeatedly shifting from one side to the other. On many questions, the "line" of the magazine was hard to follow because it expressed itself, not in articles or editorials, but in the "digests" of some obscure books ("Sowjetunion-Koexistenz," *Loc. cit.,* January 19, 1955 p. 28.) which presumably agreed with the editor's opinions on that day. Yet, apart from a generally right-of-center tendency, two consistent aspects appear in the magazine: hatred of Adenauer and militant nationalism. The second aspect has found expression in a rather belligerent assertion of German rights, "fits" over the Saar, a certain superciliousness towards

England, and a definite contempt for France. Above all, this nationalism showed itself in hostility to Adenauer's foreign policy, and in particular to EDC and Western defense strategy. Thus in foreign affairs, the position of *Der Spiegel* was in some ways comparable to the neutralist nationalism of the SPD.

105. Schumacher speech, "Das stumme Volk muss reden," *Neuer Vorwärts,* October 12, 1951. "Unsicherheit und Staatskrise," *Loc. cit.,* November 9, 1951. See especially "Deutsche Einheit–Sache der Weltdemokratie," *Loc. cit.,* December 28, 1951, and "Neue Phase im Kampf um die Einheit," *Loc. cit.,* January 11, 1952. "Kampf der Zerreissung–Hilfe den Opfern," *Loc. cit.,* June 20, 1952. "Soll 1945 verewigt werden?," *Loc. cit.,* July 11, 1952. Ollenhauer speech, "Wiedervereinigung–oberstes Ziel," *Loc. cit.,* February 15, 1953. "Einheit, Freiheit und soziale Gerechtigkeit," *Loc. cit.,* December 24, 1953. "Wiedervereinigung hat Vorrang," *Loc. cit.,* February 5, 1954. Ollenhauer statement, *V.D.B.,* 269th sitting, June 10, 1953 (Vol. 10), pp. 13253-4. *Ibid., II. Wahlperiode,* 16th sitting, February 25, 1954 (Vol. 1), pp. 524-5. See especially Ollenhauer statement, *Loc. cit., I. Wahlperiode,* 255th sitting, March 10, 1953 (Vol. 15), pp. 12317-9. *Annahme bedeutet nicht Ratifizierung!* p. 3. Heinrich Siegler, *Deutschlands Weg, 1945-1955; Von der Kapitulation bis zur Moskau-Reise Adenauers,* Cologne: Koenig (1956), p. 163.

106. Wilhelm Wolfgang Schütz, *Die Stunde Deutschlands; Wie kann Deutschland wiedervereinigt werden?* Stuttgart: Deutsche Verlags-Anstalt, 1954. W. W. Schütz, *Deutschland am Rande zweier Welten,* pp. 88-101.

107. Schumacher statement, *V.D.B.,* 98th sitting, November 8, 1950 (Vol. 5), pp. 3571-2. "Die Wahrheit muss ans Tageslicht," *Neuer Vorwärts,* March 23, 1951.

108. Ollenhauer statement, *V.D.B., II. Wahlperiode,* 16th sitting, February 25, 1954 (Vol. 1), p. 525.

109. *Ibid.,* pp. 524-5.

110. *Annahme bedeutet nicht Ratifizierung!,* pp. 2, 8, 11. Ollenhauer statement, "Kampf der Verzichtpolitik," *Neuer Vorwärts,* April 11, 1952. Schumacher's open letter to Adenauer, "Schicksalsfrage für den Frieden," *Loc. cit.,* May 2, 1952. "Am Abgrund der Illegalität," *Loc. cit.,* May 23, 1952. "Nicht Ratifizieren!," *Loc. cit.,* May 30, 1952. "Kampf der Zerreissung–Hilfe den Opfern!," *Loc. cit.,* June 20, 1952. Ollenhauer speech in Berlin, "Kalter Krieg fordert feste Demokratie," *Loc. cit.,*

October 17, 1952. "Koalition gegen Viererverhandlungen," *Loc. cit.,* July 5, 1953. "Einheit, Freiheit und soziale Gerechtigkeit," *Loc. cit.,* December 24, 1953. E. Ollenhauer, "Reise nach Moskau," *Loc. cit.,* May 21, 1954. Ollenhauer statement, *V.D.B., II. Wahlperiode,* 16th sitting, February 25, 1954 (Vol. 1), p. 525. On this, see also the statement of Frau Wessel (Federalistische Union and currently of the SPD), *Loc. cit., I. Wahlperiode,* 191st sitting, February 8, 1952 (Vol. 10), pp. 8171-2.

111. "Im Zeichen des Friedenwillens,"*Neuer Vorwärts,* June 5, 1953. Ollenhauer statement, *V.D.B.,* 255th sitting, March 10, 1953 (Vol. 15), pp. 11323-4, especially 11326. Heinrich Siegler, *Op. cit.,* pp. 103, 154, 170. See also Hermann Rauschning, *Die Deutsche Einheit und der Weltfriede,* pp. 63-4, 70-3, 88-94.

112. *Annahme bedeutet nicht Ratifizierung!,* p. 10. Ollenhauer statement, *V.D.B.,* 255th sitting, March 10, 1953 (Vol. 15), p. 12329.

113. *Ibid.; Annahme bedeutet nicht Ratifizierung!,* pp. 8, 9, 11. Ollenhauer interview, "Einheit, Freiheit und soziale Gerechtigkeit," *Neuer Vorwärts,* December 24, 1953.

114. Ollenhauer statement, *V.D.B.,* 190th sitting, February 7, 1952. (Vol. 10), p. 8110. In an exchange with the supporters of Adenauer, Dr. Arndt, speaking for the SPD, denied that his party advocated an *Ohne Uns* atittude. But the discussion brought out the fact that the party propaganda made use of this sentiment: Dr. Arndt statement, *Loc. cit.,* 191st sitting, February 8, 1952 (Vol. 10), pp. 8155-6.

115. Schumacher statement, *V.D.B.,* 98th sitting, November 8, 1950 (Vol. 5), pp. 3571-2. Concerning the idea that EDC and the *Generalvertrag* would not provide Germany with military security, see Erler statement, *Loc. cit.,* 242nd sitting, December 5, 1952 (Vol. 14), pp. 11478-80.

116. This point was especially developed by Hermann Rauschning, *Deutschland zwischen West und Ost,* and Christian Harwick, *Deutschland zwischen Ja und Nein; Prognose unter dem Fallbeil,* Kreuzlingen: Neptune, 1951. For a moderate statement of the position, see Wilhelm Wolfgang Schütz, *Die Stunde Deutschlands; Wie kann Deutschland wiedervereinigt werden?,* Stuttgart: Deutsche Verlags-Anstalt, 1954.

117. Ollenhauer statement, *V.D.B.,* 255th sitting, March 10, 1953 (Vol. 15), p. 12324.

118. Hermann Rauschning, *Die Deutsche Einheit und der Weltfriede,* pp. 43-51, 63-4, 88-94.

119. This demand for the neutralization of Germany (see also the writings of Hermann Rauschning, of the Nauheimer Kreis, of Christian Harwick, Rudolf Laun, etc.) went far beyond the idea of non-rearmament as expressed in newspaper opinion in 1950: Deutsches Büro für Friedensfragen (in Überleitung), *Die Wiederaufrüstung Deutschlands im Spiegel der Presse,* n.l. roneotyped, May, 1950, pp. 18-24.

120. Wilhelm W. Schütz, *Deutschland am Rande zweier Welten,* pp. 33-4, 44-8, 63-6, 68-74, 88-101.

121. Hermann Rauschning, *Die Deutsche Einheit und der Weltfriede,* Hamburg: Holstein, 1955, throughout but especially pp. 48-51. Nauheimer Kreis, *Die Nauheimer Protokolle; Diskussionen über die Neutralisierung Deutschlands,* pp. 55-7. Wilhelm W. Schütz, *Deutschland am Rande zweier Welten.*

122. Charles W. Thayer, *The Unquiet Germans,* pp. 151-2, 266-70.

123. Wilhelm W. Schütz, *Deutschland am Rande zweier Welten,* p. 108. Hermann Rauschning, *Deutschland zwischen West und Ost,* pp. 99 ff. See also Note 99.

Along the lines of this argument, the SPD also claimed that Germany could not meet the high costs of rearmament without precipitating a serious dislocation of the economy: Erler statement, *V.D.B.,* 241st sitting, December 4, 1952 (Vol. 14), pp. 11329-33; *Ibid.,* 242nd sitting, December 5, 1952, p. 11476. See also Ollenhauer statement, *Loc. cit.,* 255th sitting, March 10, 1953 (Vol. 15), p. 12321; and Schumacher's position: "Die Wahrheit muss ans Tageslicht," *Neuer Vorwärts,* March 23, 1951.

124. Deutsches Büro für Friedensfragen (in Überleitung), *Die Wiederaufrüstung Deutschlands im Spiegel der Presse,* pp. 18-24. Hermann Rauschning stated that an independent, neutral Germany must be armed: *Die Deutsche Einheit und der Weltfriede,* pp. 70-3. Schumacher statement, *V.D.B.,* 98th sitting, November 8, 1950 (Vol. 5), pp. 3571-2. See also Ollenhauer's speech to the Bundestag, cited as "Bedrohung der Demokratie," in the *Neuer Vorwärts,* February 15, 1952.

125. Some German "neutralists" predicated, as Gilson had done for France, an independent policy for Germany based on the re-insurance of a powerful Atlantic defense system: Wilhelm

Wolfgang Schütz, *Die Stunde Deutschlands; Wie kann Deutschland wiedervereinigt werden?* Schütz made it clear that if he hoped for Western support of a free and united Germany, the latter could not contribute militarily to either bloc and must fulfill its role essentially as a neutral, balancing factor: W. W. Schütz, *Deutschland am Rande zweier Welten,* pp. 63-6, 68-74, 78-82, 85-7.

For a similar attitude in the SPD, see: *Annahme bedeutet nicht Ratifizierung!,* p. 9.

126. Hermann Rauschning, *Deutschland zwischen West und Ost,* especially p. 197.

127. Christian Harwick, *Deutschland zwischen Ja und Nein; Prognose unter dem Fallbeil.* Rudolf Laun, *Das Völkerrecht und die Verteidigung Deutschlands,* Heidelberg: Vorwinkel, 1951. Hermann Rauschning, *Die Deutsche Einheit und der Weltfriede,* pp. 48-51.

128. Hermann Rauschning, *Deutschland zwischen West und Ost,* pp. 83, 99. H. Rauschning, *Die Deutsche Einheit und der Weltfriede,* p. 41. Wilhelm W. Schütz, *Deutschland am Rande zweier Welten,* p. 47.

129. Martin Niemöller, *Deutschland Wohin? Krieg oder Frieden?,* p. 9.

130. Wilhelm W. Schütz, *Die Stunde Deutschlands, Wie kann Deutschland wiedervereinigt werden?* W. W. Schütz, ed., *Bewährung im Widerstand; Gedanken zum deutschen Schicksal,* Stuttgart: Deutsche Verlags-Anstalt, 1956 [a series of essays, mostly by university professors, emphasizing German "unity" in all its aspects.] "Deutsche Einheit—Sache der Weltdemokratie," *Neuer Vorwärts,* December 28, 1951. "Neue Phase im Kampf um die Einheit," *Loc. cit.,* January 11, 1952.

131. Königsteiner Kreis—Vereinigung der Juristen, Volkswirte, Beamten aus der Sowjetischen Besatzungszone, *Untersuchungen zur Lösung der deutschen Frage; Bericht über die Tagung des Verfassungsausschusses des Königsteiner Kreises in Bonn am 27. und 28. März 1952,* Göttingen: Schwartz, 1952. Der Nauheimer Kreis, *Die Nauheimer Protokolle; Diskussionen über die Neutralisierung Deutschlands.*

132. Nonetheless, Ollenhauer did stress the idea that Germany should stop kowtowing to the U.S.: Ollenhauer statement, *V.D.B.,* 255th sitting, March 10, 1953 (Vol. 15), p. 12323. He also accused

Adenauer of being excessively pro-American, "Für ein Friedensprogramm des Westens," *Neuer Vorwärts,* May 22, 1953.

133. There was, of course, some implicit Socialist criticism of McCarthyism and of American policy in the Far East: "Im Geiste Mc Carthy's," *Neuer Vorwärts,* March 26, 1954. "Passion ohne Ende? Krise vor Genf," *Loc. cit.,* April 15, 1954; "Die Dulles Doktrin," *Loc. cit.,* May 1, 1954 p. 4. See also the criticism of the rearmament of Japan: H. Altner, "Der Kampf gegen die Wiederaufrüstung in Japan," *Loc. cit.,* June 25, 1954, p. 5. Finally, note the critical comments about American foreign trade policies, suggesting that low tariff levels in the U.S. are forgotten about as soon as they begin to cost Americans money: "Europas Exporte werden unbequem," *Loc. cit.,* September 3, 1954, pp. 6-7.

134. Wilhelm Wolfgang Schütz, *Die Stunde Deutschlands, Wie kann Deutschland wiedervereinigt werden?* Of course criticism of American policies and motives could be found: Martin Niemöller, *Deutschland Wohin? Krieg oder Frieden?,* p. 7. See also the writings of Hermann Rauschning.

135. Wilhelm W. Schütz, *Deutschland am Rande zweier Welten,* pp. 85-7.

136. Rudolf Laun, *Das Völkerrecht und die Verteidigung Deutschlands.*

137. *Ibid.* Wilhelm W. Schütz, *Die Stunde Deutschlands; Wie kann Deutschland wiedervereinigt werden?*

138. "A Socialist Egypt is Nasser's Goal; He Repeats Determination to Keep Country Free of Alien Influences," *The New York Times,* December 6, 1957, p. 5.

Bibliography

France

A. *Periodical Sources*

Action, Paris. Weekly newspaper, organ of the French section of the international pro-Communist movement of the *Combattants de la Paix*. Voiced primarily the position of the Communist-front *Progressiste* group centered around Pierre Cot. Officially "neutralist" but in the strictly pro-Soviet interpretation of the term. Edited by the Stalin-Prize winner and CGT leader, Yves Farge. Ceased publication in 1952.

L'Aurore, Paris. Daily paper founded after the war, under the direction of Robert Lazarick. Represents the extreme right, colonialist point of view, favorable to the conservative element in the Radical-Socialist party associated with Léon Martinaud-Déplat. In the early postwar years strongly favorable to Gaullism. Militantly anti-neutralist and pro-Western, though highly sensitive of any foreign "interference" in French overseas territories. A sensationalist morning paper aimed largely at the lower middle class, it is one of the largest mass-circulation dailies (competing neck-and-neck with *Le Figaro*), circulation: 498,579.* The foreign policy comments of Robert Bony were widely cited in political circles.

Cahiers du Communisme, Paris. Official doctrinal monthly of the French Communist Party.

Carrefour, Paris (and for a time also Montreal). Political-literary weekly newspaper born of the Free French movement during the Occupation. Edited by Félix Garas;

* The circulation figures cited here are taken from Walter H. Mallory, ed., *Political Handbook of the World, 1957,* New York: Council on Foreign Relations, 1957, pp. 74-5.

featuring the political comments of André Stibio. For many years the unofficial but most popular voice of the RPF. Supported Gaullism especially during the time that movement maintained itself as the rallying point of the French right and the defender of a "hard" foreign policy. Ultra-nationalist, militant defender of French "presence" overseas.

Combat, Paris. Left-of-center morning daily issued of the Resistance. At one time edited by the independent Marxist, Claude Bourdet. Oscillating editorial line on foreign affairs in regard to the Cold War but generally neutralist, especially in the crucial years 1953-1955. Controlled by financier Henry Smadja. Generally reflects independent Socialist opinions. A major source for the present study. The paper's shift back to neutralism in the editorials of Jean Fabiani and Marcel Gimont appear characteristic of the French non-Communist left's reaction to the evolution of United States policy during those years. Circulation: 62,000.

Courrier d'Information Politique; Le Rassemblement, Paris. Semi-monthly of the RPF, launched in 1955 after that movement had become politically moribund, intended to succeed the paper *Le Rassemblement.* Represented a hopeless attempt to revive interest in political Gaullism, but succesfully continues the mystique of that movement.

Le Crapouillot, Paris. Famed politico-satirical monthly magazine published by Jean Galtier-Boissière. Strongly anti-Communist, but especially known for its old-fashioned left-Radicalism in the tradition of Alain, that is to say violently anti-clerical, militantly pacifist, opposed to "big shots," plutocrats, and all representatives of Order. Strongly anti-EDC. Its political perspective remains that of the interwar years. Three issues were used in this study: "Scandales de la IVe République" (New Series, No. 27), "Les Gros—Tome II" (New Series, No. 23), "Le Pour et le Contre: Pétain—de Gaulle" (New Series, No. 17).

Documents et Informations Parlementaires, Paris. Roneotyped weekly on parliamentary activity and political news, with special background material on major political movements. Edited by G. Bérard-Quelin. Small circulation but widely cited as an authoritative source.

Les Documents Politiques, Diplomatiques et Financiers, Paris. Monthly roneotyped publication, edited by R. Mennevée. Continuation of the prewar publication of the same title noted for its sensationalist revelations of "secret" information, interspersed with useful studies—it is unfortunately difficult to distinguish the one from the other. Anti-everything, but particularly anti-EDC. Sees the world in terms of mysterious plots. Issue used here: "L'Extension de la synarchisation de la France et de l'Europe; le Vatican, la synarchie et l'unité européenne; Histoire de M. Jean Monnet, dictateur occulte de la France et 'Imperator' de l'Europe," 1953.

Esprit, Paris. Intellectual-literary monthly founded in 1932 by Emmanuel Mounier. Presently directed by Albert Béguin and Jean-Marie Domenach. Strongly left in politics; predominantly Catholic though open to various shades of left-wing opinion, particularly to Protestant-socialist and Marxist views. Cooperation between Marxists and Christian-socialists sought in order to bring about fundamental change in French society. Originally expressed the Christian mysticism of Mounier's "personalist" philosophy which appeared related to the thought of Péguy. In the postwar period, critical of American foreign policy and neutralist. Small circulation but influential among idealist leftists, especially idealist Christian youth and students.

L'Express; Les Echos du Samedi, Paris. Political weekly converted into a daily for a few months during the 1955 election campaign; subsequently reverted to its weekly status. Edited by Françoise Giroud and Jean-Jacques Servan-Schreiber. Moderately left-of-center, ardent supporter of Mendès-France and the principal voice of "Mendèsisme." Regular articles by François Mauriac, also frequent contributions from former Gaullist leaders Gaston Palewski, Jacques Soustelle and André Malraux. Represents merger of former Gaullist right with "New Left" of Mendès-France. Accepts Western alliance, but generally critical of American foreign policy; seeks a new approach to East-West relations, wants France to be a bridge between the U.S. and the U.S.S.R. Moderately neutralist.

Le Figaro, Paris. Leading French conservative daily, edited by Pierre Brisson, featuring Raymond Aron and François Mauriac among its major columnists. Pro-American, staunchly anti-neutralist; audience among business and government leaders and the upper bourgeois elements of the *classes dirigeantes*. Once involved in an acrimonious dispute with *Le Monde* over the latter's neutralism. Circulation: 498,995.

Franc-Tireur, Paris. Independent Socialist daily born of the Resistance. Originally pro-Communist, then underwent basic editorial change; the foreign policy comments of Charles Ronsac strongly supported the Western alliance, although a survey indicated that its readers tended to remain very suspicious of American foreign policy. Circulation of 140,000 largely among workers of left-Socialist inclination, minor functionaries and some intellectuals.

France-Illustration, Paris. Well-known illustrated weekly magazine. Distinctly conservative, colonialist and nationalist. Anti-neutralist, opposed to EDC. Audience largely among the *bien-pensants* of the upper bourgeoisie. Used here for the articles by General de Monsabert attacking the proposed European Defense Community.

France-Observateur. See *L'Observateur.*

L'Humanité, Paris. Official daily organ of the French Communist Party. Circulation: 121,000.

Jours de France, Paris. Illustrated, "popular"-type weekly, launched in 1955. Gaullist tendency, but in the sense of the extreme right nationalism and social conservatism characteristic of the early years of the RPF. It represented the anti-Mendèsist tendency among the ex-Gaullists.

Libération, Paris. Daily independent postwar left-wing paper which became the voice of the pro-Communist *Union Progressiste.* Edited by Emmanuel d'Astier de la Vigerie. Violently anti-American; technically neutralist. Circulation 130,490.

Le Monde, Paris. Evening paper. Most influential French daily, edited by Hubert Beuve-Méry who frequently contributed leading neutralist editorials under the pen-name of "Sirius." Among the paper's staff of well-known foreign correspondents and regular contributors are to be noted the names of Maurice Duverger, Jean-Jacques Servan-Schreiber, André Fontaine, Henri Pierre, Alain Clement,

Georges Penchenier and Raymond Barillon. The paper became the center of an international incident when it published the apocryphal "Fechteler Report." The articles of Etienne Gilson which it published in 1950 marked the first major expression of neutralist opinion from a source that was definitely not pro-Communist. Limited circulation but highly influential among political and intellectual elites. Moderately left-of-center, anti-colonialist. Supporter of Mendèsisme. Strongly anti-American both on foreign policy and on "cultural" levels. Most significant publication of neutralist tendency. Circulation: 155,000.

La Nef, Paris. Monthly journal edited by Lucie Faure. Featured significant special issues and major commentaries on a wide range of political and intellectual questions. Contributors are usually well-known figures in their respective fields. Various political tendencies are reflected but the "center of gravity" is generally left and neutralist.

L'Observateur, Paris. Political weekly of independent left-wing Marxist tendency, founded and animated by Claude Bourdet. Has appeared under various titles, including: *L'Observateur politique, économique et littéraire; L'Observateur d'Aujourd'hui;* and *France-Observateur*—its present name. On its editorial board and among its contributors are well-known figures of the non-Communist left: Roger Stéphane, Gilles Martinet, Jacques Armel, Claude Estier, H. de Galard and others. Magazine aimed specifically at left-wing intelligentsia. Advocated a new Popular Front to be created by the merger of an independent New Left, of Socialist militants, and of Communists. Violently critical of all French governments issued of the right-center majority, especially on colonial, economic and foreign-policy matters. Militantly anti-American and neutralist.

Le Populaire, Paris. Official daily organ of the French Socialist Party. With an extremely small circulation, the paper which in the interwar years was a major voice of the French left has repeatedly been on the verge of bankruptcy, and once was saved only by the funds supplied by Léon Blum's friend, the American labor leader David Dubinsky. Even so, the paper has been reduced to a single sheet. Represented the pro-EDC orientation of party leader Guy Mollet.

Le Rassemblement, Paris. Former weekly organ of the RPF. Ceased publication in 1954, after the collapse of the movement as a political force. Voiced nationalist opposition to United States influence in France and in French territories. Especially violent in its hostility to EDC. The evolution of the paper, which moved from a position of uncompromising opposition to appeasement of the Communist powers to one of pseudo-neutralist policy "independent" of the U.S., seeking a new line on West Germany and calling for France to become a "bridge" between Washington and Moscow, is symptomatic of the evolution of a major wing of the Gaullists themselves. It also indicates the increasing antagonism of the French right towards the United States, an antagonism that came to a head with the Suez crisis.

La Revue Socialiste, Paris. Official Socialist Party monthly. New Series begun in 1947 takes up name and tradition dormant since first World War and the days of Benoit Malon. Doctrinal and intellectual articles. Small circulation among left-wing intelligentsia and the party militants of an older generation. The pages of this journal were open to all shades of Socialist attitudes; consequently it gives an indication not only of the range of opinion on doctrinal issues but also of the intensity of intra-party conflicts on such matters as EDC.

Sondages, Paris. Quarterly publication of the *Institut Français d'Opinion Publique.* Public opinion polls on public affairs, politics and international questions. Techniques used are reported to be essentially those of the Gallup Institute on which it is modelled. Particularly useful were a poll on French attitudes towards the United States published in 1953 (and also brought out in the monthly review *Réalités* under the title: "Ce que les Français pensent de l'Amérique) and one on attitudes towards EDC, also published in the fall of 1953.

Les Temps Modernes, Paris. Famed literary monthly under the aegis of Jean-Paul Sartre. Politically pro-Communist until the Hungarian crisis of 1956. Represented extreme anti-American elements among neutralists, virtually in the *Progressiste* category. Considerable circulation for this type of review among left-wing intelligentsia.

La Tribune des Nations, Paris. Weekly newspaper devoted to international affairs, edited by André Ulmann, published by Joseph Dubois. *Progressiste,* shading from anti-American neutralism into avowed support of the Soviet Union. Small circulation but fairly significant.

B. *Sources*: *Books, Documents and Articles*

"Ce que les Français pensent de l'Amérique," *Réalités,* Paris, (No. 91) August, 1953, pp. 18-22. (See *Sondages,* section A).

Europa; Dokumente zur Frage der europäischen Einigung, Auswärtigen Amt, Bonn: Bonner Universitäts Buchdruckerei, 1953.

France. Assemblée Nationale; Deuxième Législature, Session de 1951, No. 2283, Annexe au Procès-verbal du 29 décembre 1951, *Proposition de Résolution sur l'organisation d'une Confédération européenne,* Paris: Imprimerie Nationale, 1951.

——— ——— No. 2284, Annexe au Procès-verbal du 29 décembre 1951, *Proposition de Résolution présentée par M. Billotte et les membres du groupe du Rassemblement du peuple français tendant à inviter le Gouvernement à soutenir devant les instances internationales un projet de Communauté militaire européenne dans un cadre confédéral,* Paris: Imprimerie Nationale, 1951.

——— Assemblée Nationale; Deuxième Législature, Session de 1952, No. 4916, Annexe au Procès-verbal du 2 décembre 1952, *Proposition de loi tendant à l'établissement des contrats d'association capital-travail, présentée par M. Louis Vallon et les membres du groupe du Rassemblement du peuple français,* Paris: Imprimerie Nationale, 1952.

——— *Journal Officiel de la République Française, Débats Parlementaires, Assemblée Nationale,* Paris: Imprimerie Nationale, 1950-1955. Referred to as *J.O.*

de Gaulle, Charles, *Mémoires de Guerre,* Vol. I: *L'Appel, 1940-1942,* Paris: Plon, 1954.

——— *Press Conference of General de Gaulle Held in Paris, 7th of April 1954,* Paris: Imprimerie Ed. Dauer, [1954].

Malraux, André, "The New Left Can Succeed," *Yale French*

Studies, No. 15: "Social and Political France," Winter, 1955, pp. 49-60.

——— and Burnham, James, *The Case for de Gaulle; A Dialogue Between André Malraux and James Burnham,* New York: Random House, 1948.

Mollet, Guy, "France and the Defense of Europe; A Socialist View," *Foreign Afairs* (XXXII, 3) April, 1954, pp. 365-73.

Rassemblement du Peuple Français, *La France sera la France; Ce que veut Charles de Gaulle,* Paris: R.P.F., 1951. Referred to by title.

Soustelle, Jacques, "France and Europe," *Foreign Affairs* (XXX, 4) July, 1952, pp. 545-53.

C. *Special Studies and Commentaries*

Ambassade de France [in the U.S.], Service de Presse et d'Information, *Euratom; Six Nations to Pool Atomic Research and Development,* European Affairs, No. 11, New York, June, 1957.

——— ——— *A New Step in Building Europe; A Common Market for 175 Million Consumers,* European Affairs, No. 10, New York: June, 1957.

Aron, Raymond, "France and the Cold War," *The Political Quarterly,* London (XXXII, 1) January, 1951, pp. 57-66.

——— "French Public Opinion and the Atlantic Treaty," *International Affairs,* London (XXVIII, 1) January, 1952, pp. 1-8.

——— "Historical Sketch of the Great Debate," in D. Lerner and R. Aron, eds., *France Defeats EDC.*

Baum, Warren C., "The Marshall Plan and Foreign Trade," in Earle, E. M., ed., *Modern France.*

Bouscaren, Anthony Trawick, "The MRP in French Governments, 1948-1951," *The Journal of Politics,* Gainesville, Fla. (XIV, 1) February, 1952, pp. 104-31.

Blum, Léon, *A l'Echelle Humaine,* Paris: Gallimard, 1946 (first published in Montreal).

Brogan, Denis W., *France Under the Republic; The Development of Modern France (1870-1939),* New York: Harper, 1940.

Brown, William A.; and Redvers, Opie, *American Foreign Assistance,* Washington: The Brookings Institution, 1953.

Buthman, William C., *The Rise of Integral Nationalism in France,* New York: Columbia University Press, 1939.

Carroll, Eber Malcolm, *French Public Opinion and Foreign Affairs, 1870-1914,* New York: The Century Co., 1931.

Churchill, Winston S., *The Second World War,* Vol IV: *The Hinge of Fate,* Boston: Houghton-Mifflin, 1950.

Courtin, René, "French Views on European Union," *International Affairs,* London (XXV, 1) January, 1949, pp. 8-22.

Duroselle, Jean Baptiste, "The Crisis in French Foreign Policy," *The Review of Politics,* Notre Dame, Ind. (XVI, 4) October, 1954, pp. 412-37.

——— Grosser, Alfred; and Megret, Maurice, *French Opinion and the United States,* Waltham, Mass.: World Peace Foundation–Brandeis University Conference on France, June, 1956 (mimeographed).

Earle, Edward Mead, ed., *Modern France; Problems of the Third and Fourth Republics,* Princeton: Princeton University Press, 1951.

Einaudi, Mario; and Goguel, François, *Christian Democracy in Italy and France,* Notre Dame, Ind.: University of Notre Dame Press, 1952, Pt. II.

Fauvet, Jacques, "Birth and Death of a Treaty," in D. Lerner and R. Aron, eds., *France Defeats EDC.*

Florinski, Michael T., *Integrated Europe?,* New York: Macmillan, 1955.

Furniss, Edgar S., Jr., "French Attitudes Towards Western European Unity," *International Organization,* Boston (VII, 2) May, 1953, pp. 199-212.

Galimand, Lucien, *Origine et déviations du Gaullisme; de Gaulle, Agent de Reynaud?,* Paris: Edit. de la Couronne, 1950.

Gavin, Catherine, *Liberated France,* New York: St. Martin's Press, 1955.

Godfrey, E. Drexel, "France: Collapse of a Class," *The Antioch Rveiew,* Yellow Springs, O. (XIV, 2) June 1954, pp. 131-48.

——— *Fate of the French non-Communist Left,* New York: Random, 1955.

Goguel, François, *France Under the Fourth Republic,* Ithaca: Cornell University Press, 1952.

——— *Géographie des Elections françaises de 1870 à 1951,*

Cahiers de la Fondation Nationale des Sciences Politiques, No. 27, Paris: A. Colin, 1951.

——— *La Politique des Partis sous la Troisième République, 1871-1939,* 2 vols., Paris: Edit. du Seuil, 1946 (2 vols. in one, 1947).

——— *Christian Democracy . . .*: see Mario Einaudi.

Grosser, Alfred, "Germany and France; A Confrontation," in D. Lerner and R. Aron, eds., *France Defeats EDC.*

——— see also this entry under section E.

Hadsel, Fred Latimer, "France Among the Powers," in Earle, E. M., ed., *Modern France.*

Hayes, Carlton J. H., *France, A Nation of Patriots,* New York: Columbia University Press, 1930.

——— *The Historical Evolution of Modern Nationalism,* New York: Macmillan, 1950 (1st edit.: 1931).

Hill, Henry Bertram, "The Reliability of France in the European System," in Earle, E. M., ed., *Modern France.*

Hughes, H. Stuart, "Gaullism," in Earle, E. M., ed., *Modern France.*

Hoffmann, Stanley, "The Postmortems," in D. Lerner and R. Aron, eds., *France Defeats EDC.*

Jaurès, Jean, *L'Organisation socialiste; L'Armée nouvelle,* Paris: J. Rouff, 1911.

de Kerillis, Henri, *I Accuse de Gaulle,* New York: Harcourt-Brace, 1946.

Kohn, Hans, *The Idea of Nationalism; A Study of Its Origins and Background,* New York: Macmillan, 1944.

Krieger, Leonard, "The Horizons of History," *The American Historical Review* (LXIII, 1) October, 1957, pp. 62-74.

Langer, William L., *Our Vichy Gamble,* New York: A Knopf, 1951.

Lerner, Daniel, "Reflexions on France in the World Arena," in D. Lerner and R. Aron, eds., *France Defeats EDC.*

Lerner, Daniel; and Aron, Raymond, eds., *France Defeats EDC,* New York: F. A. Praeger, 1957.

Lipsedge, M. S., "The Poujade Movement," *Contemporary Review,* London (No. 1082) February, 1956.

Luethy, Herbert, *France Against Herself,* New York: F. A. Praeger, 1955.

——— "Poujade: Hitler or Pierrot?," *Commentary,* New York (XXI, 4) April, 1956, pp. 301-10.

Mallory, Walter H., ed., *Political Handbook of the World, 1957,* New York: Council on Foreign Relations, 1957.

Marchand, Jean José, "A Tableau of the French Press," in D. Lerner and R. Aron, eds., *France Defeats EDC.*

Matthews, Ronald, *The Death of the Fourth Republic,* New York: F. A. Praeger, 1954.

Micaud, Charles A., *The French Right and Nazi Germany, 1933-1939; A Study of Public Opinion,* Durham, N. C.: Duke University Press, 1943.

Muselier, Emile H. D., *De Gaulle contre le Gaullisme,* Paris: Edit. du Chêne, 1946.

The New York Herald Tribune, European Edition, Paris, reports by George Slocombe were used in this study.

The New York Times, New York. Reports by Robert C. Doty and Harold Callender as well as special articles have been referred to.

Pickles, Dorothy, *French Politics, The First Years of the Fourth Republic,* New York: Oxford University Press, 1953.

Pierce, Roy, "De Gaulle and the RPF—A Postmortem," *The Journal of Politics,* Gainesville, Fla. (XVI, 1) February, 1954.

Philip, André, "The Interplay of Interests and Passions," in D. Lerner and R. Aron, eds., *France Defeats EDC.*

Price, Harry Bayard, *The Marshall Plan and Its Meaning,* Ithaca: Cornell University Press, 1955.

Rémond, René, *La Droite en France de 1815 à nos Jours; Continuité et Diversité d'une Tradition Politique,* Paris: Aubier, 1954.

Robertson, A. H., *The Council of Europe: Its Structure, Functions and Achievements,* New York: F. A. Praeger, 1956.

Rose, Arnold M., "Anti-Americanism in France," *The Antioch Review,* Yellow Springs, O. (XVIII, 4) December, 1952, pp. 471-82.

Salvin, Marina, *Neutralism in France and Germany,* New York: Carnegie Endowment for International Peace, 1951.

Schoenbrun, David, *As France Goes,* New York: Harper & Bros., 1957.

Shafer, Boyd C., *Nationalism: Myth and Reality,* New York: Harcourt-Brace, 1955.

Siegfried, André, "History of the Mendès-France Government,"

Yale French Studies, New Haven, No. 15: "Social and Political France," Winter, 1955, pp. 61-7.

Snyder, Louis L., *The Meaning of Nationalism,* New Brunswick, N. J.: Rutgers University Press, 1954.

Soltau, Roger H., *French Political Thought in the Nineteenth Century,* London: E. Benn, 1931.

Stoetzel, Jean, "The Evolution of French Opinion," in D. Lerner and R. Aron, eds., *France Defeats EDC.*

Taylor, Alan J. P., *The Course of German History; A Survey of the Development of Germany since 1815,* New York: Coward-McCann, 1946.

Taylor, Edmond, "The Communists' 'New Look' in France," *The Reporter,* New York, March 30, 1954, pp. 19-22.

Thomson, David, *Democracy in France; The Third Republic,* New York: Oxford University Press, 1946.

——— *Democracy in France; The Third and Fourth Republics,* New York: Oxford University Press, 1952 (revised edition of previous entry).

——— *Two Frenchmen: Pierre Laval and Charles de Gaulle,* London: Cresset Press, 1951.

Turtledove, Harry L., "Why the French Act That Way," *Harpers' Magazine,* New York (CCXII, 1272) May, 1956, pp. 71-6.

United States Department of Commerce, Office of Business Economics, Clearing Office for Foreign Transactions, *Foreign Aid by the United States Government, 1940-1951,* Washington: U.S. Government Printing Office, 1952.

Van Dyke, Vernon, "The Communists and the Foreign Relations of France," in Earle, E. M., ed., *Modern France.*

Vernant, Jacques, "European Politics Faces French Economics," in D. Lerner and R. Aron, eds., *France Defeats EDC.*

Weinstein, Harold, *Jean Jaurès; A Study of Patriotism in the French Socialist Movement,* New York: Columbia University Press, 1936.

Werth, Alexander, *France, 1940-1955,* New York: H. Holt, 1956.

Wright, Gordon, *The Reshaping of French Democracy,* London: Methuen, 1950.

Yale French Studies, New Haven, No. 15: "'Social and Political France," Winter, 1955.

Zartman, I. William, *De la Résistance à la Révolution: Post-*

war French Neutralism, MSS: Yale University Thesis, 1956.

Britain

D. *Sources and Selected Secondary Comments*

Balogh, Thomas, "Political Economy in the Cold War," in McKitterick, T. E. M.; and Younger, Kenneth, eds., *Fabian International Essays.*

Beloff, Max, "The American Role," in *World Perspectives.*

Bevan, Aneurin, *In Place of Fear,* London: Wm. Heinemann —New York: Simon & Schuster, 1952.

Crossman, R. H. S., "Britain and the Outside World," *The Political Quarterly,* London (XXIV, 1), 1953, pp. 28-38.

——— "Towards a Philosophy of Socialism," in Crossman, R. H. S., ed., *New Fabian Essays.*

——— editor, *New Fabian Essays,* London: Turnstile Press, 1952.

——— and Younger, Kenneth, *Socialist Foreign Policy,* Fabian Tract No. 287, London: Fabian International Bureau, 1951.

Epstein, Leon, *Britain—Uneasy Ally,* Chicago: University of Chicago Press, 1954.

Fitzsimons, M. A., *The Foreign Policy of the British Labour Government, 1945-1951,* Notre Dame, Ind.: Notre Dame University Press, 1953.

Foot, Michael; and Bruce, Donald, *Who Are the Patriots?,* London: Gollancz, 1949.

Freeman, John; and Healey, Denis, *Rearmament—How Far?,* Fabian Tract No. 288, London: Fabian International Bureau, 1951.

Gellman, Norman Ira, "Bevanism: A Philosophy for British Labour?," *Journal of Politics,* Gainesville, Fla. (XVI, 4) November, 1954.

Going Our Way?, London: Tribune pamphlet, [1951]. (Followed *One Way Only.*)

Great Britain, *Parliamentary Debates (Hansard), House of Commons, Official Report,* London: H. M. Stationery Office. Referred to as *Hansard.*

Healey, Denis, "Power Politics and the Labour Party," in Crossman, R. H. S., ed., *New Fabian Essays.*

Hughes, Emrys, *Arms and Mr. Bevan,* Glasgow: Unity Press pamphlet, 1952.

——— *Bomb over Britain,* Glasgow: Civic Press pamphlet, 1953.

In the Shadow of the H-Bomb: A Reprint of the News Chronicle Articles of March 1st-11th with Additional Material, London: News Chronicle Book Department, 1955 (pamphlet).

Keep Left, by a Group of Members of Parliament, London: New Statesman and Nation, 1947 (pamphlet).

Labour Party, *In Defence of Europe,* London: Labour Publications Department, June, 1954 (pamphlet).

Lichtheim, George, "Behind the 'Anti-Americanism' of Mr. Bevan; How Far Will It Take Him—and British Labour?," *Commentary,* New York (XIV, 7) July, 1952, pp. 15-20.

Manchester Guardian Weekly, Manchester. Weekly collection of articles and editorials from the daily paper.

The New Statesman and Nation, London. Socialist weekly, edited by Kingsley Martin; assistant editor, R. H. S. Crossman.

McKitterick, T. E. M., *Conditions of British Foreign Policy,* Fabian Tract No. 289, London: Fabian International Bureau, 1951.

——— and Younger, Kenneth, eds., *Fabian International Essays,* London: Hogarth Press, 1957.

Morris, Stuart, *Neutrality, Germany's Way to Peace,* London: Peace News Pamphlet, 1953.

One Way Only, London: Tribune pamphlet, [1951]. (First of the special pamphlets issued by the Bevan group after his break with the Labour government.)

Orwell, George, *England Your England, and Other Essays,* London: Secker & Warburg, 1953.

Powell, Enoch, "The Empire of England," in *Tradition and Change.*

Quo Vadis?, London: Tribune pamphlet, [1951]. Third of the series begun with *One Way Only.*

Roche, John B., "The Crisis in British Socialism," *The Antioch Review,* Yellow Springs, O. (XII), pp. 387-97.

Sellon, Hugh, "Peace with Honour," in *Tradition and Change.*

Socialist Union, *Socialism and Foreign Policy,* London: Book House, May, 1953, (pamphlet).

Strachey, John, "British Defence Policy," in McKitterick, T. E. M.; and Younger, Kenneth, eds., *Fabian International Essays.*

The Times, London.

Tradition and Change; Nine Oxford Lectures, London: Conservative Political Centre, 1954.

Tribune, London. Left-socialist weekly. Editors include Jennie Lee, wife of Aneurin Bevan. Magazine also brought out series of pamphlets in 1951 defending Bevan's position.

Wilson, Harold, *Today They Die, The Case for World Cooperation,* Peace Aims Pamphlet, No. 54, London: National Peace Council, 1953.

——— *Two out of Three; The Problem of World Poverty,* Peace Aims Pamphlet, No. 57, London: National Peace Council, 1953.

——— *The War on Poverty; An Appeal to the Conscience of Mankind,* London: Gollancz, 1952.

Windrich, Elaine, *British Labour's Foreign Policy,* Stanford, Cal.: Stanford University Press, 1952.

World Perspectives; Seven Oxford Lectures, London: Conservative Political Centre, 1955.

Germany

E. *Sources and Selected Secondary Comments*

Barth, Karl, " 'Ne craignez point,' Lettre ouverte de Karl Barth sur la Remilitarisation de l'Allemagne," see "Les Protestants allemands et le réarmement," *Esprit.*

Büttner, Walter, *Verschwörung gegen Deutschland,* Kahl: Hohe Warte, 1953.

Carr, E. H., *The Romantic Exiles; A Nineteenth Century Portrait Gallery,* Harmondsworth, Middlesex: Penguin Books, 1949 (1st published 1933).

Deutsches Büro für Friedensfragen (in Überleitung), *Die Wiederaufrüstung Deutschlands im Spiegel der Presse,* s.l.: roneotyped, May, 1950.

Germany, Federal Republic, *Verhandlungen des Deutschen Bundestages, I. Wahlperiode 1949, Stenographische Berichte,* Bonn: Bonner Universitäts-Buchdruckerei, 1951-1953. Referred to as *V.D.B.*

——— ——— *II. Wahlperiode, 1954, Stenographische Berichte,* Bonn: Bonner Universitäts-Buchdruckerei, 1954.

——— ——— Auswärtigen Amt, *Europa.* See title under section B.

Grosser, Alfred, *La Situation en Allemagne en 1955; Rapport du Congrès International de Bruges, 1955,* Brussels: Institut des Relations internationales, 1955.

——— *West Germany from Defeat to Rearmament,* London: Allen & Unwin, 1955.

Harwick, Christian, *Deutschland zwischen Ja und Nein; Prognose unter dem Fallbeil,* Kreuzlingen: Neptune, 1951.

Königsteiner Kreis—Vereinigung der Juristen, Volkswirte, Beamten aus der Sowjetischen Besatzungszone, *Untersuchungen zur Lösung der deutschen Frage; Bericht über die Tagung des Verfassungsausschusses des Königsteiner Kreises im Bonn am 27. und 28. März 1952,* Göttingen: Otto Schwartz, 1952.

Laun, Rudolf, *Das Völkerrecht und die Verteidigung Deutschlands,* Heidelberg: Vorwinckel, 1951.

Marx, Karl, *The Eastern Question; A Reprint of Letters Written in 1853-1856 Dealing with the Events of the Crimean War,* ed. by Eleanor Marx Aveling and Edward Aveling, London: S. Sonnenschein, 1897.

——— and Engels, Friedrich, *The Russian Menace to Europe; A Selection of Articles, Speeches, Letters and News Dispatches,* Selected and Edited by Paul W. Blackstock and Bert Hoselitz, Glencoe, Ill.: The Free Press, 1952.

Mettmann, Rudolf, "Carlo Schmid, Revolutionär oder müder Troubadour?," *Das Neue Journal,* Wiesbaden, (VI), October 9, 1957.

Nauheimer Kreis, *Die Nauheimer Protokolle; Diskussionen über die Neutralisierung Deutschlands,* Wurzburg: Nauheimer Kreis—Dr. Ulrich Noak, 1950.

Neuer Vorwärts; Zentral Organ der Sozialdemokratischen Partei Deutschlands, Hanover, 1950-1955.

Niemöller, Martin, *Deutschland Wohin? Krieg oder Frieden?,* Darmstadt: Jupiter, 1952.

Perlacky-Kasa, *Report to the Mutual Security Agency,* Office of the Special Representative (Paris), Information Division, Research and Analysis Branch, Paris: MSS, 1953.

"Les Protestants allemands et le réarmement," *Esprit,* January, 1951.

Rauschning, Hermann, *Die Deutsche Einheit und der Weltfriede,* Hamburg: Holstein, 1955.

——— *Deutschland zwischen West und Ost,* Berlin: Christian Verlag, 1950.

Roegele, Bernhard, "Herbst der Illusionen," *Neues Abendland,* (XII, 2) 2nd quarter, 1957.

Schütz, Wilhelm Wolfgang, *Deutschland am Rande zweier Welten; Voraussetzungen und Aufgabe unserer Aussenpolitik,* Stuttgart: Deutsche Verlags-Anstalt, 1952.

——— *Die Stunde Deutschlands; Wie kann Deutschland wiedervereinigt werden?,* Stuttgart: Deutsche Verlags-Anstalt, 1954.

——— ed., *Bewährung im Widerstand; Gedanken zum deutschen Schicksal,* Stuttgart: Deutsche Verlags-Anstalt, 1956.

Salvin, Marina, *Neutralism in France and Germany.* See under Section C.

Siegler, Heinrich, *Deutschlands Weg, 1945-1955; Von der Kapitulation bis zur Moskau-Reise Adenaurs,* Cologne: G. Koenig, 1956.

Siemsen, Reimer, "Des Kanzlers geistiger Standpunkt," *Die Kultur,* Stuttgart (VI, 91) September, 1957.

S[ozialdemokratische] P[artei] D[eutschlands], *Annahme Bedeutet nicht Ratifizierung! Der Kampf um die Verträge geht weiter!,* Bonn: Vorstand der SPD [1953]. Referred to by title.

Der Spiegel, Hamburg. Political weekly.

Thayer, Charles W., *The Unquiet Germans,* New York: Harper & Bros., 1957.

*** "Auf dem Prüfstand; Zur Pathologie des politischen Denkens der Deutschen," *Wort und Wahrheit; Monatsschrift für Religion und Kultur,* Freiburg in Breisgau (XII, 2) February, 1957.

Index